RESTORATIVE THEORY IN PRACTICE

by the same author

Just Care
Restorative Justice Approaches to Working with Children in Public Care
Belinda Hopkins
Foreword by Jonathan Stanley
ISBN 978 1 84310 981 5
eISBN 978 0 85700 087 3

Just Schools
A Whole School Approach to Restorative Justice
Belinda Hopkins
ISBN 978 1 84310 132 1
eISBN 978 1 84642 432 8

of related interest

The Forgiveness Project
Stories for a Vengeful Age
Marina Cantacuzino
Foreword by Archbishop Emeritus Desmond Tutu
Foreword by Alexander McCall Smith
ISBN 978 1 84905 566 6
eISBN 978 1 78450 006 1

Restorative Justice
How It Works
Marian Liebmann
ISBN 978 1 84310 074 4
eISBN 978 1 84642 631 5

The Psychology of Emotion in Restorative Practice
How Affect Script Psychology Explains How and
Why Restorative Practice Works
Edited by Vernon C. Kelly, Jr. and Margaret Thorsborne
ISBN 978 1 84905 974 9
eISBN 978 0 85700 866 4

Implementing Restorative Practice in Schools
A Practical Guide to Transforming School Communities
Margaret Thorsborne and Peta Blood
Foreword by Graham Robb
ISBN 978 1 84905 377 8
eISBN 978 0 85700 737 7

RESTORATIVE THEORY IN PRACTICE

INSIGHTS INTO WHAT WORKS AND WHY

EDITED BY
BELINDA HOPKINS

Jessica Kingsley *Publishers*
London and Philadelphia

Parts of Chapter 3 are reproduced with permission from Hart Publishing, an imprint of Bloomsbury Publishing PLc: Vaandering, D. (2013) 'A window on relationships: Reflecting critically on current restorative justice theory.' *Restorative Justice: An International Journal 1*, 3, 311–333.

First published in 2016
by Jessica Kingsley Publishers
73 Collier Street
London N1 9BE, UK
and
400 Market Street, Suite 400
Philadelphia, PA 19106, USA

www.jkp.com

Library of Congress Cataloging in Publication Data
Restorative theory in practice : insights into what works and why / edited by Belinda Hopkins.
    pages cm
Includes bibliographical references and index.
ISBN 978-1-84905-468-3 (alk. paper)
1. Restorative justice. 2. Juvenile delinquency--Psychological aspects. I. Hopkins, Belinda, 1956- editor.
HV8688.R497 2016
364.6'8--dc23
                                    2015012620

British Library Cataloguing in Publication Data
A CIP catalogue record for this book is available from the British Library

ISBN 978 1 84905 468 3
eISBN 978 0 85700 847 3

Printed and bound in Great Britain

Contents

Introduction

BELINDA HOPKINS

Who is the book for?

This is a book for all those who are fascinated by restorative practice and especially by what makes it so effective, often in situations where without it things may have got much worse. This fascination may have come for professional reasons, from the desire to gain a deeper understanding of what is actually going on when people come together in what are called 'restorative encounters'. Might there be some essential elements to such an encounter without which the process would fail to address the needs of all those present? Might there be other factors that enhance the process in certain cases but not others? Is there a set of necessary, if not always sufficient, conditions under which restorative interventions are more likely to be successful in the eyes of those involved? All these are questions for restorative practitioners and for those who, like myself, combine hands-on restorative practice with training and trainer development. For all of us, on-going professional development involves deepening our understanding of what we do, how we do it, and how we can do it better, for the sake of those we serve – whether those harmed or those responsible for the harm (or both, as is so often the case).

This book is not simply for practitioners however. Some readers will be among the rapidly growing community of restorative academics, evaluators and researchers, keen to deepen their own understanding of the theoretical underpinnings of restorative practice, and perhaps make links to other fields and other practices. New ways to look at restorative practice can shed light on so many aspects of the human condition. Such readers may view restorative processes through the lens of criminology, psychology, psychiatry, sociology, biology, neuroscience, linguistics, anthropology or any combination of these. All these lenses, and more besides, can help us to understand what people are going through in the aftermath of harmful behaviours. It may become clearer how restorative responses provide the answer to questions not previously even fully understood.

A brief history of restorative justice

The field of restorative justice, approaches and practices is so diverse these days that it becomes difficult to find a single overarching definition on which everyone can agree. Indeed, the on-going debates and controversies keep the field dynamic, self-critical and in constant development, which I believe to be a healthy thing. However, I subscribe to the belief that there are some critical core ingredients to effective restorative practice and these can be found in the ancestral lineage of the field, which this section briefly summarises.

As is often the case, a professional field develops its own creation myths about how 'it' all began, and restorative justice is no different. Innovatory approaches to youth offending in Ontario in the 1970s informed the development of victim-offender mediation across North America, which in turn spread to Europe (Liebmann 2007). Centuries-old community problem-solving circles used by Maori people inspired what has become known as family group conferencing circles in New Zealand (Drewery 2004). Indigenous peoples in North America have influenced the development of sentencing circles and other circle practices (Pranis 2005).

Subsequent commentators have warned against over-simplification of these apparent 'golden age' myths (Cunneen 2007). Nevertheless their influence can be felt in the diverse ways in which restorative practice has developed and continues to develop around the world. New Zealand's experience with family group conferencing influenced justice professionals in New South Wales, Australia, for example. The original model developed by O'Connell (known as the 'Wagga Wagga' model after the city in New South Wales, where he was working as a police officer), identified some critical language and key stages to follow to help to repair the damage done after an offence (Moore and O'Connell 2003). This 'scripted approach', as it has become known, is widely used in one form or other, across the globe. At some point both the practice of bringing victim and offender face-to-face in dialogue, and the practice of including friends and family members in the dialogue became collectively known as 'restorative justice'.

In fact as victim-offender mediation, sentencing circles and family group conferences developed it became evident that such practices had been used informally in many parts of the world. Worldwide, in places where a sense of family and a sense of community remain key to social organisation, circle problem-solving and face-to-face dialogue have a role in addressing issues of offending behaviour. Sometimes these more reparative processes have been used alongside exclusionary or punitive responses as well. However, it is important to acknowledge that restorative approaches in themselves are not new, and neither are they unique to a particular culture.

The essential elements of restorative practice

The various approaches to addressing offending behaviour, developed on opposite sides of the globe, appear to share common values, beliefs, core elements and intended outcomes. Herein lie what I referred to earlier as core ingredients. These include a recognition of the importance of strong, respectful relationships as the 'glue' that keeps communities safe, and of the importance of repairing these relationships when things go wrong; a commitment to putting things right and moving on rather than stigmatising and punishing those responsible for any harm caused; the importance of face-to-face encounter between those affected by the harm or wrongdoing in a community; the need for everyone affected to be able to tell their story and to do this with reference to their innermost thoughts and feelings before, during and after the incident; the belief that it is those affected who can and must be the ones to find the ways forward, and the importance of dialogue in finding ways forward that are mutually acceptable.

Despite the commonality of core values and essential elements there is also diversity, in part connected to what people believe a restorative encounter is about, should be about and could be about. This is why continuing discussions about what may be happening during such a meeting are so important. Theory inevitably informs practice.

The growth of different practices and explanatory theories

Restorative practice evolved initially as a practice without a theory. Victim-offender mediation and family group conferencing in the 1970s and 1980s, and sentencing circles in the 1990s, developed and spread because they 'worked'. In other words the practices appeared to reduce re-offending, victims expressed satisfaction in the process and all participants generally appeared to consider the practice fair and positive. In order to disseminate the practice further two things needed to be developed – first, a way of replicating the good practice so that more people could be trained to use it, thereby spreading the benefits more widely, and second, some kind of explanatory theory for what was going on.

In fact over time practice has evolved and developed, and in different parts of the world restorative practice differs according to which model is most favoured. Some people lean more towards the face-to-face mediation model, others more to larger group circles. To some extent the choice of model can be dictated by the context and the more flexible practitioners will adapt their process to address the needs of those involved.

Another very important factor governing one's choice of model is one's beliefs about what is actually happening in a restorative encounter, and indeed what makes a specific encounter restorative or not. Over time the application of the word 'restorative' to various processes has grown. For some people a restorative process is something that has day-to-day applications – insofar as it involves people coming together to listen to each other after something has gone wrong between them, expressing their feelings and needs to each other and then working together to find a mutually accepted way forward. With such a definition the process called *mediation*, when both sides are in conflict (with neither accepting responsibility but both blaming the other) can also be classed as restorative. Again, if 'restorative' includes encounters where the intention or the outcome is the healing of relationships following a breakdown in these relationships, then the term could also be applied to conversations between folk in conflict without the need for a third party to facilitate. Indeed it could also be argued that the values, skills, mindset and language implicit in these restorative encounters provide a recipe for social cohesion and respectful society in general. They can provide strategies for pro-active team and community building, and act as a template for leaders at middle and senior management level in any context. For some, restorative practice offers a 'way to be' and a framework for daily interaction with family, friends, colleagues and indeed the general public (Hopkins 2007, 2013; Sullivan and Tifft 2001; Wachtel and McCold 2001).

In contrast to this maximalist position are those who caution against widening the net of what 'restorative justice' might mean, and where it might be used. It is believed that applying the word restorative too widely leads to confusion. Walgrave (2003) warns:

> Paradoxically, one could even say that the most important threat to restorative justice is the enthusiasm with which it is being implemented. Enthusiasm leads to poorly thought-out implementation, an overestimation of possibilities, negligence of legal rights, and the blurring of the concepts and confusion with the aims and limits of restorative justice. (p. ix)

To get around this some proponents suggest that the phrase 'restorative justice' be used in criminal matters and the word 'approaches' or 'practice' should be applied for wider community applications, whether in schools, care settings and the workplace. The debates continue and will continue as the field expands.

The rationale for this book

Since the use of restorative practices has spread into schools and care settings many more people have begun to recognise how theoretical models from the fields of child development, social care and neuroscience may help to explain and indeed endorse the benefits these practices bring to such settings. Advances in research and understanding about brain function, socialisation and emotionality continue to shed light on what may be happening when people in conflict or in the aftermath of harmful behaviour find themselves face-to-face in a constructive dialogue.

For many years now I have been keen to learn more about what may be happening during a restorative encounter; to deepen my own understanding about this; to improve my own practice as a facilitator and to help deepen the insights and understanding of those whom I train in restorative practice. Over the years I have developed my own unique model of practice by seeking inspiration from many different sources. The 'Hopkins' model, as it is sometimes known, has elements of humanistic psychology, cognitive behavioural therapy, Nonviolent Communication (the focus of Chapter 5) – to name but a few of the many influences on my practice (Hopkins 2004, 2007, 2013). I also have a background of practical experience in community building using democratic circle processes, in interpersonal conflict resolution, community mediation and restorative justice conferencing based on the original Wagga Wagga model from New South Wales. Indeed, my eclectic approach barred me from being a contributor to this book.

I was seeking to learn from people who regularly facilitate restorative encounters in their day jobs and have a very specific psychological or sociological theory informing their own practice. I sought people whom, while they may draw from other models to some degree, are nevertheless able to name a single theory that has most influence, in some cases a unique influence, on their practice. It is the 'lens' through which they look to understand what is happening in a given situation, to understand those involved or affected, and to assess how best to approach this situation as a facilitator. Some contributors are psychologists working in educational and care settings, some are researchers and teachers, some are trainers in restorative practice, and some work in youth justice settings. They are all informed by a specific theoretical approach in their work. The two exceptions support conflict resolution in other ways, or have done in the recent past. I invited their contributions because their insights can also deepen the understanding of those using more recognisable models of restorative practice. They certainly have done mine.

Each of the contributors explore what they mean by a restorative meeting or encounter. They do not necessarily share the same view about what does and does not classify as a restorative meeting. Each suggests what they believe are the key components of a restorative encounter and why, offering an explanation from their own theoretical perspective. Each explains what they believe to be happening during the restorative encounter and what elements are key to its success, explaining what they mean by a successful outcome. Some contributors offer alternatives to the more familiar restorative models, adding elements they believe to be important from their particular theoretical model and experience.

The design of the book – a Circle Process in book form

I have worked as a classroom teacher over the years that the popularity and the use (and misuse) of Circle Time has developed, and have been inspired by the work of Bliss, Robinson and Maines (1995) and Mosley (1993, 1996, Mosley and Tew 1999). Like many restorative practitioners I have also been moved by my experience of using Circle Process for meetings, problem-solving groups, community building and on training courses (Boyes-Watson and Pranis 2010, 2014; Pranis 2005).

In my own work I have integrated best practice from both Circle Time and Circle Process and am now almost 'hard-wired' to use circles in training, seminars, meetings and indeed whenever more than a few people get together. This explains the design of the book – possibly the first book about restorative practice that itself embodies this Circle Process.[1]

Circle Time and Circle Process share some common principles. All participants sit in a circle, ideally on chairs of an equal height. One person has the responsibility of facilitating or 'holding' the circle – instigating each round of contributions; being sensitive to when to continue going round, when to stop and perhaps what new questions to pose. Everyone has the opportunity to contribute and a talking piece is passed around the circle to each person in turn. This visual symbol serves as a reminder to the whole group of whose turn it is to speak, and indeed whose turn it is to listen. As a listener everyone is invited to keep an open mind and endeavour to remain non-judgemental, or at least to silently examine any judgements that surface. Some circles have, as an intention, to reach consensus or find resolution to a problem; some to heal broken relationships or build new connections based on mutual understanding; some to explore new ideas and open people's minds to other perspectives on an issue or topic; some to build community and strengthen connections.

There are different designs for Circle Process, but many involve an initial Check-in stage, where everyone has the chance to introduce him- or her-self and share some personal information

---

1   I was encouraged to be more explicit about the book's Circle design after a conversation with my friend and colleague Joelle Timmermans in Belgium. She recognised the Circle structure in the way I was describing what I wanted to do and I am grateful to her for this.

or anecdote to begin to build safety and trust. Next comes a series of Go-rounds on the topic that has brought everyone together. At some point there may be some *collaborative work* on the issue to find common ground, or at least to seek understanding of each others' differing perspectives. Finally there is a Check-out stage where people say how they are feeling and what they have learnt, or are taking away from their experience of the Circle.

How to read the book

You, the reader, will be invited to join the circle by first reading our 'Check-in', in which all the contributors, including me, the volume editor, introduce ourselves. If you would like to find out more about each of the contributors you are encouraged to begin with this section, in the spirit of the book's design. However if you are keen to get to the theories section first then it is possible to skip this initial Check-in.

The ten contributing authors will then engage in a 'Go-round', each one taking a chapter to introduce their particular theoretical model and explain, by example, how it informs their practice. This is the lens through which they see the world, and their work in particular.

Next comes some initial *practical work,* in the sense that each contributor was given the same two case studies and asked to reflect on how they would think about them, and then approach them as a facilitator. It is true that this stage did not involve live discussion and so is not as collaborative as a real circle would have been, but at least everyone worked on the same issues.

Behind the scenes, however, something very exciting was happening and did involve everyone engaging with each others' ideas. Once all the chapters were in, and after an initial bit of editing on my part, I circulated them all to everyone and invited all the authors to read them, in an open-minded non-judgemental way. In the final 'Check-out' stage everyone reflects on their experience of taking part in this Circle Process in a book and shares what they have learned, from each other, and from the process.

I believe this has been a very rich and exciting way to engage a group of wise and experienced practitioners in reflecting on their own practice and that of others, and I share my own learning from the endeavour at the Check-out stage, with everyone else.

As you will see from this final section all the contributors attest to having learnt a great deal from their involvement in the project of bringing this book to fruition. It has been rather like an action research project and feels like the beginning of something, rather than an end in itself. We all hope that you will feel the same kind of excitement that we do from this collaborative venture and will get involved in taking things further. There is no doubt that there are many more theoretical perspectives that can help us understand better this powerful and effective way of helping people find ways through what have often been such appalling experiences. If our understanding grows then surely our practice will benefit and we can do even more effective work and reach even more people.

References

Bliss, T., Robinson, G and Maines, B. (1995) *Developing Circle Time.* Bristol: Lucky Duck Publishing.

Boyes-Watson, C. and Pranis, K. (2010) *Heart of Hope: A Guide for Using Peacemaking Circles to Develop Emotional Literacy, Promote Healing and Build Healthy Relationships.* Boston, MA: Centre for Restorative Justice, Suffolk University.

Boyes-Watson, C. and Pranis, K. (2014) *Circle Forward: Building a Restorative School Community.* Saint Paul, MN: Living Justice Press.

Cunneen, S. (2007) 'Reviving Restorative Justice Traditions?' In J. Johnstone and D. W. Van Ness (eds) *Handbook of Restorative Justice.* Cullompton, Devon: Willan.

Drewery, W. (2004) 'Conferencing in schools: Punishment, restorative justice, and the productive importance of the process of conversation.' *Journal of Community Applied Social Psychology, 14,* 332–344.

Hopkins, B. (2004) *Just Schools – A Whole School Approach to Restorative Justice.* London: Jessica Kingsley Publishers.

Hopkins, B. (2007) *Just Care.* London: Jessica Kingsley Publishers.

Hopkins, B. (2013) *The Restorative Classroom.* Milton Keynes: Optimus Publishing.

Liebmann, M. (2007) *Restorative Justice: How it Works.* London: Jessica Kingsley Publishers.

Moore, D. B. and O'Connell, T. A. (2003) 'Family Conferencing in Wagga Wagga: A Communitarian Model of Justice'. In G. Johnstone (ed.) *A Restorative Justice Reader.* Cullompton, Devon: Willan.

Mosley, J. (1993) *Turn Your School Round.* Wisbech: LDA.

Mosley, J. (1996) *Quality Circle Time.* Wisbech: LDA.

Mosley, J. and Tew, M. (1999) *Quality Circle Time in the Secondary School.* London: David Fulton.

Pranis, K. (2005) *The Little Book of Circle Process: A New/Old Approach to Peacemaking.* Intercourse, PA: Good Books.

Sullivan, D. and Tifft, L. (2001) *Restorative Justice: Healing the Foundations of our Everyday Lives.* Monsey, NY: Willow Tress Press.

Wachtel, T. and McCold, P. (2001) 'Restorative Justice in Everyday Life' in H. Strang and J. Braithwaite (eds) *Restorative Justice in Civil Society.* Cambridge: Cambridge University Press.

Walgrave, L. (ed) (2003) 'Introduction' in *Repositioning Restorative Justice.* Cullompton, Devon: Willan.

Check-in

Circle process begins with everyone sitting in the circle having the opportunity to introduce themselves and perhaps share what they would like those present to know about them. This is often referred to as the *Check-in*, as we have seen. At the end of a circle participants all take part in a *Check-out*, sharing something they have learned from the process or will take away as a new idea, or thought.

Although I have not personally contributed a chapter for the reason I explain below I am, as editor, convening and facilitating the circle, and so contribute both here at the Check-in stage and again at the end, in our Check-out.

Belinda Hopkins

I had been a secondary school teacher of modern languages for over twelve years when I first received training in conflict resolution and mediation, in the early 1990s. I had finally found what I wanted to do with my life.

I learned how to facilitate circles for tutor groups and taught modern languages using circles in many of my classes, developing social and emotional skills as well as communication skills. I used my conflict resolution and mediation skills when students fell out. After a few years I become a freelance trainer in circles and peer mediation but felt something was missing. The traditional power structures in school stayed the same and the values and principles implicit in circle work and mediation were not consistent across any school I knew.

Hearing Australian police officer Terry O'Connell speak about restorative justice was transformative. Here was not just a process – one I recognised as very similar to my mediation experiences, but a philosophy that challenged the punishment paradigm in both schools and the criminal justice system.

I trained as a restorative justice conferencing facilitator and a community mediator, and soon became a trainer myself. I founded my own small organisation, offering training and consultancy to schools with a wonderful team of associates. I began to write and publish books about creating a restorative ethos and culture across a whole establishment or institution. I am privileged to be working with, and meeting, so many people who share this vision of change.

Margaret Thorsborne

I came to this restorative work through my high school teaching (biology and science) followed by post-graduate study to become a school counsellor. Along the way (years in both careers) I developed skills and expertise in mediation and conflict resolution, and organisational responses in the wake of traumatic incidents, whole of school approaches to bullying, drug and alcohol education, special education. It seemed to me then, in 1994, when I stumbled across restorative conferencing while working in a high school in Queensland, it was as if everything I had ever done and learned was in preparation for this restorative problem solving – this BIG thing. I became, with other colleagues, a true pioneer of restorative justice (RJ) in a school and workplace context, and have been both boggled and delighted with the uptake of restorative practice in schools, workplaces, other agencies and communities and the extent of innovation in all fields of RJ. These days, basic skill development in restorative facilitation is my bread and butter, but I am increasingly interested in culture change and leadership development in the pursuit of sustainable practice and a relational ethos. In the early days, I was so excited I could barely sleep. My excitement and passion has not waned 20 plus years down the track, but I sleep better now!

Juliet Starbuck

There was a time, many years ago, when I had the misfortune to be involved in two court cases. Both ended in my favour but neither left me feeling as if 'justice had been done'. While the outcome mattered enormously to me I remember being caught up in a process in which I didn't matter: only the law mattered. Issues of right and wrong or justice were unimportant. My voice, my views, my hurt weren't relevant. I wasn't relevant.

So, when I discovered restorative justice (RJ) I was determined to become involved. I was working as a senior educational psychologist in a youth offending service (YOS). I volunteered to manage 'RJ' because I wanted to make it more than just something that happened at a referral order panel (where young offenders are made to attend a meeting with community volunteers who decide what 'activities' the young person should do as part of their referral order). I was already managing Education, Parenting and Prevention but thought I could expand RJ into each of these areas to truly make a difference. So I did. I attended training. I recruited some RJ staff to set up and run RJ conferences. I appointed staff to introduce RJ into schools. I trained the police, education colleagues and children's home staff in RJ. I travelled around Europe with some school and police colleagues 'spreading the word'. And I completed my doctorate.

I've left the YOS now but I hope that I've left a legacy and that the good work is continuing. I now teach my university students about RJ and I seek opportunities to introduce it into 'my schools'. I also try to 'live' RJ. Life throws conflict at me (I'm afraid I've got an opinion on everything and I like to 'get involved') and so I use RJ to guide me and to keep me 'out of trouble'. I often run the RJ questions through my head as a little 'self check' to help me think about what I'm about to say or do. It brings me a kind of peace which, sadly, was not brought to me all those years ago when, as just a youngster really, I became 'nothing' in something that was, for me, everything.

Dorothy Vaandering

I am blessed that my work encapsulates what I am passionate about in life. After years of teaching in primary-elementary education, and curriculum writing in Ontario and Alberta, I formally moved into the world of theorising where I am now a researcher and teacher-educator at Memorial University in Newfoundland.

In reflecting back, I realise my life has been about finding 'better ways' to disagree, to address conflict, and to prevent and repair harm. What began as a search for practices that would make a difference in education, faith community, and family contexts turned into a curiosity about what makes some approaches more effective than others, and what makes some approaches effective sometimes and not at others. Ultimately in digging deep into the philosophical origins of restorative justice I discovered a set of core beliefs and values that resonated with my understanding and experience of what it is to be human. Without a clear understanding of the root, it is difficult to know how to nurture the plant and flower. Thus, I make every effort as a practitioner to hold the entire experience within a space where my attention is always conscious of the root – the back-story – of restorative justice as well as all involved in a circle meeting. When I do this, the outcome is much less mysterious, yet full of wonder.

I love my artist spouse who has taught me to see, my two grown boys who have taught me unconditional love, and my large family and community that are always full of intrigue.

Ann Shearer

I started my working life as a journalist on *The Guardian*, and soon began to specialise in aspects of social welfare. This led to becoming particularly involved with people with intellectual disabilities, and I spent quite some time as an internationally-travelling campaigner and consultant on the kind of services that would help to end their often cruel exclusion from the most ordinary of social opportunities. For the last two decades, I've been a Jungian analyst and psychotherapist, again travelling to teach in different countries as well as in Britain. Around ten years ago, my imagination was seized by the ideas of restorative justice, and since 2013 I've given workshops on the continuing professional development programme of the Restorative Justice Council.

What holds all these interests together? One consistent thread has been a preoccupation with what might make for a more just society. That seems to me – the second thread – crucially to involve a greater ability to live with people who seem 'different', instead of rejecting them and denying their social dignity. One of the many reasons I became an analyst was to try to understand more about this – and I soon learned that what we do to others is also and first of all what we try to do to the 'unacceptable' parts of ourselves. So the third thread is about trying to help people *come together*, to lessen divisions both within, and between themselves and others. And so to my interest in restorative process, as another way of working towards just that.

Shona Cameron

My life as an educational psychologist was changed when I started exploring Nonviolent Communication (NVC) in 2003. By how much, I realised a few months later when I met Dr Marshall Rosenberg, the originator of the process, for the first time. I was shocked to discover that I had been working as a psychologist but had no idea how I was feeling. I was, at that time and from then on, able to feel the benefits of the power of empathy as explored using NVC. I began exploring self-empathy and self-compassion as ways to improve my practice as an applied psychologist in schools, as well as sharing what I had learnt in my communities.

I soon realised what NVC could bring to restorative approaches and vice versa. In my daily practice as a psychologist I am privileged to work with so many different people so I can practise putting relationships at the heart of what I do. As I work in this way during consultations, meetings and in supervision I notice more and more the powerful alchemy that occurs when people are fully heard and they are offered a space to explore. In this space much healing and creativity is co-created and plans can be made to move forward with kindness.

Pam Denicolo

Now tentatively trying to retire but happily not succeeding, I have had a lovely life full of opportunities to view the world from many different perspectives. At a personal level, these have covered most female family roles as well as being, at different life stages, a 'kept woman' while both a young mum and studying and a main bread-winner and carer on occasions in later life. Professionally I have been a both a scientist and a psychologist, a teacher and an academic researcher. In that last role and as a practising, chartered psychologist I have explored through constructivist approaches the different constructions of reality that others hold, as well as contemplating alternative ways in which I could interpret my own and others' worlds. In both roles I have had opportunities to travel the world and live and work with people from diverse backgrounds, learning not just about the infinite variety of human beings but also about how much we all have in common, hopes and fears, sorrows and joys.

Mark Vander Vennen

I am the Executive Director of the Shalem Mental Health Network, a community-based mental health organisation in Ontario, Canada. One of Shalem's key areas of service is offering restorative practice supports especially in schools, faith communities and workplaces. I have worked as a restorative facilitator for ten years and am a restorative practice trainer. I consider it a privilege to be invited into spaces of deep pain, and to there be humbled again and again by the extraordinary courage and resilience of people.

Prior to coming to Shalem, I worked for 14 years as the service co-ordinator for Children's Case Coordination Services for Northumberland County, which took me directly into all sectors of the child service delivery system, including youth justice, child welfare, children's mental health, special education, developmental services and health. I have also practised as a marriage and family therapist for over 25 years.

I am the Founding Board Chair of Wrap Canada, a non-profit dedicated to supporting WrapAround initiatives across Canada, and I serve as the co-director of its Canadian WrapAround Training Institute. I have been active in the peace movement in the U.S. and Canada for over 30 years. My wife is a professional artist, and we are proud of our three adult children. I love canoeing and fishing in Ontario's Algonquin Park, not to mention driving my car on waste vegetable oil.

Pete Wallis

I started my career as a geography teacher in a large comprehensive school in Oxford. I enjoyed many aspects of the work, particularly when I took my classes out on field trips, when I could share my love of people and places. When it went well it was the best job in the world. However, I struggled with certain classes where I wasn't able to capture young imaginations sufficiently for them to remain sitting happily in rows for an hour, and was embarrassed every time the ex-army history teacher in the classroom next door had to enter my classroom to command my students to be silent. How I wish I had known about restorative justice, or better still, worked in a restorative school.

I left teaching to manage a Quaker outreach centre with my wife, but returned briefly to a school for young people with emotional and behavioural difficulties, hoping to appease the feelings that I had failed to provide a good experience for some of my previous students. This school was even less enlightened than the comprehensive. I went on to run a relapse prevention programme in a drug agency, worked in a homeless day centre and with the Prison Phoenix Trust (a national charity which teaches yoga and meditation to prisoners) and finally joined Oxfordshire Youth Offending Service in 2000. Even though, over the past 15 years, I have facilitated hundreds of restorative meetings between young people who offend and those they have harmed, I still feel like a relative beginner, and take fresh learning and insight from every restorative encounter.

Having become concerned for young people who struggle to cope and recover following an experience of victimisation, my manager, Gordon Richardson and I set up the charity *SAFE! Support for Young People Affected by Crime* in 2011.

With my colleague Eric Fast, I designed the new restorative justice facilitator training course for the Youth Justice Board based upon Belinda's model of restorative practice, and I have recently became an assessor for the new Restorative Services Quality Mark. I draw particular inspiration from my grandfather, Corder Catchpool, who dedicated his life to peace-making. Corder learnt German when imprisoned as a conscientious objector during the First World War, and caused controversy when he moved to Germany in the 1930s and tried to engage people on opposing sides in dialogue.

I live in Oxford with my wife Marguerite, and have two daughters, Thalia who is studying psychotherapy and Freya who is completing her masters in social work.

Wendy Drewery

In my early-middle adulthood I found myself a single mother of four sons. In those days there was a huge amount of social bias against people in my situation, and I was very conscious of the injustice of this. I had a master's degree in philosophy straight from school, and when it became possible I went back to university to study developmental psychology and counselling, with the intention of becoming a school teacher when my children were old enough for me to go full time. The University of Waikato was a wonderful place to be at that time (late 1980s and early 1990s). It was a hot-bed of Māori protest, feminist poststructuralist seminars were the highlight of my week, and I did not need much encouragement to become a feminist counsellor. I was lucky enough to get a job as counsellor educator at the university, located in the Faculty of Education. In the counselling programme we were aware of the injustices wrought by a middle-class, Western psychological model of the well-functioning individual, and we embraced narrative therapy as an approach that seemed to us to respond to these critiques. We were fortunate to have a Māori student, a kuia (respected female elder) who initially challenged us, and then committed herself to supporting us ever since to bring understanding of Te Ao Māori (the Māori world) into our teaching. This sometimes uncomfortable, precious relationship with Hinekahukura Aranui has been very important in developing my understanding of the ravages and insidiousness of the colonising mentality.

In the late 1990s our group was awarded a contract to develop and trial a process for restorative justice conferencing in schools (The Restorative Practices Development Team 2003). By this time I had seen enough examples of injustice towards me and my boys, and others, by teachers to recognise that restorative practice was something that just had to happen in schools. I enjoyed the practice, but over time my mind has turned to the theoretical ideas behind, first, narrative therapy, then restorative justice. I figure that this is an appropriate thing for someone in a university to do. It is a tricky line to tread, being a theorist who is very mindful (and, dare I say it, capable) of practice: some people seem to think theory and practice are fundamentally opposed.

Now I teach a postgraduate paper on restorative practices in education, and support student research on restorative practices. I do have another 'string to my bow': I teach and am co-author of a popular New Zealand text for first-year university human development – otherwise known as developmental psychology, or lifespan development. The two lines of thought are converging as I think about the rights of all persons in this world to flourish, and the role of respect in that process.

Mo Felton

I am a training and supervising transactional analyst psychotherapist, and consultant to a local authority home for young people in the West Midlands. I became interested in restorative approaches (RA) when the staff team were required to attend some skills training and to integrate this knowledge into their practice and parenting of the teenagers in their care. While initially I was keen to point out that the approach and skills of RA were already established in the training in transactional analysis (TA), I soon realised that the two approaches had much to offer each other, and I made a subtle shift in perspective from competition to cooperation.

My background as a Relate counsellor and trainer, and a professional foster parent, provided a psychodynamic foundation, and further training in transpersonal psychology and Gestalt led me to my later qualifications in TA, which, for me, holds the bigger picture.

As a trainer and supervisor I have discovered and embraced the theories and philosophy of Deep Democracy and open forums, which link directly for me with the restorative conference, where my goal is to enable all parts of the 'system' to be heard and accounted in order for healing or integration to take place and move on. More recent influences have been in neuroscience and I constantly revisit attachment theory.

Reference

The Restorative Practices Development Team (2003) *Restorative Practices in Schools: A Resource.* Hamilton, NZ: School of Education, University of Waikato.

CHAPTER 1

Affect and Script Psychology

Restorative Practice, Biology and a Theory of Human Motivation

MARGARET THORSBORNE

Introduction

In this chapter, I will explain the links between restorative process and a theory, Affect and Script Psychology (ASP), otherwise known as Human Being Theory, based firmly in our neurobiology. My hypothesis, even taking into account cultural differences, is that *our biology is always at work.* If an approach of any sort that involves people coming together in dialogue is effective for all sides then it is because it is biologically sound and following some basic principles. Part of the success of these emotionally transformative processes can be explained by a 'central blueprint' – a set of biological rules that direct and govern our sense of emotional wellbeing. In this chapter I seek to explain, in brief, how this blueprint works and how the restorative process obeys these rules.

The encounter process I use to explain how and why restorative practice (RP) works is a restorative 'conference'. This refers to the coming together of people involved in an incident of harm to tell their stories and in doing so transforming strong negative emotions of conflict to more positive emotions of cooperation. The conference, used in order to resolve an issue, is one of several processes on a continuum ranging from formal to informal. Finally in this chapter I will outline the sequence of emotions that occurs during the stages of a restorative process, explained in terms of ASP.

Defining restorative process

This story about ASP has its origins in processes variously referred to as family group conferences, community conferences, restorative conferences, workplace conferences, or classroom conferences. Howard Zehr (2002) refers to an 'encounter' – a coming together of two or more people who are participants in the crime or incident(s) or conflict. In this chapter this means those responsible, those harmed and their respective supporters. The focus of this encounter is on:

- reaching an understanding of what happened and why
- appreciating the context in which the incident happened
- acknowledging what harm the situation/incident has caused to the community of people affected
- holding those responsible for the harm done
- encouraging acceptance by them of that responsibility
- planning to fix the damage as far as possible
- planning to solve underlying issues to minimise future offending/harmful behaviour
- seeking an opportunity for healing for all parties *including the person responsible*.

A restorative process works best when all key parties are present (but even when certain players are absent for unavoidable reasons), focusing on the issues listed above, and meeting the needs of those present, the process can still qualify as restorative.

The encounter can be achieved through a variety of processes: from conferences, circles and restorative/transformative mediation to restorative conversations. They can be a one-off or a series of processes that gradually build trust and enhance the degree of vulnerability that participants are prepared to express. Only through sincere expressions of vulnerability are people able to truly re-connect with each other after harm has been done.

The model: Affect and Script Psychology

It is helpful to explain the history of why the theory explained in this chapter has been so compelling. New Zealand was the first nation to legislate for a different approach to youth justice, in response to a call for more culturally sensitive approaches to dealing with young offenders. The legislation was intended to reflect Māori dispute resolution models (Bowen, Boyack and Calder-Watson 2012). This initiative motivated police officers in New South Wales to implement a pilot in the city of Wagga Wagga, using an adapted version of the New Zealand Family Group Conference process (Moore 2004). It was the similarities in emotional transformation observed in these processes that began a search for an explanation of why and how these processes worked (Moore with Forsythe 1995).

Criminologist John Braithwaite (1989) draws a distinction between processes of 'shaming' that stigmatised offenders and those that reintegrated them back into their communities. The restorative approach seemed to fit the reintegrative end of the continuum. Braithwaite's theory of reintegrating shaming allowed researchers such as Moore (2004) to reflect on, and analyse, what they were seeing.

Convenors ask questions in a particular sequence, encouraging participants to paint a picture of what happened and how people have been affected, before considering how the situation might be improved. As these questions are asked and answered, the group as a whole seems to move through a series of stages. Each of these stages is dominated by a small number of emotions (Moore 2004, p.77).

Moore noted that in a well-facilitated restorative process there seemed to be a common turning point in the latter half of the process when participants became more cooperative and could work constructively to develop a plan to make things better. This was not limited to the changes within an individual – more a collective event involving all participants. This point of the process, where participants' feelings and perspectives changed towards each other, and themselves, led to the use of 'transformative' to describe the effectiveness of restorative practices.

But there was interest in the notion of shame as a motivating factor in the reduction of offending rates that prompted further research into the transformative qualities of restorative processes. Later in this chapter I will provide a framework for understanding the biological underpinnings of shame and seek to show that it is, when understood and used constructively, a useful motivator for change.

Moore and McDonald (2001) recognised there was a need for an explanation about the transformational nature of the conference process which involved:

- emotional 'contagion' seen as people sharing their emotions
- the consistency of the sequence of emotions expressed and observed during a process
- the power of feelings to change the way people think
- the universality of the emotions seen and expressed in these processes (no matter the cultural diversity of participants).

The restorative process is marked by three general stages where particular emotions are expressed:

- Stories about what happened (the past) trigger very strong feelings of anger, fear, contempt (dissmell)[1] and shame directed at the individuals responsible.
- The sharing of stories of harm that have been generated (both past and present) triggers strong feelings (and their expression) of disgust, distress, shame and surprise.
- As plans for the future are negotiated, more pleasant emotions of relief and interest begin to emerge, a sign that goodwill and cooperation are likely outcomes.

The research done during this trial led to the work of Silvan S. Tomkins (1962, 1963, 1987, 1991, 1992, 2008). Tomkins described a theory about the biology of emotion and motivation drawing initially from the work of Charles Darwin (1920) who had written about the *motivational function of emotions* and how critical these were to survival. Tomkins described nine basic affects that each of us are born with, explaining that the wiring for these emotions

---

1   Dissmell, a word created by Silvan Tomkins, refers to the innate human reaction to offensive, unpleasant smells. The closest we would understand about this look would be the 'sneer' of contempt. This response is to guard against the ingestion of drink, food, gases that would be poisonous to us – rejection before sampling. As dissmell can also be present in terms of our connections/relationships with others, not just our relationship with food or drink, it is also thought to be the biological basis of racial and cultural prejudice (Kelly 2012).

is inherently 'human', and are the same at birth across races and cultures.

These affects are part of an evolved, information-gathering system that allows the brain to process the overwhelming amount of data from all our senses, and enables us to respond in a way that will enhance the likelihood of survival. This affect system is a mechanism for amplifying sensory messages about changes taking place outside and inside the body so that the brain can attend to that which is urgent, rather than flitting haphazardly from one stimulus to another against the backdrop of excessive data. Each affect is triggered when there is change in the rate and density of neural firing in the Central Nervous System (CNS). The face (and its fine blood supply, nerves and musculature) is the main site for the display of these affects – the purpose of the system is to amplify the information, and bring it to our conscious awareness (Kelly 2012).

Race, culture, family, community or religion do not determine the mechanisms that are wired into our brains, but will impact on how we respond to the information – particularly in the way we have been socialised. Our socialisation explains differences in the *expression* of these affects as emotions, not whether or not they exist. The terms affect, feeling and emotion in strict ASP terms are defined as:

- *Affect*: the biological and innate response that occurs in our CNS as a result of a change in the rate and density of neural firing as sensory information is received.

- *Feeling*: this occurs when we become aware that an affect has been triggered. We have an enormous vocabulary to describe all these feelings.[2]

- *Emotion*: a learned response (developed over time) 'scripted from our life experience with our affects, the responses of others to our affects, and our observations of the affects of those around us' (Kelly 2012, p.168). Emotion then is our biology combined with our biography.

---

2   Research into oral language competence and the extent of a person's vocabulary has shown that those who are not orally competent or do not have a wide range of words to tell what happened, or what they were thinking and feeling at the time (alexithymia), are more likely to end up in more trouble with the law (Snow and Powell 2008).

One of the characteristics of the highly evolved human brain is its capacity for cognitive functioning – memory, problem-solving, recognition of patterns, learning, analysing data and planning – and how this is intimately linked with the affect system. However we choose to behave in the moment will *be triggered by an affect* or a script.[3] Hence, *affect* is the birthplace of all motivation.

Table 1.1 shows the nine basic emotions (affects) and describes the way each motivates our behaviour.

Table 1.1: The nine basic affects and associated motivations

Affect	Motivation
Interest	Engage with person or thing
Enjoyment (relief, satisfaction, through to joy)	Affiliate with others or the task as it is such a source of feeling good
Surprise	Stop. Look. Listen. Pay attention to what comes next
Shame	Seek to restore that which was feeling good but was interrupted
Distress (sadness)	Trigger comforting behaviour in others
Anger	Attack (fight)
Fear	Run (flight)
Disgust	Reject after sampling (get rid of) – 'you make me sick'
Dissmell (contempt)	Reject before sampling (stay away) – 'I want nothing to do with you'

Adapted from Abramson and Beck 2011

---

3   'Script' refers to an affect management mechanism learned over time from experiences that repeat themselves – a kind of 'shorthand' or neural pathway that prevents similar experiences producing 'new' responses each time they occur. When people come to therapy, they are usually seeking ways to do and think about things differently. Successful counselling and therapeutic interventions can be explained in terms of ASP as the long term change in a person's scripts that have been damaging the individual and relationships (through adverse life experiences of one sort or another). Changes of culture withing organisations, families, communities, classrooms and schools can also be explained as changes to the dominating scripts that groups have adopted. Restorative processes also have the power to change a person's or group's scripts.

As can be seen in the table, two of the affects (interest and enjoyment) are positive and constitute the biology of goodwill, respect, trust, affection, attachment, collaboration and cooperation. One affect, (surprise), is neutral and serves the purpose of 'clearing the decks' in order to pay attention to what might come next. The remainder are affects that are experienced as negative or punishing, and are triggered in the immediate wake of an incident experienced as negative or harmful, and beyond the event, via memory. These emotions that feel so bad are what we experience and speak about as *emotional harm*. While they feel awful, it is important to remember that they are simply information about the state of our connections to each other, and sometimes our relationship with our own 'better' or inner selves. What we make of this information and what we do about it is usually determined by how we have been socialised and thus the behaviours, or 'scripts' as they are known, that we have developed. The emotional competencies we might have developed in order to manage these very difficult feelings also influence our responses. Kelly (2014, p.28) states 'that affect motivates everything human beings do and think'.

The affect of shame

Most of us understand the word 'shame' usually in the sense of being ashamed of something we have done, or a body part we don't like, or a result in an exam that was disappointing. Sometimes we tell others 'they should be ashamed of themselves' when they have done something we think is wrong, bad or mean. Building on the writing of Tomkins (Vol ii and iv, 1962, 1963, 1991 and 1992) and Nathanson (1992), Kelly (2012) urges us to re-think the meaning of the word from a *biological* perspective. Shame, then, in ASP terms, is defined as a 'recently' evolved (in evolutionary terms) mechanism (affect) that lets us know when something that has been good has been interrupted – when an impediment of some sort has blocked our positive affects of interest and/or enjoyment. In its most intense expression, shame becomes visible with a dropped head and loss of eye contact with others and possibly a blush. What cannot be seen, but is certainly felt, is a state of cognitive shock (Nathanson 1992), causing an inability to think clearly or express oneself, in other words feeling 'flustered'.

Shame can be triggered in many different circumstances on a daily basis by events both major and minor. The more intense the positive feelings that have been interrupted, the more intense the signal of shame as the affect system amplifies in order for us to 'mind' what's happening. Words we use to describe the fact that shame has been triggered and that we have become aware of it include: frustrated, confused, embarrassed, humiliated, uncomfortable, rejected, disrespected, diminished, remorseful, powerless, hurt, inadequate, foolish, isolated, helpless, worthless, wounded, awkward, shy, excluded, patronised, insulted.

The emotional competence needed to recognise the motivational nature of shame is rare. We are socialised primarily in our families and cultures of origin and many of us have learnt scripts that help reduce the difficult feelings of shame without using them as a spur to restore and reconnect. These behaviours can be illustrated in a diagram called the Compass of Shame first developed by Nathanson (1992). See Figure 1.1.

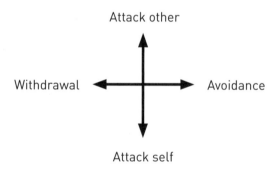

Figure 1.1: Scripted behaviours for managing the feelings triggered by shame affect
Adapted from Nathanson 1992

Each pole of the Compass represents a *family* of behaviours we can employ in order to manage these punishing feelings. In the extreme, these scripts are maladaptive. In short summary (Kelly 2012; Kelly 2014; Nathanson 1992), the four poles are:

- *Withdrawal*: shutting down, pulling away from others, solo activities, silence, sexual withdrawal, agoraphobia.

- *Avoidance*: alcoholism and other addictions such as gambling, workaholicism, promiscuity and infidelity, chronic lying, over-intellectualisation, obsessive accumulation of wealth and property, refusal to accept responsibility.

> (Both withdrawal and avoidance are families of behaviours where one *runs away from* the feeling, putting distance between self and self, and self and other, as one retreats.)

• *Attack self:* self-recrimination, sexual masochism, self-mutilation and suicide.

• *Attack other:* angry put-downs, abusive recrimination and blaming others, competitiveness and jealousy, violence, sarcasm, hatred, sadism and murder.

> (Both forms of attack behaviours are how we *fight the feeling*, rather than running away from it – and both of these do not allow reconnection with others.)

In summary, these behaviours interfere with connection and reconnection, isolating people from self, family, friends and community (Kelly 2007). Imperative then that a process such as the restorative conference can make it possible to work through such feelings, rather than ignoring or trying to minimise them.

Anger and shame

It is worth mentioning briefly here the relationship between anger and shame. When anger is triggered due to overwhelming negative affect of one sort or another, the physiological response in the body includes the pumping of adrenaline preparing us for fight or flight. This allows us to feel much more powerful than the feelings associated with shame, fear and distress. It is thought that the manifestation of anger scripts might be a result of trying to overcome these very difficult moments in ways that allow a person to feel less helpless. If this is indeed the case, then anger is a *mask* for the other punishing affects. In a restorative process the question 'What's been the worst of it for you?' is designed to uncover the extreme feelings of vulnerability that lie below the mask of anger. It is a very useful question for those who cannot seem to move past strong expressions of anger, that, if continued, push people away. Anger blocks emotional connection while expression of the vulnerable feelings beneath the anger enhances it (Kelly 2007).

Shame and guilt

The words shame and guilt are often used interchangeably but in fact they are experienced differently. The distinction lies in whether the feelings about self are internalised into an image of who we are as being fixed and unchangeable ('I have done a *bad thing*, so I am a *bad person*) versus a view of self that includes the possibility of change – separating the deed from the doer. (I have done *a bad thing* to others – what can I do to *change* this?). Whereas the latter might be motivated to repair the harm they have done, the shame-prone person (and so less resilient around moments of shame) may well remain deeply rooted in the scripts described in Figure 1.1. It is also likely that in a restorative process the person responsible for the harm to others is likely to feel both shame and guilt. As the process unfolds, redemption in the eyes of both self and others (developed through explanation, empathy and compassion for each other as stories of harm are told) becomes possible through acknowledgement of responsibility, apology and planning to fix the problem.

From the perspective of those harmed by crime and wrongdoing, it is easy to interpret their feelings and behaviours through the lens of the four poles of the Compass of Shame, since crime triggers such deep shame. Victims of family violence may well default to *withdrawal, avoidance* and *attack self* as they suffer the deep shame (along with fear, distress and anger) of being violated.

Reflecting on the crime and wrongdoing itself and the behaviours that led the person responsible to do what they did, it is possible to understand that it could be their *own shame* that triggered their harmful behaviours. For example, feelings of helplessness and powerlessness might trigger '*attack other*' behaviour in the case of family violence referred to above. Far from *shaming* wrongdoers, the restorative process assists the biological need of *everyone involved* to express these very punishing feelings, to explain how and why it happened, to tell their stories of harm done, to express regret and remorse. This needs to be done in order to *reduce* the shame, distress, fear and anger, disgust and contempt. Then they can move towards reconnection, cooperation and goodwill as interest, relief and hope are triggered as the group plans for the future. As Moore and Abramson (2002) noted, there is a moment of collective vulnerability obvious in the process where everyone's heads are dropped to avoid eye contact with each other.

'This moment is the fulcrum of the process, the point at which the general tone is poised to shift from negative to positive' (p.135), and it is only when interest, relief and enjoyment are triggered that participants lift their heads and look at each other. This is the visible evidence of the power of the transformative nature within the restorative process.

The central blueprint

The affect system directs our attention to what is going on around and in us. Anything that triggers the positive affects of interest and enjoyment will be inherently rewarding, and anything that triggers the negative affects of shame, distress, anger, fear, disgust and dissmell will be inherently punishing. Working in conjunction with memory and analysing systems in the brain, rules about how to manage the balance between positive and negative are explained in a simple framework called the 'central blueprint', designed to enhance our survival both as individuals and within the species. The simple principles (Tomkins 1962) are:

- positive affect should be maximised
- negative affect should be minimised
- affect inhibition should be minimised (in other words, talk things through, do not let these feelings back up)
- the power to maximise positive affect, to minimise negative affect and to minimise the inhibition of affect should be maximised.

When these central blueprint rules are adapted to describe our relationships with others and indeed the restorative process itself, they look like this:

- We should come together to share and maximize positive feelings.
- We should come together to share and minimize negative feelings.
- We should come together to express our feelings in order to maximize our ability to do the first and second bullet points.

- ✦ We should encourage and share the ability and power to do the above three things.

(George 2014, p.213)

Kelly writes:

> Wellbeing results from a life lived with numbers 1–3 as balanced as circumstances permit. When that is the case, number 4 progressively generates more and more advanced skills to carry out 1–3. Whereas, some physical illnesses or negative life events such as abuse can create distortions in central blueprint balance, leading to unhealthy behaviours. For instance, a chronically abused person might resort to a life dedicated solely to maximizing positive affect through addictive behaviours without regard for the consequences that lead to negative affect. Or someone who has had an experience that harmed them deeply might turn solely to behaviours dedicated to minimizing negative affect – perhaps by withdrawing from all social contact – thereby limiting what they used to do maximize positive affect and have fun. […] effective restorative practices restore the ability of individuals and communities to live and function in emotionally balanced ways consistent with the biological directives of the Central Blueprint. (Kelly and Thorsborne 2014, p.30)

To illustrate this regaining of balance between positive and negative: A participant of a victim-offender conference[4] says, of meeting with the person responsible for the death of his daughter ten years earlier, that having been given the chance to tell the perpetrator how the incident had affected him and his family, he felt later like a new person, that a cloud had been taken away. There is a shift away from the relentless negative affect triggered by the crime and a return to a life that can be lived more positively – when the balance described in the central blueprint is achieved. And this only becomes possible with dialogue with the person responsible, and others, within a careful process such as a restorative encounter, as outlined by to the central blueprint above.

---

4   These comments are contained in a testimonial sheet supplied to victims of crime who are considering participation in a restorative conference, by the NSW (Australia) Government, Corrective Services, Restorative Justice Unit.

Affective resonance and the phenomenon of contagion

Because human beings are social animals who do best when we are living in right, robust and healthy relationships with each other, the human brain is exquisitely attuned, not only to our own affective/ feeling state, but also, with maturity, to the affective state of others. We must be able to 'read' the other, and to do that, we 'see' affect on the other's face and in their other body language. Display of affect on the face is a physiological response as a result of a change in neural firing – and as a result of this, the pattern of neural firing in our own brain when we see the face of other changes. This explains why when we are around angry people it becomes increasingly easy to become angry, when we see distress in others it distresses us too, and when we are around people who are terrified we become afraid. We call this *contagion* or affective resonance. What is happening in terms of biology is that *each* affect causes facial and other bodily responses that reflect that affect and become sensory triggers for that same affect in others. This is the biological basis for empathy and compassion. In a restorative intervention, the development of empathy for each other in the group is what allows us to reach a shared understanding of the harm done to each and every one in the room.

Affect and the restorative process

The process can be broken into three distinct phases: preparation, facilitation of the process, and follow-up, shown best as a representation of three distinct keystones[5] which are held together by their shape (Jansen and Matla 2011). See Figure 1.2.

---

5   A keystone is the wedge-shaped stone piece at the apex of a masonry vault or arch, which is the final piece placed during construction and locks all the stones into position, allowing the arch to bear weight: http://en.wikipedia.org/wiki/ Keystone_%28architecture%29.

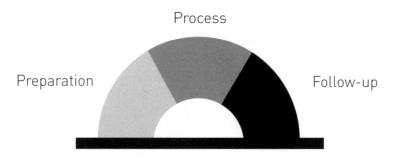

Figure 1.2: Three stages of restorative encounter: the Restorative Keystones
Adapted from Jansen and Matla 2011

The following is an outline of each of these phases and the flow of affect that occurs in each.

Preparation

There are two primary goals of preparation. The first is to brief each participant so they understand what is likely to happen. This will help align them to the structure and purpose of the process, to minimise anxiety (fear and shame) about the process and to prepare them for the inevitable mixture of fluctuating emotions during the process. For example, for those harmed, it pays to tell them that the early part of a restorative process might be hard for them, as they listen to the person responsible describe and explain their actions. While this can be very painful it does allow some relief from strong negative feelings about what happened as they gain perspective.

The second goal is to develop trust between the facilitator and each participant. This is achieved through a number of channels. First, the facilitator listens keenly and respectfully to the story – showing interest in each participant. As a result the participant experiences relief (a mild version of the affect of enjoyment). The interest shown by the facilitator is returned by the participant becoming interested in the facilitator as a person, and also their interest in the process, despite possible misgivings. Again, this is our affect system at work, even in this first stage of the process. If the facilitator is experienced as trustworthy and competent then this increases trust in the process.

Facilitation

Any truly restorative encounter should start with an introduction of participants to each other, some ground rules and a reminder about the purpose of the process and what it hopes to achieve. In some cultures, facilitators use song and/or prayer to settle people and help them settle their very strong feelings as they wait for the process to get underway. I have represented the stages of a restorative conference (formal or informal) in the table on the next page.

Table 1.2: Restorative process stages

Restorative process stages	Affects (and feelings) triggered and expressed
Introduction: Introductions, ground rules, clarifying purpose of process.	With adequate preparation this stage should hold no *surprise*; the calmness of the facilitator is contagious (*affective resonance*); *interest* in what happens next will be present, despite very strong negative feelings of *shame, distress, anger, fear and dissmell (contempt)*.
Telling the story of what happened: Exploring facts and the 'story behind the story', the 'what' and the 'why'. This stage is about the *past*.	At this point, intense almost overwhelming feelings of *shame, distress, anger, fear and dissmell (contempt)* are likely for some participants. However, the shared stories will gradually trigger *interest*. New perspectives about the incident and the person responsible may bring *surprise* and some degree of *relief* as people move away from *shame* default behaviours such as *attack self*.
	First signs of empathy and understanding from the person responsible, a show of *interest* in those harmed, can trigger some *relief from the distress and shame* of being harmed.
	Sensing the *interest* by others in their story the person responsible will also experience some *relief* that comes with being understood and respected.

Exploring the harm: Sharing how people have been affected, and what has been the worst thing. This stage is about the *past* and the *present*.	The opportunity to 'unload' strong feelings associated with emotional harm (*distress, fear, anger, disgust, dismell and shame*) provides tremendous *relief* for each person, and triggers compassion and empathy in others (affective resonance), as well as *surprise* as they hear about the harm to others. This stage is usually marked by a moment of collective vulnerability, (it's not just 'me', who feels this way). The impact of these stories will trigger a range of affects in those responsible: *interest* in these stories of harm, *shame* in their role in these harms – and possible 'compass of shame' behaviours (Nathanson 1992), *distress, self disgust,* possibly *fear* of exclusion from their community of care. In summary, it is the *mutualisation of affect* – ie being able to talk freely about the issues.
Acknowledgement of harm caused (and possibly) apology:	Genuine apology is motivated by *shame, guilt* and the need to restore 'other' and 'self'. Apology need not mean saying 'sorry' – acknowledging the harm caused can suffice. This can provide those affected with the sense of *relief* at finally being understood. Acknowledgement of harm caused can also come from others understanding the role they may have played. This part of the process is characterised by a sense of *collective shame/vulnerability* and the *contagion of affect* in others.

cont.

Restorative process stages	Affects (and feelings) triggered and expressed

Developing a plan: focusing on the *future*.
All participants contribute ideas about how to:
 	
  ♦ repair the harm
 	
  ♦ prevent further harm
 	
  ♦ support participants in order to address identified needs
 	
  ♦ plan for follow-up with the agreement and check on participants' wellbeing.
	This stage is characterised by displays of *interest* in each other and in the plan. Empowerment of the person harmed is achieved by direct questioning about how their needs might be met. This is a powerful trigger for *interest* and *relief* as the group shows their care for them. The democratic and inclusive approach to problem-solving is another source of *interest and relief*, sometimes bordering on actual enjoyment. As plans are made for follow-up and responsibilities for various parts of the plan are delegated, hope and optimism (*both interest and enjoyment*) continue to be triggered.

Conference close: Final comments by everyone; followed by refreshments while the plan is being written up.	This provides a final opportunity to mutualise positive affects of *interest and enjoyment* – sometimes expressed as gratitude for the process, and comments which may mean that healing is underway. The provision of food ('breaking bread with the enemy') draws people together for longer and in a much less formal way that keeps the intensity of negative affect low – building and re-building connections between participants and triggering more feelings of goodwill and cooperation.

Follow-up

There are two areas that need attention in the wake of a restorative process. The first is an evaluation of whether or not the process was experienced as fair, whether people felt sufficiently heard and understood, whether the facilitation was experienced as competent, and whether the plan was considered appropriate. In other words, did the process satisfy all participants' needs? This evaluation can be done by electronic or paper survey, or a phone call. The willingness by the facilitator to accept feedback about the process and its facilitation continues to trigger the affects of interest and enjoyment in participants.

The second part of the follow-up relates to whether or not there has been compliance with all parts of the agreement, that is, whether or not people have kept their promises. If agreements are breached, this will trigger shame, anger, distress, fear and disgust in those with the greatest investment in the plan, negating the positive feelings of goodwill and cooperation generated in the process. In my experience, sloppy preparation and inadequate follow-up destroy the possibilities of healing that good process provides.

Conclusion

I have been very conscious of the weight of responsibility as an author to paint a simple picture here of the biological underpinnings that explain why restorative practice works. I urge you to read further in order to deepen your understanding of our biology and how it explains why healthy positive relationships are so critical to our survival. I have found that my own understanding has come in layers over many years, as I have persisted in my immersion of the ASP theory and how it links not only to my own restorative practice and the teaching of it, but more widely to my relationships with my own self and others. If we all understood what it takes to connect and reconnect in the face of impediments to relationships, of crime and wrongdoing, then maybe we might be able to spend our energies at developing peace with each other. For me it has been truly a Human Being Theory.

I would like to conclude with a quote from Vick Kelly, my co-editor in Kelly and Thorsborne (2014):

Restorative interventions work because human beings *care*. Amongst other things: people care about what others feel and think about them; they care that others have been harmed and are in need of repair; they care that they may have harmed others and don't know how to fix it; they care that others care for them; they care if others act as if they don't care for them; and they sometimes care to act as if they don't care because they have been harmed. Furthermore, all human behaviour is motivated by what we care about. (Kelly and Thorsborne 2014, p.26)

References

Bowen, H., Boyack, J. and Calder-Watson, J. (2012) 'Recent Developments within Restorative Justice in Aotearoa/New Zealand.' In J. Bolitho, J. Bruce and G. Mason (eds) *Restorative Justice Adults and Emerging Practice.* Sydney: Sydney Institute of Criminology Monograph Series.

Braithwaite, J. (1989) *Crime, Shame and Reintegration.* Cambridge: Cambridge University Press.

Darwin, C. (1920) *The Expression of the Emotions in Man and Animals.* New York, NY: Appleton-Century-Crofts.

George, G. (2014) 'Affect and Emotion in a Restorative School.' In V. Kelly, and M. Thorsborne (eds) *The Psychology of Emotion in Restorative Practice: How Affect Script Psychology Explains How and Why Restorative Practice Works.* London: Jessica Kingsley Publishers.

Jansen, G. and Matla, R. (2011) 'Restorative Practice in Action.' In V. Margraine and A. Macfarlane (eds) *Responsive Pedagogy: Engaging Restoratively with Challenging Behaviour.* Wellington, NZ: NCER.

Kelly, V. (2007) Workshop: *Existential Issues: Who am I? How did I get here? Where am I going?* Presented at Inaugural Restorative Practices International Conference: Best Practice in Restorative Justice – Transformational Change. Twin Waters, Australia.

Kelly, V. (2012) *The art of Intimacy and the Hidden Challenge of Shame.* Maine, USA: Maine Authors Publishing.

Kelly, V. (2014) 'Caring, Restorative Practice and the Biology of Emotion.' In V. Kelly and M. Thorsborne (eds) *The Psychology of Emotion in Restorative Practice: How Affect Script Psychology Explains How and Why Restorative Practice Works.* London: Jessica Kingsley Publishers.

Kelly, V. and Thorsborne, M. (eds)(2014) *The Psychology of Emotion in Restorative Practice: How Affect Script Psychology Explains How and Why Restorative Practice Works.* London: Jessica Kingsley Publishers.

Moore, D. (2004) 'Managing social conflict: The evolution of a practical theory.' *Journal of Sociology and Social Welfare XXXI,* 1, 77.

Moore, D. and Abramson, L. (2002) 'The Psychology of Community Conferencing.' In J. Perry (ed) *Restorative Justice: Repairing Communities through Restorative Justice.* Maryland: American Correctional Association.

Moore, D. with Forsythe, L. (1995) *A New Approach to Juvenile Justice: An Evaluation of Family Conferencing in Wagga Wagga.* Report compiled for the Criminology Research Council. Available at www.criminologyresearchcouncil.gov.au/moore/chapter6.pdf, downloaded on 21st May 2015.

Moore, D. and McDonald, J. (2001) 'Community Conferencing as a Special Case of Conflict Transformation.' In J. Braithwaite and V. Strang (eds) *Restorative Justice and Civil Society.* Cambridge: Cambridge University Press.

Nathanson, D. (1992) *Shame and Pride: Affect, Sex, and the Birth of the Self.* New York, NY: W.W. Norton and Company.

Snow, P. C. and Powell, M. B. (2008) Oral Language Competence, Social Skills, and High-risk Boys: What are Juvenile Offenders Trying to Tell Us? *Children and Society 22,* 16–28.

Tomkins, S. S. (1962) *Affect/Imagery/Consciousness, 1: The Positive Affects.* New York, NY: Springer

Tomkins, S. S. (1963) *Affect/Imagery/Consciousness, 2: The Negative Affects.* New York, NY: Springer.

Tomkins, S. S. (1987) 'Script Theory.' In J. Aronoff, A. I. Rabin, and R. A. Zucker (eds) *The Emergence of Personality.* New York, NY: Springer.

Tomkins, S. S. (1991) *Affect/Imagery/Consciousness, 3: The Negative Affects – Anger and Fear.* New York, NY: Springer.

Tomkins, S. S. (1992) *Affect/Imagery/Consciousness, 4: Cognition – Duplication and Transmission of Information.* New York, NY: Springer.

Tomkins, S. (2008) *Affect, Imagery, Consciousness: The Complete Edition.* New York, NY: Springer.

Zehr, H. (2002) *The Little Book of Restorative Justice.* Intercourse, PA: Good Books.

CHAPTER 2

Attribution Theory

JULIET STARBUCK

Introduction

The following chapter outlines a theory of restorative justice conferencing that will contribute to improved practice and more psychologically focused research. Causal attribution theory, and in particular Weiner's theory of social motivation, justice and the moral emotions (2006), is drawn upon to explain what is going on in a restorative conference. Weiner proposes a staged model of motivation. This is mapped against the stages of a restorative conference as outlined in Bazemore and Schiff (2005) so that the psychological changes that stakeholders in a restorative conference go through can be better understood. The value of each stage of the conference is, therefore, emphasised.

The theory

Causal attribution theory is a psychological theory that deals with how we use information to explain the causes of events. Weiner (2006) proposed an attribution theory of interpersonal or social motivation that explains behaviours such as help-giving, aggression, achievement evaluation, and compliance to commit a transgression. This builds on his earlier studies (Weiner 1985) and in particular his interest in the explanations people give for success or failure on achievement tasks. The theory has been applied in various fields including sport, politics, education and advertising. I am proposing that this theory can also help to explain what is going on in a restorative encounter.

What is causal attribution theory?

Attribution theory is a cognitive theory of motivation. The theory states that humans are conscious, rational decision makers. The theory is based on two fundamental assumptions, the first of which is that people are motivated to understand and master their environment and themselves. That is to say, they try to make their environment predictable and controllable. The second assumption is that individuals are naïve scientists, who try to understand the causal determinants of their own behaviour and the behaviour of others.

A typical example of the theory in use is when sports players give explanations for their wins and losses. Attributions are made to effort or skill, to the behaviour of the opponents and the state of the pitch or equipment. A fundamental part of attribution theory introduced here is bias. Attributions to internal attributes such as effort and skills are more likely following a victory, whereas a loss is more likely to be attributed to problems with the pitch or the referee's decisions.

Social motivation, justice and the moral emotions

Weiner's theory of interpersonal motivation is an attribution theory that distinguishes between the roles of thinking and feeling in determining action. The theory can explain the process individuals go through before giving help to a person who is homeless, attacking someone who has 'looked at them in the wrong way' or punishing them because they've committed a crime, for example. The theory includes an assumption that the motivation process following an interaction moves *from* an understanding about cause and perceptions of intent *through to* inferences about personal responsibility and emotions of anger and sympathy *leading to* social reactions that might include help-giving, reprimand, aggression and retaliation.

Weiner's attribution approach to motivation and social justice shares the assumption with the criminal justice system that we are responsible for the choices we make, and that these choices lead to actions we undertake freely. Broadly speaking he proposes that:

- actions are determined by the causes of events

- causes can be grouped on the basis of having three fundamental properties – locus, controllability and stability

- the causal assessment and inferences of intent produce responsibility inferences about the person

- these cognitive appraisals of personal responsibility are linked to feelings of anger and sympathy

- beliefs about responsibility and associated feelings are significant determinants of aggression, help-giving, and so forth

- moral beliefs are a key part of this theory of social motivation and justice.

Weiner's theory is based on the assumption that the 'person is a judge' (2006, p.4). He suggests that people will interpret evidence and make their own minds up. Perceptions of intent and judgements about responsibility affect the decision and any subsequent actions made.

Responsibility is the cornerstone of this theory. It is also a cornerstone of restorative justice theory. Weiner asks whether there's a similarity between *control*, a causal property generally accepted by attribution theorists, and perceptions of *intent*. He suggests that control and intent are not equivalent but that they share a property – they are both antecedents of personal responsibility. He writes:

> the essence of responsibility is moral accountability, whether through an act of omission or commission. A person must answer to others regarding an outcome, particularly when that outcome is aversive. (Weiner 2006, p.32)

This could also describe restorative justice. Weiner suggests that intentionality is a crucial element regarding perceptions of responsibility – a person is held more responsible if they intended to do something rather than if they did something by accident. He proposes that a judgement of responsibility with intent in relation to a negative event, for example an aggressive act, will produce an anti-social behavioural reaction. This might include a reprimand, a condemnation or retaliation. However, if the negative event occurs but the instigator is not thought to be responsible, a pro-social reaction will occur. This might involve help-giving. There will be no aggressive retaliation. Indeed, Weiner suggests that the theory addresses how we 'psychologically represent sin versus sickness and the motivation process to which these construals are linked' (2006, p.33).

Interestingly, although Weiner believes that most people will react angrily if another person causes them harm on purpose, he notes that people can be talked out of feeling angry. He suggests that this indicates the close connection between feelings of anger and thoughts about the event. Restorative justice questioning specifically asks the wrongdoer and victim to describe their thoughts about an event and then their feelings about an event. Weiner also invites the reader to consider what thoughts promote certain emotions. He suggests that answering these questions will show that inferences of personal responsibility, controllability and intentionality during 'situations of transgression' make people angry.

A typical example of wrongdoing that the theory could address is a serious foul on an opponent in football. If the wrongdoer were known to dislike the opponent, if they were usually a skilful defender, and if they didn't go over and check if their opponent was OK, then they would probably receive a harsh punishment because they would be deemed to be responsible. They would be thought to have done it on purpose, since they did not show remorse. However, they would receive a less harsh punishment if they were a clumsy forward trying to make a match-saving tackle when no team mate was around to help, and who looked distraught as they saw their opponent carried off the football pitch, even if the outcome for the opponent was the same. They would be thought to have done it by accident – it wasn't really their fault because they were unskilled at defending, and showed remorse.

Weiner's model can be represented as follows:

Aggressive act of another → (*is perceived as*) intentional → (*is thought to be*) responsible → (*resulting in feelings of*) anger → (*and actions of*) reprimand/retaliation.

We could say that most people watching the football game would reach a similar conclusion, with some variation depending on which team you supported (a typical bias). But there are some occasions when individuals or groups of individuals will interpret the same events differently. Understanding these differences helps us to understand why people behave as they do and, importantly, helps us to intervene with those whose perceptions lead to difficult and anti-social behaviours.

Weiner offers an example in which aggressive children perceive that others provoke them on purpose and so they are justified in retaliating. That is to say, they perceive the act of the other as aggressive and intentional. In an early experiment, Dodge (1980) showed that 'aggressive' children retaliated against clearly hostile behaviours, as did 'non-aggressive' children, and they behaved with restraint following an accidental behaviour. However, when the cause of the behaviour was ambiguous the aggressive children reacted with hostility, whereas the non-aggressive children did not. This, and other research, shows an intent–retaliation linkage. Later, Dodge and Crick (1990) showed that aggressive adolescents also have 'an attribution bias to infer hostile intent following a peer-instigated negative event' (p.180).

Graham and Hudley (1994) argue that aggressive and non-aggressive children differ in their attributions in terms of how accessible the constructs stored in their memory are. They suggest that aggressive children are more likely to infer intentionality because their own life experiences include more instances of giving and receiving blame. They also suggest that aggressive young people who have been both victims and perpetrators of anti-social behaviour might be quick to blame. This response might indeed have become a coping strategy and will become part of the way the young person sees the world. They will then react in this way even when the social situation makes it inappropriate.

Encouragingly, attributions can be altered. For example, Hudley *et al.* (1998) developed an attribution-retraining programme called the BrainPower Programme. This programme was introduced in four elementary schools in the U.S. Significant reduction in aggressive behaviour was demonstrated, and a causal relationship between attributions made and aggression was suggested.

Wrongdoers can also influence the judgements made against them by their subsequent behaviour; if the wrongdoer confesses to their wrongdoing then the consequences will be less severe. Weiner (2006) believes that confessing and showing remorse both help to repair an individual's social identity. This is because 'the confessor asserts guilt but remains a moral person' (Weiner 2006, p.119). If there is no confession or remorse it might be concluded that the act was due to some sort of enduring personality trait. If there is a confession (or the football player puts up his hand after a bad tackle and says sorry), then the link between the act and attribution to some enduring personality characteristic is broken and the wrongdoer may not be thought of as 'all bad'. Furthermore, the wrongdoer should feel more positive about themselves, perhaps less ashamed. Indeed, Weiner describes confession as a 'conversational move' that aims to improve interpersonal relationships. He points to experimental and observational evidence to show that confessions work. That is, they result in greater positive moral impressions, reduced feelings of anger, increased feelings of sympathy, decreased belief that the person will offend again, and forgiveness. This is, it will be noted, an ambition of restorative practices.

What is a restorative encounter?

For me, restorative justice (RJ) is a value-based approach to responding to wrongdoing and conflict. It focuses on the person harmed, the person causing the harm, and the affected community. It transforms wrongdoing by healing the harm caused, particularly to relationships. Restorative justice can be seen in various practices including in restorative conversations and discussions (Hopkins 2004). Whatever the approach used, key factors should be present. These factors are, arguably, most visible in a restorative conference – I regard the conference as a 'microcosm of restorative justice'. The conference (a meeting that follows a structured format) has the following five elements or stages, each of which should be present to a greater or lesser extent in any restorative encounter:

- *Introducing and creating a safe place*, which aims to clarify the purpose of the meeting, establishes the ground rules and creates an atmosphere where the stakeholders feel safe.

- *Storytelling*, which allows the group to take 'collective inventory' of the harm caused by the offence or wrongdoing; gives the wrongdoer the opportunity to give an account of his or her behaviour and acknowledge some acceptable degree of responsibility; and gives the person harmed and his or her supporters the opportunity to describe the impact that the incident has had on their lives.

- *Mutual acknowledgement by key players of each others' account*, which has as its aims to create a transition between the storytelling and the agreement stages; to clarify the statement of harm; to give the wrongdoer an opportunity to apologise and indicate remorse; to allow community members to elaborate on the harm caused; to create a space in which those harmed may acknowledge the wrongdoer's honesty or question their sincerity. (At this stage there may be some shift in the relationship between wrongdoer and harmed.)

- *Agreement*, a stage that needs to be preceded by the facilitator having a sense of the harm caused and of the needs of the harmed and wrongdoer, and also the acceptance of responsibility. This stage has as its aims the reaching of an agreement where a plan is made that defines specific roles for stakeholders in repairing harm.

- *Celebration*, the final stage, which has as its aim to provide an informal chance for participants to build relationships by sharing refreshments.

(Bazemore and Schiff 2005, p.147)

How do causal attribution theory and Weiner's motivation process inform how to prepare for and facilitate a restorative encounter?

Weiner (2006) proposes that we go through a process from understanding the causes and perceptions of intent of an event (or act of another) to a social response such as retaliation or help-giving. It is argued that the phases of a restorative conference described above facilitate a repeat of this process in a safe and controlled environment. Stakeholders revisit the motivation process so that perceptions of intent and degrees of responsibility can be discussed and understood. This affects subsequent feelings and behaviour. Most important, the restorative process gives the wrongdoer the opportunity to 'confess' and to show remorse. This severs the 'act to disposition' link. It changes the nature of the judgement that is made against them.

How does each phase of the restorative conference contribute to the stakeholders' pathway through Weiner's motivation process?

As previously stated, Weiner's motivational process moves from an understanding about cause and perceptions of intent to inferences of personal responsibility. From this the process allows for emotions of anger and sympathy and moves to social reactions which might include help-giving, reprimand, aggression and retaliation.

He states that a confession has a number of components:

- acceptance of responsibility for the action

- expression of an associated emotion such as shame

- indication of remorse or regret

- an offer of compensation or reparation

- the promise not to engage in such actions in the future.

How the phases or stages of the conference support the attribution process and how they give the wrongdoer the opportunity to confess is described briefly below.

Introducing and creating a safe place

An atmosphere of safety will encourage honesty. This will make it possible for the wrongdoer to confess, a fundamental part of Weiner's theory. During the introduction to the conference the facilitator emphasises that the focus is not on the intrinsic worth of the wrongdoer as a 'good' or a 'bad' person but on the impact of their behaviour and on how things can be put right. This severs the 'act to disposition' link. The wrongdoer will effectively separate their 'bad' behaviour from themselves as a person. The wrongdoer is given the opportunity to repair their social identity.

Storytelling

Weiner's theory is based on the idea that the 'person is a judge' (2006, p.4). He suggests that people will 'interpret evidence and reach a decision regarding an alleged transgression of another' (2006, p.4). During storytelling the evidence is revisited. The motivational process is, therefore, revisited. An understanding about the causes and intentions of events can be established. Inferences of responsibility can be revisited and feelings of anger, and possibly sympathy, can be felt.

The wrongdoer will have the opportunity to confess. They'll have the opportunity to accept responsibility for their actions. It is important, therefore, that the wrongdoer tells their story first. This allows the harmed to hear that responsibility is accepted. It lessens the likelihood that the wrongdoer will be defensive and make excuses.

Mutual harmed/wrongdoer acknowledgement

This phase is an opportunity for the wrongdoer to show remorse and to apologise. This reaction is made more likely because the harmed has an opportunity to expand on the pain and upset that was caused. The harmed also has the opportunity to probe the wrongdoer to ensure themselves of the sincerity of the wrongdoer's responses.

Agreement

This phase allows for the confirmation of acceptance of responsibility. An offer of compensation or repair can be made. New ideas and constructs can be introduced as alternative thoughts and behaviours should future incidents arise. Reaching an agreement together symbolises a shift in the social relations between parties and is an indication to the wrongdoer that they are not regarded as a 'bad' person.

Celebration

This phase offers the stakeholders the opportunity to demonstrate a shift in their relationship and to build confidence in their view of the other as a reasonable person.

How does causal attribution theory explain what is occurring in a restorative conference?

An empirical study of two restorative justice conferences examined five propositions[1] to try and explain what is happening before, during and after a conference from a psychological perspective (Starbuck 2008). Multiple sources of evidence were used, including pre- and post-conference interviews with all the participants, the use of 'before' and 'after' measures, and observation to demonstrate whether the predictions were correct and, therefore, whether causal attribution theory can explain what is happening in a restorative conference.

In the first restorative conference it was alleged that a Year 8 (about 13 years old) boy approached a Year 10 boy (about 15 years old) in the playground one lunchtime and punched him repeatedly in the face. This was reported to the school by witnesses. The older boy was excluded for five days. The school's police community support officer was asked to investigate the incident. The case was also passed to a police officer responsible for restorative interventions in that school to assess whether it would be appropriate to run a restorative conference. In the second restorative conference it was alleged that R., a Year 9 girl (about 14 years old), had posted malicious and threatening comments about V., another Year 9 girl, in an internet chat room called Bebo, and that this was the most serious of a number of attacks that had been made against V. by R.

In both of these restorative conferences the police officer responsible for restorative justice in the school spoke to all parties and decided that it was appropriate to proceed on the basis of the following criteria:

◆ a specific (aggressive) act had occurred between two members of the school community

◆ a wrongdoer had been identified

◆ the wrongdoer had acknowledged some degree of responsibility and was willing to take part in the conference

◆ the harmed was willing to take part in the conference.

---

1   Propositions are predictions based on theory, the theory states what 'should' happen.

Let's now look at the five propositions and show how what's going on in a conference can be explained by causal attribution theory.

Proposition 1

> The harmed (and their supporters) will describe feelings of anger and thoughts of reprimand, and/or other negative reactions, following an initial causal act against them. (Starbuck 2008, p.99)

This prediction is made because Weiner's theory tells us that the motivation process following a causal event (in these examples an aggressive act) develops from thinking to feeling to action or from 'causal understanding and perceptions of intent to inferences about personal responsibility, and then to emotions of anger and sympathy which generate social reactions involving reprimand, help-giving, aggression…' (Weiner 2006, p.38). He also states that 'cognitive appraisals of personal responsibility are linked with anger and sympathy' (p.42), and that responsibility is distinct from intention (p.32). These thoughts and feelings are elicited during a pre-conference preparatory interview using the restorative questions:

'What were you thinking?' and 'What were you feeling?'

They are revisited during the storytelling phase of the restorative conference.

It is critical that the restorative intervention can effect positive change for all parties involved in a conflict. It is important, therefore, that causal attribution theory can explain how the harmed makes sense of what happened to them and, if it is likely to result in negative feelings, how this perception can be changed. In both the case studies mentioned above the person harmed questioned the degree of responsibility they apportioned to the wrongdoer. This tempered their reaction. Both the person harmed and their supporters thought that the act against them was intentional, but neither felt the wrongdoer in each case to be entirely responsible. The harmed in the first conference thought that he was partly to blame because he had had a run-in with the wrongdoer's brother. His father thought the wrongdoer had not had a good upbringing and so it was not entirely his fault. Weiner's theory helps us to understand the importance of separating perceptions of intention and perceptions of responsibility. It also emphasises how important it is to explore the view of the person harmed, and to address any feelings of misplaced responsibility they might have for wrongdoing that has been committed against them.

Proposition 2

The wrongdoer who perceives the harmed as responsible for an act of antagonism will, during the pre-conference preparatory interview, describe feelings of anger and thoughts of reprimand in response to an initial 'antagonistic act' from the harmed. (Starbuck 2008, p.100)

This is also informed by Weiner's theory. The proposition focuses attention on the wrongdoer. These thoughts and feelings will be elicited during the pre-conference interview. They will be revisited during the storytelling phase of the conference. Causal attribution theory can explain how the wrongdoer makes sense of what was happening to them since they instigated a hostile act against the harmed. It may inform the extent to which opportunities are made prior to a face-to-face meeting for wrongdoers to reflect on the way their thinking and feeling influenced how they acted.

Proposition 3

(i) The wrongdoer will make fewer inferences of hostility and intention following attendance at an RJ conference'.

They will therefore:

(ii) react less angrily and propose fewer hostile behavioural responses after attendance at an RJ conference. (Starbuck 2008, p.102)

This proposition is based on research by Dodge and Crick (1990) which suggests that aggressive adolescents 'have an attribution bias to infer hostile intent following a peer-instigated negative event' (p.180). They're also based on findings from research conducted by Graham and Hudley (1994) that suggest that aggressive and non-aggressive children differ in terms of the 'accessibility of constructs from their memory storage' (p.370). Graham and Hudley go on to suggest that the accuracy of such attributions and inferences can be altered through interventions that increase the availability of attributions of unintentionality. The restorative conference is one such intervention. Attendance at a conference can change the attributions that wrongdoers make for their victim's behaviour. If wrongdoers don't interpret the hostile behaviour of others as intentional then their thought processes, and subsequent behavioural choices, will not follow Weiner's model as shown in the diagram below and they may make different choices.

> Aggressive act of another → (*is perceived as*) intentional → (*is thought to be*) responsible → (*resulting in feelings of*) anger → (*and actions of*) reprimand/retaliation.

It is proposed that when a wrongdoer participates in a conference they will hear the story of what happened from the perspective of the person harmed, which will offer them an alternative interpretation of this person's behaviour. In addition, discussion about alternative choices and behaviours following a provocation during the storytelling and agreement phases of the conference will give the wrongdoer improved access to more pro-social examples of behaviour. They will now draw on more pro-social constructs (Graham and Hudley 1994) when, for example, deciding whether or not to retaliate aggressively against a peer following a 'provocation'.

Proposition 4

There are five elements to this proposition. Each is informed by Weiner's description of 'confession'. Weiner sees 'confession' as forming an additional step from 'judgements about the act of responsibility' and 'subsequent actions' (such as reprimand). He suggests that if the wrongdoer confesses following a judgement of responsibility then this will result in thoughts about the character of the wrongdoer that may lead to different emotions and, therefore, action.

1. The wrongdoer will 'confess' during the restorative conference (it was predicted that participation in a restorative conference provides a space to confess, as described by Weiner).

2. The harmed and their supporters will report during the post-conference interview that they perceive that the wrongdoer

is not an inherently bad person, and that they are not likely to commit the causal act again.

3. The harmed and their supporters will have a more positive moral impression of the wrongdoer following the conference.

4. The harmed and their supporters will have reduced feelings of anger and increased feelings of sympathy when interviewed after attendance at a conference compared with before attendance at a conference.

5. The harmed will acknowledge the increased likelihood of restored interpersonal relations between themselves and the wrongdoer.

(Starbuck 2008, p.102)

Data were collected which showed that the wrongdoers were able to confess, as predicted by Proposition 4.i. They accepted responsibility, indicated remorse, offered reparation, and promised not to do it again. It is important that the conference facilitator ensures that the conditions that allow this to happen are in place. The remaining four elements, Proposition 4.ii–iv, describe the changes in feeling and thinking that stakeholders will experience as a result of the restorative conference (confession). This proposition relates to Weiner's core assumption: that 'confession (an act which it is argued takes place during a restorative justice conference) with remorse signals recognition by the transgressor that a moral rule has been violated and the value of that rule validated' (Weiner 2006, p.119). This means that they will repair their social identity. The wrongdoer should feel more positive about themselves, perhaps less ashamed. Weiner points to experimental and observational evidence to show that confessions work. That is, they result in greater positive moral impressions; reduced feelings of anger; increased feelings of sympathy; decreased belief that the individual will offend again, and in forgiveness. Furthermore, Abel (1998 in Weiner 2006), defines confession as a 'means for the offender to accept 'moral inferiority', leaving the victim the decision to accept the confession, which then equalises the status of the transgressor and the victim, or to reject it, in which case the imbalance remains' (1998 in Weiner 2006, p. 113).

This proposition focuses on the harmed and their supporters and the changes that occur in their perception of the wrongdoer as a result of attendance at the restorative conference. It is hoped that, as an outcome of the conference, they will feel less fearful of further incidents occurring in the future. It should be noted that one stakeholder, a victim's supporter, did not perceive the wrongdoer's apology as sincere. While Weiner's model only requires that an indication of remorse is given, and Bazemore and Schiff (2005) only suggest that a space is provided where the wrongdoer can apologise and indicate remorse and the harmed can challenge their sincerity, it is arguable that this may mean that the victim's supporter continues to see the wrongdoer as a bad person. This may lead him to think that an attack could happen again. It would be interesting in further studies, therefore, to see if there is a relationship between the extent to which any restorative encounter provides 'the space' in which a wrongdoer can indicate remorse, the extent to which the harmed and their supporters feel that the remorse is sincere, and the subsequent thoughts and feelings of the harmed.

Proposition 5

> Comparison of the wrongdoer's pre-conference interview and post-conference interview responses shows that the wrongdoer feels better about themselves and feels that they are not a bad person following participation in the conference. (Starbuck 2008, p.103)

Weiner proposes that if the wrongdoer confesses, they will effectively separate their 'bad' behaviour from themselves as a person. As already explained a restorative conference begins with the facilitator doing precisely this in their opening introductory lines. The wrongdoer is given an opportunity to repair their social identity. The wrongdoers were much more positive about themselves after the conference. They knew they had done something wrong but they also knew they had admitted it and said sorry. They had absolved themselves of their wrongdoing.

Of course the outcome here is dependent on whether or not the harmed accepts the wrongdoer's confession and regards them as remorseful. The facilitator must, therefore, feel confident that the confession is likely to be 'heard' by the harmed, and that the wrongdoer is likely to show remorse. This can be achieved during conference preparation and through careful facilitation through each stage of the conference. Proposition 5 is supported by Pranis

(2001) who suggests that giving the wrongdoer the opportunity to tell their story, and be listened to, encourages them to realise that they have 'intrinsic worth as a human being' (p.28).

Conclusion

Weiner's model accounts for the behaviour of individuals within social situations and he describes how the punishment-oriented culture of Western society impacts on both the wrongdoer and the harmed in a conflict situation. As a consequence, wrongdoers may try to deny responsibility for their actions. If a wrongdoer is deemed responsible they will evoke negative responses in the harmed, and this may result in additional conflict. However, Weiner suggests that some individuals may confess and apologise, and this usually results in a more favourable response. Restorative practices make it more probable that individuals will accept responsibility and confess because they offer a respectful and safe environment in which to address the consequences of a wrongful act. This chapter has described how the phases of a restorative conference support wrongdoers and harmed through a motivational process in which the attributions they make affect the subsequent thoughts, feelings and behaviours they will experience.

However, it must be acknowledged that more research is needed. For example, the model cannot necessarily account for irrational thoughts or feelings. In addition, Weiner's theory, though described as 'a more complete theory of social behaviour' (2006, p.42), arguably focuses on an intrapersonal level of psychology. So it cannot yet account for the full impact of a restorative justice conference on the stakeholders and the wider community, particularly over a sustained period. A broader systemic analysis is required and it is probable that reference to organisational theory (Brofenbrenner 1979) will usefully contribute to an explanation of any longer term impact. Reference to other theories, including social learning theory (Bandura and Walters 1963) will enhance an understanding of the effects of restorative justice at both an intra- and inter-personal level.

References

Bandura, A. and Walters, R. H. (1963) *Social Learning and Personality Development.* New York, NY: Holt, Rinehart and Winston.

Bazemore, G. and Schiff, M. (2005) *Juvenile Justice Reform and Restorative Justice: Theory, Policy and Practice.* Collumpton, Devon: Willan.

Bronfenbrenner, U. (1979) *The Ecology of Human Development: Experiments by Nature and Design.* Cambridge, MA: Harvard University Press.

Dodge, K. A. (1980) 'Social cognition and children's aggressive behaviour.' *Child Development, 51,* 162–170.

Dodge, K. A. and Crick, N. (1990) 'Social information biases of aggressive behaviour in children.' *Personality and Social Psychology Bulletin, 16,* 8–22.

Graham, S. and Hudley, C. (1994) 'Attributions of Aggressive and Nonaggressive African-American male early adolescents: A Study of Contract Accessibility.' *Developmental Psychology, 30,* 365-373.

Hopkins, B. (2004) *Just Schools – A Whole School Approach to Restorative Justice.* London: Jessica Kingsley Publishers.

Hudley, C., Britsch, B., Wakefield, W., Smith, T., Demorat, M. and Cho, Su-Je. (1998) 'An attribution retraining programme to reduce aggression in elementary school students.' *Psychology in the Schools 35,* 3, 271–282.

Pranis, K. (2001) 'Restorative Justice, Social Justice, and the Empowerment of Marginalised Populations.' In G. Bazemore and M. Schiff (eds) *Restorative and Community Justice: Repairing Harm and Transforming Communities.* Cincinnati, OH: Anderson Publishing.

Starbuck, J. (2008) *How do Restorative Justice Conferences Work? Can the impact of an RJ Conference be explained by Causal Attribution Theory?* Unpublished thesis. University College London.

Weiner, B. (2006) *Social Motivation, Justice and the Moral Emotions – An Attributional Approach.* New Jersey, NJ: Lawrence Erlbaum Associates, Inc.

CHAPTER 3

Critical Relational Theory[1]

DOROTHY VAANDERING

We are broken within relationships;
we need to be healed within relationships.

OJIBWAY ELDER: HILDA NADJIWAN (2008)[2]

Introduction

I have come to recognise the intricacies and wonder of relationship as an educator, parent and more recently a researcher as I journey to understand the potential of restorative justice for bringing about healing. Though who we are as human beings is complex and often confounding, restorative justice, in returning to the wisdom of ancient and contemporary indigenous and spiritual traditions, taps into a profound simplicity – that *all* people are worthy and relational (Bianchi 1994; Pranis 2007; Zehr 2005).

In this context, Nadjiwan's insight in the quote above (graciously spoken in 2008, shortly after she and other indigenous peoples of Canada received an official public apology for the destruction of their cultures through residential schooling), creates a framework that sounds like common sense. However, this framework counters our current Western ideologies that have sanctioned the removal of responding to harm from those directly involved, and given it

1   Thanks are due to Hart Publishing, an imprint of Bloomsbury PLc for permission to re-print sections of the paper that originally appeared in *Restorative Justice: An International Journal 1*, 3, 311–333 entitled: 'A window on relationships: Reflecting critically on current restorative justice theory' by Dorothy Vaandering.

2   The online link to this speech (given in the references) is no longer active.

over to third parties to be addressed at arm's length (Christie 2013, p.15–19). As a member of this dominant Western society – white, middle class, educated, able-bodied, heterosexual, Christian – I easily took on the role of educator, blind to the power I wielded and the ease with which I felt entitled to *fix* other people's problems (Sensoy and DiAngelo 2012, p.51). When I confronted yet again the brick wall of conflict personally and institutionally, learning of restorative justice and catching a glimpse of its potential through the healing of some of my relationships with students and my children, I explored its indigenous and spiritual foundations more closely. I donned different lenses (Zehr 2005) and discovered anew (or perhaps for the first time) that *all* people, including myself, are worthy and honourable, and that our wellbeing is nurtured through relationship. As I adjust to these new lenses, I recognise the harm perpetuated by my 'dominator' lenses and I am gradually coming to engage with the world in more nurturing and relational ways.

This awareness is grounded in critical theory (Freire 2005; hooks 1994), a framework that recognises people as positioned in social contexts that value individuals and groups differently. To address the resulting, deeply embedded and inequitable access to resources which creates injustice, critical theory challenges presumed superiority by questioning who benefits and who bears the burdens of societal and institutional norms and decisions (Franklin 2006, p.73). The ultimate goal of critical theory is to create a just, rational, humane and reconciled society (Jensen 1997).

Expanding on Zehr's (2005) analogy of changing lenses, critical theory creates an awareness of the frames holding the lenses – the dominant social groups which I am born into, and privileged to be a part of. The lenses held in place by the frames are those characteristics unique to me that colour my view of the world. Through critical questioning (e.g. *Who benefits? Who bears the burden?*) I have come to see that the frames and lenses interact and discover the power held by myself and my dominant social groups (Sensoy and DiAngelo 2012, pp.21–22; Vaandering 2010).

Dominant ideologies have a history of, and the potential for, co-opting new ones (Morris 1998) and it is important for me to be alert to this possibility for restorative justice in its various contexts – first for myself and then in contributing to the field more generally (Vaandering 2010). To that end, a critical relational theory emerged that combines critical theory with early theoretical explorations of how restorative justice engages with foundational concepts of right relationship (Bianchi 1994; Zehr 2005) and the more recently proposed relational theories (Llewellyn 2012; Llewellyn and Howse 1998; Morrison 2012; Pranis 2007; Ross 2012). In addition to '*Who benefits?*' and '*Who bears the burden?*' I developed three more questions to further serve as a filter challenging me to critically reflect on my actions and the practice of educators implementing restorative justice: '*Am I honouring the people I am engaged with? Am I measuring them? What message am I sending them when we are together?*' (Vaandering 2011). Using these questions creates an awareness of how my interactions are influenced by and set in the broader socio-cultural context of my inherited privileged position and I am able to explicitly resist unconsciously perpetuating harm.

In addition to the questions, I created a matrix to further explain critical relational theory. Influenced by the work of McCold and Wachtel (2003) who developed the Social Discipline Window, the development of the Relationship Window occurred as a means for confronting the hierarchical, power dynamics that I experienced in using the Social Discipline Window. For a full discussion of the differences between the two different models and the theoretical development of the Relationship Window see Vaandering 2013.

What follows is a description of the model that informs my approach and an example of how I would facilitate a restorative encounter with youth involved in causing harm at school.[3] I conclude by reviewing the aspects of the approach that I believe are key for bringing about healing as well as critically reflecting on the institutional structures that often perpetuate much of the harm done to and by individuals. The Relationship Window (Figure 3.1) informs and illuminates the relational essence of restorative justice.

Focusing on *relationship* among people and their environments invites users of the Relationship Window to reflect on interpersonal interactions first and foremost, which can include individual relationships that harm others. The basic design of a matrix has two axes or continuums that intersect. The vertical indicating low to high levels of '*expectations*' *one gives another for being human* (where expectation includes accountability); the horizontal indicating low to high levels of '*support*' *one gives another for being human*. The four resulting quadrants clearly identify the varied responses given by

---

3   This slightly modified description and example were first published by Hart Publishing in Vaandering 2013. Reprinted with permission.

people in relationship for which the terms TO (punitive), FOR (permissive), NOT (neglectful) and WITH (restorative) serve as apt descriptions. Unlike McCold and Wachtel's (2003) Social Discipline Window in which these categories describe the manner of interaction between a person and an authority figure, in the Relationship Window, these interactions describe how relationships at any level can either diminish or nurture one's inherent worth as a human being. This perspective of humanity is foundational to the broader concept of justice, as Bianchi (1994), Llewellyn (2012), Pranis, Stuart and Wedge (2003) and Zehr (2005) put forth as being the ultimate goal of restorative justice – that of justice being understood as honouring the inherent worth of all, where people meet with the intent of fulfilling 'their vocation of becoming more fully human' (Freire 2005).

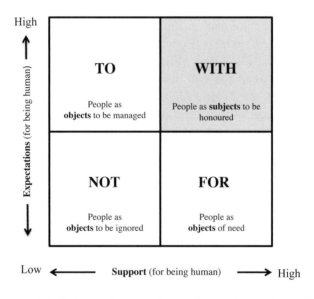

Figure 3.1: The Relationship Window: subject–object relationship

Specifically, when people provide each other with high support and high expectations and accountability they treat each other as *subjects*, as humans, and relate *with* each other. Buber (1958, pp.24–25) explores this in his famous *I-Thou* and *I-It* relational orientations. Here, as humans we strive for relationships among each other where *I* am understood in relation to *You* and vice versa. *I-It* involves distancing, where we separate ourselves from the other. Freire (2005) identifies this in his call for humanisation and states that 'No one can be authentically human while he prevents others from being so' (p.69). The reciprocal nature of relationships is central to our ability to thrive. By combining a high level of expectation for the other and a low level of support, a hierarchical power relationship results. Disagreement, dominance and disruption characterise the relationship, as people are turned into *objects* that are acted upon so that they contribute to what the giver wants. The relationship is characterised by what is done *to* another. High support and low expectations result in unhealthy interactions as well. Though it may begin well, in time the relationship deteriorates as people are seen as *objects* of need who also fulfil the giver's need to be needed. The relationship is characterised by what is done *for* another. In situations where there is no support or expectation the result is a non-existent relationship or an extreme form of objectification. This relationship is characterised by what is *not* done – neglect of relationship. In the latter three responses, it is important to notice that harm is perpetuated, not repaired. When these quadrants are entered into, one is working against the paradigm shift needed for restorative justice. It is also important to note that *expectation* and *support* can be given and received by anyone of any age or status, not just by an adult to a student, or a manager to an employee, as in the Social Discipline Window.

Another way of thinking about this Relationship Window is to use Simon's (1991) self-esteem terms, *lovable* and *capable*, as axes (Figure 3.2). If one is seen as not lovable or capable, one is neglected and ignored. If they are capable but not lovable, their skills are *used* to benefit the other. If they are lovable but not capable, they are *used* for the other's comfort. Only when I engage with someone believing that they are lovable *and* capable can I support and encourage them to be who they are becoming, and only here am I nurtured to be more fully human myself.

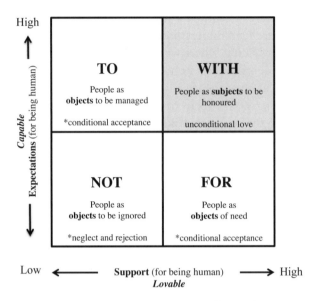

Figure 3.2: The Relationship Window: as influenced by Simon (1991) and Kohn (2005)

Kohn (2005) identifies with this restorative quadrant as a place of unconditional love, where unconditional teaching and learning occurs – it does not matter what you say or do, I am still going to love you AND hold you accountable to be all you can be. The other three quadrants represent places of conditional acceptance, teaching and learning. In this regard, it becomes clear that if we are committed to honouring one another as human beings, it is not acceptable to move to any of the other three quadrants. Glasser (1985) identifies the importance of maintaining a supportive role as a teacher and uses the terms *with, for* and *to* in his discourse as well. He states:

> Warmth and care are done *with* students, not *to* or *for* them… If students reject warmth and care, they do so because they do not believe it is sincere. (p.244)

He encourages educators to continue to offer warmth and care until the student is convinced of the sincerity of commitment. Glasser's work is grounded in the understanding that we cannot control another human being. Satisfying relationships in satisfying environments are what are needed to influence people (Glasser 1990). Though Glasser's work is grounded in individualism and rationalism rather than the social, interconnected, relational foundation of restorative justice, his emphasis on the need to be sincere and consistent is helpful for preventing people in authority from becoming authoritarian and perpetuating the thought that adults can *control* youth.

A Relationship Window grounded in the principles of restorative justice provides the framework that Morrison (2007) identifies as necessary for schools that are looking for a way to embed responses to behaviour in the broader context of relationship, as

> many of the problems encountered in a typical school day are frequently misdiagnosed if (they are) not viewed through a relational lens (nor involve) an exploration of factors contributing to relationship breakdown. (p.348)

This framework also allows for the organic growth of a relational school culture where participants in school communities explore together the fundamental principles of living in community so that a growth towards humanisation occurs. This common commitment from people within the school is critical for its growth and development (Glasser 1985).

Finally, the Relationship Window is also supported by contemporary educational research (Kohn 2005; Morrison 2007; Noddings 2005; Palmer 1998; Van Manen 2002), which calls clearly for the foundational role of relationship, care and trust in school cultures to be developed so that environments that are conducive to learning can be nurtured, and democratic citizenship can be encouraged.

Beyond the theoretical foundation that the Window on Relationship provides, what would it look like in an institution, organisation, work environment, family, community or any group engagement where people are committed to practising restorative justice. How would it inform a specific restorative justice encounter?

Using the Relationship Window to guide a restorative justice encounter

The Relationship Window illustrates how institutional and societal culture is nurtured by the way people engage with each other. Broadly speaking, a restorative justice encounter is *any* relational encounter where the wellbeing and worth of the one(s) I am with are a priority. It is grounded in a comprehensive definition of justice 'as honouring the inherent worth of all and being enacted through relationship' (Vaandering 2011), which involves consciously using language and actions that humanise (Freire 2005). This creates the framework for times when something occurs that undermines the wellbeing of some. At that point, a restorative justice encounter can be characterised as providing 'a space... for dialogue whereby the dignity of all involved and affected can be restored so that each can once again become a fully contributing member of the community of which they are a part' (Vaandering 2011, p. xx).

In a school context, for example, adults need to commit to living this out in their relationships with each other before or while expecting the students to engage with it meaningfully, as it is critical that students see this modelled for them each moment they are at school. The Relationship Window, though not able to stand alone in terms of supporting educators seeking to abandon a punitive approach, can challenge restorative justice proponents critically to reflect on how their use of language might be nuanced and politically saturated. In my personal experience both within and outside of school contexts, with youth and with adults alike, such reflection moved me beyond blind acceptance of 'expert' knowledge and served as an impetus for significant change. Figure 3.3 provides a visual reminder of the importance of living together in relationship in such a way that everyone is honoured and supported as a human being who is using and discovering their unique gifts that contribute to the wonder of life.

When we do this we live *with* each other as human beings. If we only support each other but don't expect each other to be human, then we treat one another like a stuffed toy – an object that we do things *for* so *we* feel good about ourselves. If we expect lots from each other but don't support each other, then we turn each other into machines and do things *to* another so that we get what *we* want. If we don't support or expect anything from each other, we ignore each other and treat each other like dirt – as if they don't exist so *we* do *not* have to care for them. When we treat each other or ourselves like toys, machines or dirt, we need to remind each other that we are human or we will never become the people we could be.

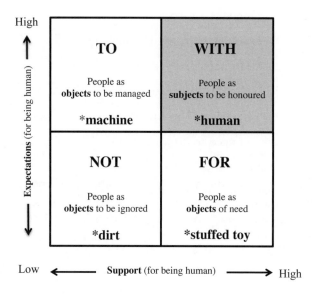

Figure 3.3: The Relationship Window: relationship analogies

Here is an example from a school context of using the Relationship Window when something has gone wrong. Imagine a situation in which one of the bathrooms ('toilets' in the UK) has been vandalised by someone who has written graffiti on the wall. In such a situation, the Relationship Window will be used as a guide for working *with* the people responsible to remind them that in the vandalism they forgot that their actions impacted others' ability to be human. They have ignored other people's need for a clean facility, treating them like dirt, and they expected the custodian ('caretaker' in the UK) to be a machine who has to clean up your mess. They have also forgotten that they are capable of doing things that support others, and in this way have forgotten that they themselves are human. Lots of people have been impacted and they have caused harm (a problem).

To move forward, all those involved will remind themselves that human beings can repair harm. Because those involved and affected were in a relationship that has now been broken it is within that relationship that healing will be sought. To help repair the harm, everyone affected by this will come together, and everyone will be given a chance to tell their story, including those responsible by responding to some key questions. These include a variation of some or all of the following:

- ◆ What happened?
- ◆ What were you thinking and/or feeling?
- ◆ Who has been impacted and how?
- ◆ What is the hardest thing for you?
- ◆ What do you need for healing to occur?
- ◆ What do you need to do to encourage healing to happen?

In this way, everyone involved will have a chance to understand how to better support and have expectations of each other that help them to be human.

This example shows how the Relationship Window keeps everyone focused on the relationship and humanity of the people involved rather than on the behaviour and on the incident. It is a reminder that the people involved are capable and worthy of support, regardless of what has been done. It also reminds those in authority that, for reparation or healing, all stakeholders are required for the dialogue as each has needs and each has contributions that can be made towards restoration of the dignity of all. Finally, it clearly illustrates that moving into the *to* or *for* quadrants is not an option, as those in authority would then be objectifying the very people they are seeking to support and encourage.

To further elaborate on what the circle conference involves, as the facilitator of the encounter arising from the vandalism described above, I would first identify those directly and indirectly involved and affected (the person or people responsible for the graffiti, the custodian (caretaker), someone responsible for building maintenance, other people who use the facility, an administrator); I would then meet in a pre-conference with each; ask them the key questions to hear their story; explain the process; invite them to participate; allow them to ask any questions they might have. If they agree, I would ask if they would like to take a support person with them to serve as an extra pair of ears and eyes, as well as tell the story from their perspective (in the case of youth, a parent is included as a supporter. However, a good friend is also a possibility). Finally, I would ask them if there are others involved or affected that they would recommend being there.

Reflecting critically on what I have heard by filtering the details through the questions such as '*Will all participants be honoured in this process? 'Will the wellbeing of all be nurtured?'* I will proceed. If I am assured that there are no power dynamics that will manipulate the outcome and cause further harm, I would then arrange for a time and place for the circle conference to occur, inform each participant and review the key guidelines and process involved with them. I would invite and respond to questions they might have. I would prepare for the meeting by thinking about the seating arrangements, and making sure small details are ready such as an opening reading/ quote; a talking piece; a card listing a few agreed upon guidelines; tissues; agreement forms and refreshments.

When everyone has arrived I facilitate by posing a few key questions to each of the participants so they can relate their point of view and its impact on them and others. The order in which the people are asked is significant. In most cases, the one causing the harm goes first, then those directly affected and harmed, next their supporters, then the ones indirectly affected, finally the supporter(s) of the one causing harm. This order requires those who have caused the harm to take responsibility and provides those harmed with details that address their need for hearing what led to the situation. When everyone has had opportunity to share and then respond or ask for clarification, the final questions are posed to each participant. Beginning with those most affected this time, each person is invited to respond to *What do you need to move on?* with specific expectations for the harm to be resolved for them personally. The one(s) causing harm conclude(s) this round by indicating what they need as they draw conclusions about what they can do to repair the harm that they caused. They then begin the last round by responding to the question, *What do you need 'to do' to move on?* This allows them to respond specifically to the needs identified by the others in the previous round and demonstrates their willingness to set things right. Then the rest of the group, with the one harmed going last, are invited to answer the same question. This provides an opportunity for others to identify and respond with offers to rectify those things that they have come to realise they may have contributed to the incident or with offers of support when they note they have resources that others might not have. The significance of the two final questions exemplifies that honouring each other includes recognising that *all* involved have needs and resources. It also creates a space so the incident is understood as being complex with various contributing factors. The possibility becomes clear that the situation might not be just one party's responsibility as it occurred within a context that may have been created beyond the control of those causing harm. From all of these responses, the group makes plans they can all agree to for repairing the harm within a designated time frame. Participants are then invited to mingle over refreshments while the agreement is written up and signed.

What about the person who refuses to participate, continues to cause harm, or is a significant threat to others? Is it not necessary to then move into an assertive, controlling role – the *to* or the *for* quadrants? Again the Relationship Window is a reminder that educators are in relationship *with* students, always supporting them, always expecting them to be human. In this way, the Window reminds us to look beyond the incident that has occurred to what it is that prevents the student from trusting us and wait, as Glasser (1985) indicates, until that trust is built. For the wellbeing of all, the student may need to be removed from the context – not as a punishment, but rather as a means for rebuilding relationship, for gaining trust, for taking time (with necessary support) simply to grow in what it means to be human.

Every stage of the restorative justice encounter held to address harm, regardless of willingness, is filtered through the critical reflective questions *'Am I honouring?', 'Am I measuring?', 'What message am I sending?'* In this way, the restorative justice encounter is never reduced to practice alone – a dangerous venture as facilitators and/or participants with power have the ability to manipulate the practice to serve their own or institutional needs. Theory and philosophy stand guard to ensure that the worth and wellbeing of all is nurtured.

Conclusion

If there is any doubt that a critical relational theory and the Relationship Window are necessary, perhaps the insights of Jaron Lanier, scholar at large and partner architect for Microsoft Research, can provide a final rationale. Lanier pioneered the technology for and coined the term 'virtual reality'. In his 2010 book entitled *You are Not a Gadget: A Manifesto*, he states:

> Something started to go wrong with the digital revolution around the turn of the 21st Century... A new generation has come of age with a reduced expectation of what a person can be, and who each person might become. (pp.3–4)

Though it is easy to point a finger in blame at this new generation, it is important to realise that this world has its roots in previous generations. The Relationship Window is grounded in the foundational understanding of justice as honouring the worth and working for the wellbeing of humanity. It creates a matrix that can guide people in their engagement with each other and their environments at *all* times rather than responding only to people's behaviour isolated from context. Herein lies the potential of restorative justice.

The Relationship Window illustrates a critical relational just theory. It guides me personally and professionally. It is showing itself to be informative for individuals, institutions, and societies. It is a reminder that in a world still rife with oppression (often ignored or unseen) it is important to re-examine our starting point. How do *I* view other human beings? How do *we* collectively view humanity? Who bears the burden? Who benefits? How can humanity reach out to each other and be nurtured to become fully who we have been made to be? I have come to recognise the intricacies and wonder of relationship as I acknowledge that we are broken through relationship and through relationship we are also healed.

References

Bianchi, H. (1994) *Justice as Sanctuary*. Bloomington, IN: Indiana University Press.

Buber, M. (1958) *I and Thou* (R. Gregory Smith Trans.). Edinburgh: T and T Clark.

Christie, N. (2013) 'Words on words.' *Restorative Justice: An International Journal 1*, 1.

Franklin, U. (2006) *The Ursula Franklin Reader*. Toronto: Between the Lines.

Freire, P. (2005) *Pedagogy of the Oppressed* (30th edition). New York, NY: Continuum (Original work published 1970).

Glasser, W. (1985) 'Discipline has never been the problem and isn't the problem now.' *Theory Into Practice 24*, 4, 241–246.

Glasser, W. (1990, 2nd Edition 1992) *The Quality School: Managing Students Without Coercion*. New York, NY: Harper Collins.

hooks, b. (1994) *Teaching to Transgress: Education as the Practice of Freedom*. New York, NY: Routledge.

Jensen, W. (1997) *Defining the Critical Theory – Application of the Critical Theory.* Available at http://www127.pair.com/critical/d-ct.htm, accessed on 5th February 2008.

Kohn, A. (2005) 'Unconditional teaching.' *Educational Leadership 63*, 1, 20.

Lanier, J. (2010) *You are Not a Gadget: A Manifesto.* New York, NY: Alfred A. Knopf.

Llewellyn, J. (2012) 'Restorative Justice: Thinking Relationally about Justice.' In J. Downie and J. Llewellyn (eds) *Being Relational.* Vancouver: UBC Press.

Llewellyn, J. and Howse, R. (1998) *Restorative Justice – A Conceptual Framework.* Ottawa: Law Commission of Canada.

McCold, P. and Wachtel, T. (2003) *In Pursuit of Paradigm: A Theory of Restorative Justice.* Restorative Practices E-Forum. Available at www.iirp.edu/article_detail. php?article_id=NDI0, accessed on 3rd May 2015.

Morris, R. (1998) *Why transformative justice?* Paper presented at the ICCPPC World Congress, Mexico City.

Morrison, B. (2007) *Restoring Safe School Communities.* Sydney: Federation Press.

Morrison, B. (2012) 'From Social Control to Social Engagement: Enabling the "Time and Space" to Talk Through Restorative Justice and Responsive Regulation.' In R. Rosenfeld, K. Quinet and C. Garcia (eds) *Contemporary Issues in Criminology Theory and Research.* Florence, KY: Wadworth.

Nadjiwan, H. (2008) *Stolen Children: Truth and Reconciliation Concert.* Available at www.cbc.ca/radio2/cod/concerts/20080605stoln, accessed on 4th March 2009. [since removed]

Noddings, N. (2005) 'Caring in education.' *The Encyclopedia of Informal Education.* Available at www.infed.org/biblio/noddings_caring_in_education.htm, accessed on 12th July 2010.

Palmer, P. J. (1998) *The Courage to Teach.* San Francisco, CA: Jossey-Bass.

Pranis, K. (2007) 'Restorative Values.' In G. Johnstone and D. Van Ness (eds) *Handbook of Restorative Justice.* Cullompton, Devon: Willan.

Pranis, K., Stuart, B. and Wedge, M. (2003) *Peacemaking Circles: from Crime to Community.* Minnesota: Living Justice Press.

Ross, R. (2012) 'Through a relational lens.' *Rethinking Justice Conference.* Pacific Business and Law Institute, Vancouver, B.C., October 25th and 26th, 2012. Available at www.youtube.com/watch?v=75HNjefhY3I, accessed on 6th May 2015.

Sensoy, O. and DiAngelo, R. (2012) *Is Everyone Really Equal?* New York, NY: Teachers College Press.

Simon, S. B. (1991) *I Am Loveable and Capable.* Niles, IL: Values Press.

Vaandering, D. (2010) 'The significance of critical theory for restorative justice in education.' *The Review of Education, Pedagogy, and Cultural Studies 32*, 2, 145–176.

Vaandering, D. (2011) 'A faithful compass: Rethinking the term justice to find clarity.' *Contemporary Justice Review 14*, 3, 307–328.

Vaandering, D. (2013) 'A window on relationships: reflecting critically on a current restorative justice theory.' *Restorative Justice: An International Journal 1*, 3, 311–333.

Van Manen, M. (2002) *The Tone of Teaching: The Language of Pedagogy.* London, Ont. Althouse Press.

Zehr, H. (2005) *Changing Lenses: A New Focus for Crime and Justice* (3rd edition). Waterloo: Herald Press.

CHAPTER 4

Depth Psychology and the Psychology of Conflict

ANN SHEARER

Introduction

This chapter explores restorative processes through the lens of depth psychology, with a particular focus on the theory of C. G. Jung. The two approaches may seem very different. The intensive and often lengthy work of individual psychotherapy is in sharp contrast with the necessarily brief, often scripted approach of restorative practice. The first focuses on the inner world of the individual, with an emphasis on unconscious processes; the second is concerned above all with restoring networks of outer relationships. Yet for psychotherapists and restorative practitioners alike, conflict is the very stuff of the work. Jungian psychology offers one model for understanding its causes and healing, whether it is expressed primarily through individual distress or disruptions in outer relationships.

A Jungian approach
Conscious and unconscious

People often consult psychotherapists because their relationships with others are painful or in disarray. Jungian theory suggests that the roots of these difficulties lie primarily in individuals' conflicted relationships with themselves, with 'the other' that is their own unconscious. Its hope is that by making the inner world more conscious, people learn to live more harmoniously with their own different and often contradictory aspects – and so to accept more easily the 'otherness' of others. Importantly, because they understand themselves better, they become more able to make moral decisions about their lives and actions, rather than being driven by unconscious energies and motivations.

Jung was far from the first to suggest that psychological distress was the result of conflict between the conscious and unconscious mind. The idea that we are unknown not just to others but to ourselves seems inescapably part of the human condition. St Paul's cry echoes down the centuries: 'I do not understand my own actions. For I do not do what I want but I do the very thing I hate!' (Romans 7:15). Explorations of this basic fact of human life were given their most influential codification by Freud. He saw psychological life as a more or less permanent tussle between conscious and unconscious. In his best-known formulation, the Ego, or rational everyday consciousness, must struggle to hold its position between the demands of the Id, the instinctual world of unconscious and repressed desire, from below, and pressure of the Super-Ego, the voices of 'oughts' and 'shoulds', from above.[1]

Jung's understanding of the relationship between conscious and unconscious was more benign. He saw psyche as purposeful, working always towards greater consciousness. And while Freud focused his attention on the personal unconscious, and on bringing its repressed memories and desires into the light of consciousness, Jung added another dimension. He posited that below the personal unconscious there lay the vast collective unconscious of humankind, made up of archetypal energies and potentials, both positive and negative, encoded like psychic instincts into each individual. These archetypes can never be experienced directly. But we can get an idea of their energy and how this might operate through the emotional charge of stories and images that recur and recur again across time, space and culture.

This is not to say that Jung saw relations between consciousness and unconscious as easy. For him, the personal unconscious is the meeting ground between archetypal energy and the deposits of life experience. Together these coalesce into 'complexes', bundles of autonomous unconscious energy that could, at any time, if triggered, usurp the rational, conscious world of ego. When we

---

1   Storr 2001, first published 1989, gives a good introduction to Freud's ideas.

bewilder ourselves with an unexpected outburst, when 'I can't think what came over me!' is our shamed response to behaviour we'd condemn in others, Jungians would suspect a complex has been at work. More generally, the complexes consistently colour attitudes and behaviours, obscuring the relationship between ego and the world's reality. We are less likely to notice this when their energy is positive – until perhaps this tips into a dangerous over-optimism and naïveté. But a negative complex can wreak havoc for the individual and their relationships. A positive 'father-complex', for instance, will tend to support a view of the world as on the whole fair, its institutions not to be questioned. At the complex's negative pole, the perception is very different. Here, the very notion of 'authority' may seem intolerable; even its most benign expression can trigger totally disproportionate resentment, fear, and even violence, with which there seems to be no reasoning. What is going on here? In Jungian terms, the rational ego seems to have been usurped by the negative complex. So a Jungian approach might hope to explore the individuals' life experiences at the hands of actual father and other authority figures, and also to uncover the archetypal image of the father – as avenging God, as terrible Judge? – that together give the complex its huge energy. The hope would be that through these explorations the individual would build the ego-strength to realise that not all authority is as negative as the complex has told them it must be.[2]

Persona and shadow

For both Freud and Jung in their different ways, then, conflict between rational consciousness and the unconscious is an inevitable part of being human: we are all self-divided. But we all also have to get up, go to work, sustain our everyday lives and relationships: we need an ego that is strong enough to maintain a reliable and consistent sense of who we are. Jung suggested that to protect and bolster our ego, psyche creates persona, the social mask that best serves us in our dealings with the outer world. We may have a whole wardrobe of these masks, each suited to particular situations and different social demands. Not all of them may be agreeable: for some people at some times, for instance, it may seem a matter of

---

2   Stevens 2001, first published 1991, gives a good introduction to Jung's ideas.

survival to appear to the world as completely tough, emotionally untouchable.

But none of us is just our persona. I am more than a Psychotherapist; you are more than a Restorative Justice Practitioner. What happens to all the parts of ourselves that don't fit? We may be self-aware enough to know that these persona masks are just that, and so able to make rational ego choices about which parts of our underlying selves to show in which circumstances. We are more likely to take off the mask of competence with our partner, for instance, than to show our underlying vulnerabilities to the bank manager when we need a loan. But where we are less aware of, or able to tolerate, our inner multiplicity, there is a danger that we become identified with our persona, unconsciously rejecting many aspects of ourselves to ensure that the mask does not slip. Someone who clings to an emotionally untouchable persona, for instance, may deny their own vulnerability and longing for love as too painful and dangerous to reveal, even to themselves.

So we disown the unacceptable parts of ourselves. In Jung's terms, they become part of our unconscious shadow. Yet they are still part of us. If the persona, the way the individual wishes to see her or himself and be seen, becomes too rigid, too estranged from the shadow, there can be some dramatic psychological eruptions. The soldier is schooled in obedience to rules, a sense of duty and clear sense of right and wrong: this is the military persona. The shadow erupts and they totally lose control in a pub brawl. The priest is disciplined in adherence to the rule of the Church and of God, to the avoidance of sin and the promotion of virtue. And then he sexually abuses children in his care. A director of public prosecutions, upholder of the rule of law, is found kerb crawling in Kings Cross. A banker who appears to be the very embodiment of prudent reliability is overwhelmed by greed and ruthlessness.

We can surely all think of eruptions from our own shadow, if less dramatic than these; we can all shock and shame ourselves by unwanted reactions and behaviours. This is a psychological law, it seems: the inbuilt urge towards psychic wholeness identified by Jung means that the shadow 'wants' to become conscious. If unacknowledged, it may force its presence on us in ever more extreme forms, to the extent of overwhelming persona and ego as well. If we can see it as such, this is actually a gift from the unconscious. It offers a chance to become more psychologically whole and to take greater moral responsibility for ourselves instead of acting out of unconscious motivation. By becoming more conscious of our shadow sides, we have the opportunity to make more conscious decisions about how to live with them.

And we may then discover that hidden in the shadow there are also many positive potentials, for in another sense, as Jung also said, it comprises the whole realm of the unconscious (1945, para. 373), a vast reservoir of potential for good and ill. Here I think of Sherman's defiance theory, his suggestion that people who commit crimes don't think of themselves as having done anything immoral: this awareness, if you like, has been banished into the shadow. Restorative process, says Sherman, invites them to reconsider this self definition, become more self-aware, and offers them the moral choice to become law abiders, members of another moral universe (Sherman and Strang 2007). It gives them the chance, put another way, to recognise and reclaim a positive aspect of themselves that until now has been lost in the shadow of the unconscious.

Working with the shadow

It is not easy to accept the shadow aspects of ourselves; they may carry too much pain, or be too shameful, too challenging to our good image of ourselves. To enable us to go about our daily lives, psyche may construct defensive barriers between them and our conscious ego. So they may be repressed into the unconscious until suddenly triggered by an outer event. At the extreme, psyche itself may even fragment or split into distinct 'personalities', each unknown to the other, but each with their own life in the world. Sometimes these barriers seem impregnable: shadow aspects may remain literally inaccessible to conscious awareness, necessary defences of a fragile ego. But very often we first get a hint of them through projection. Projection of shadow, for all that it's responsible for so much trouble within individuals, between them and in the world, can also be a first step towards greater self-awareness.

Projection is everywhere, positive and negative, with potential for both good and ill. Positive projections onto others contain the germ of our psychological growth. Falling in love must be the most common projection of them all! And falling out of love, the withdrawal of that projection of all that's good and true onto the other, may also be the beginning of a new self-awareness: these are qualities that I recognise and admire, and if that once-marvellous other isn't so special after all, then maybe I share more of their qualities than I thought. But negative projections are dangerous for both individuals and societies. At the level of intimate relationships, we 'know' that it is always *you* who picks the quarrel, when *I* want nothing but peace: the fixity of the projection fuels the conflict. The person whose emotionally untouchable persona is an unconscious defence against fearful awareness of their own vulnerability may project that vulnerability onto others: the very sight of someone seemingly weak and defenceless may be so intolerable to them that they attempt to destroy this reminder of their own weakness, in an attack that is rationally incomprehensible: this sort of projection is fuel for bullying and other interpersonal violence. The same mechanism can be seen in societies. In the columns of the popular press, the tax-evasive businessman sees nothing incongruous in excoriating the person on benefits for immorally ripping off the system: the projection feeds social divisiveness. The projection of aggression onto the 'evil empire' leaves our country blameless as it goes to war 'only' to defend 'civilised values'. Negative projections are the fuel of ideologies: think of the mass projection of all Weimar Germany's ills onto the Jews, apartheid South Africa's projection of all its shadow onto blacks and communists.

Yet in Jung's terms, projection fulfils an important psychological function: it gives us a glimpse 'out there' of shadow aspects of ourselves, positive or negative, desired or feared. If we can begin to recognise this, we may be able to start acknowledging these aspects of ourselves, whether it's our own projected creativity or our own greed or worse. Sometimes projections seem to dissolve of their own accord: we turn a psychological corner and are shocked to discover that this person is neither the monster nor the angel we took them for, but rather a human being not entirely like ourself. Sometimes the withdrawal of projection is very hard work – especially when the other provides a hook for them: it may be perfectly true that your nature is more quarrelsome than mine, that some people defraud the benefit system, that some have a level of vulnerability which seems to invite the bully. Sometimes the force of projection, sustained by outer economic and social circumstances, is such that there seems no other outcome but catastrophe, whether for individuals, states or both. The realities of the inner and outer worlds must always be in negotiation.

Jungian psychology and restorative practice

What is a restorative encounter?

From my perspective, any meeting or encounter is 'restorative' when it leads not just to a degree of healing between antagonists, but when this healing is essentially based on a shift *within* each participant in the process. This is turn means that they have learned something not only about the other person, but about the profoundly 'other' that is their own unconscious. In Jungian terms, they have withdrawn something of themselves that they have projected onto the other. The same psychological mechanism can be seen at work in any situation of conflict, from intimate squabbles to those that reach the criminal courts.

People who have lived self-consciously 'proper' lives, for instance, may bolster this pleasing view of themselves by contrasting their own life with that of a shameful 'underclass' of 'wastrels and losers'. But they may be shocked into a recognition of their own 'loser' when they become helpless victims of a crime. In accepting that they too are vulnerable, sometimes helpless in the face of what life has thrown at them, they may become more able to understand the 'victim' in their antagonist and so feel less punitive towards them. On the other side, those who may consciously feel themselves to be 'victims' of an unfair society and so justified in taking what they can, may begin to recognise how powerfully they can affect other people's lives. As Peter Woolf put it after meeting Will Riley, whom he had severely beaten and burgled in the search for money for drugs: 'I never knew I made people feel that angry, bad, depressed, isolated, guilty, and guilty about things I had done. I never realised the harm I had caused, I never realised how many people I had affected' (Morris and Usborne 2008, p.11). From this realisation that he actually had power in the world, rather than being its victim, came the start of a choice to live in another way.

What makes restorative practice work?

What is it that makes two human beings in situations of hurt and harm willing to risk coming together and facing the other? And what makes others, whether psychotherapists or restorative practitioners, willing to spend their days sitting through the pain and distress? We all have our own back-histories: individual motivation may vary from the ideological to the downright cynical.

But perhaps there is also a deeper energy at work. The yearning for justice seems to be encoded into human beings: we hear in it in the child's cry that 'It's not fair!'; we read it in the great Messianic prophecies of Isaiah; we see it inspiring countless social and political movements across history. But justice is not just a state towards which human beings continue to aspire. The very words associated with restorative process – re-store, re-pair, re-concile, re-integrate – suggest that it seeks to re-establish a *once-known state*. The search is not for something new, but to recover something that once was and has been lost.

Restorative process not only recognises this, but works from it. It has always drawn inspiration from the ways in which traditional societies have approached the resolution of conflict – whether these are Maori, Australian aboriginal or North American Indian and First Nation (Johnstone 2002). And what unites all these traditional approaches, and others too, is the belief that what is being re-stored is a pre-existent, often god-given, 'right order' of society which has been damaged by the offence. In Jungian terms, the belief in this pre-existent state is archetypal, found across time and place. This is the Golden Age of ancient Greece, the Chinese state of Tao; it is the Hindu Rama-Raya, when there was no need for laws because humans lived by the example of the god-king Rama; it is the state of Eden, when God walked with Adam in the cool of the evening. This doesn't make the theory behind restorative justice flawless; there are plenty of questions about the relevance of traditional justice systems to contemporary societies (see Johnstone 2003, Zehr and Toews 2004). But it is to suggest that the willingness to engage in restorative process, the belief that it is possible, takes its deepest psychological energy from this archetypal pattern. In a profound sense, this is what makes it 'work' (Shearer 2012).

Mainstream Western justice systems may seem a long way from those of traditional societies. But the search for 'right order' is still encoded in the very image of Justice who, with her sword and scales, stands over Western law courts and informs our social understanding of what is just and fair. The sword suggests discrimination, the proper apportioning of 'right and 'wrong', 'innocence' and 'guilt'. But the scales suggest something else: a painstaking weighing of two distinct and separate quantities until they come to balance. The familiar figure of Justice has her beginnings in another archetypal image: the classical Greek goddess Themis, whose very name means 'right order'. The overriding task of this goddess was not to apportion innocence and guilt or to punish, but to bring together in harmony gods and humans, individuals and societies. Themis's energy, the urge to 'bring together' and to find a right balance between the claims of two disparate and conflicted individuals, is written into our very idea of justice and fairness. Restorative practice can be seen as one expression of it (Donleavy and Shearer 2008).

Building restorative practice

Restorative process is not therapy, but any psychotherapist would readily recognise the healing power of story. It is when people feel that they can entrust their story to another – their history, their motives, the way they experience the world – that healing can begin. 'I was able to convey my deepest thoughts and the trauma that was affecting me from not being able to protect my family and home', said Will Riley after that brutal burglary. 'It was only on the day I got home after the meeting with Peter that the feeling had gone away. I was able to restore my sense of freedom and not being a victim' (Morris and Usborne 2008, p.11). Even in situations of continuing suffering, telling the story can itself be healing. Lucas Sikwepere told the South African Truth and Reconciliation about how he was blinded by a policeman's shot in the face. And then he added:

> I feel what… has brought my sight back, my eyesight back, is to come here and tell the story. I feel what has been making me sick all the time is the fact that I couldn't tell my story. But now …it feels like I've got my sight back by coming here and telling the story. (Quoted in Tutu 1999, pp.128–9)

Telling the story is a basic building block of restorative process. But the healing lies in it being heard and accepted in the presence of a trustworthy witness. As the major Ministry of Justice study of restorative schemes emphasised, the perceived fairness and impartiality of the facilitator is key to successful restorative process. But this is only the beginning. As the study also found, some three-quarters of participants, both victims and offenders, thought face-to-face meetings much better than indirect approaches; the authors concluded that direct meetings between aggrieved parties are likely to be the most effect form of restorative process (Shapland *et al.* 2007).

What is true for criminal justice may also be true elsewhere, not just psychologically, but at a level that is only now beginning to be understood. Neurophysiological research suggests that the attunement between individuals may actually be happening at the level of bodily process as well as conscious understanding. When someone can move from a state of frustration, distress or anger towards someone sitting nearby and find appreciation or compassion, their own heart rhythms may move into a more coherent, less erratic rhythm. But something else seems to happen too: the heart's powerful electromagnetic field may entrain the heart rhythms of the other, drawing the two hearts literally to beat as one (see Donleavy and Shearer 2008, Chapter 4). Research into mirror neurons suggests that we humans are biologically wired, at the level of single brain cells, to feel what others feel (Iacoboni 2009). The triggering of mirror neurons in face-to-face encounter may be where the recognition of 'the other' as more like me than I thought, that glimpse of my own inner 'other', may begin. This is the foundation of 'empathy' – the sense that I feel with and interact with this other human being. In time, Riley and Woolf set up a charity together to support victims of crime.[3]

In terms of Jung's psychology, restorative process encourages the withdrawal of projections. By contrast, and for all its clear and valued benefits, the more conventional adversarial approach carries quite some danger of reinforcing them. This may be particularly true in the justice system, but may apply to any adversarial process set up to 'deal with' conflict.

At the extreme, and at the risk of caricature, adversarial justice can be seen as the justice of the sword. Its overriding concern is to find clear separation between right and wrong, innocence and guilt. To this end, rather than 'bringing together' victim and offender, the very settings and conventions of the courts perpetuate their separation. Neither is heard by the other, their stories are told for them in a language that is rarely their own, or even always understood. The intensely personal nature of restorative process is lost by reframing the offence as no longer between two individuals, but rather as damage to 'the State' or 'Regina'. So both offender and victim remain disempowered, unchallenged by the belief and expectation that each has the inherent capability to make a difference to their own life or that of the other. Each side is likely

---

3   www.why-me.org.

to be reinforced in their prevailing view of themselves rather than challenged to recognise what they are projecting onto the other. Offenders are able to avoid the psychological effect of their actions on their victims; high recidivism figures attest to the fixity of their self-identity as criminal, which may also mask their own sense of themselves as victims of social circumstance. For victims themselves, court proceedings rarely bring healing: they most often feel unheard, their own feelings of helplessness, fear and anger unassuaged or even strengthened. In terms of Jung's psychology, there has been no challenge to discover what lies behind the persona of 'offender' or 'victim': in fact, the adversarial process may rely on the fixity of these social masks. And the public pressure for more and larger prisons can continue to testify to the tenacious power of shadow projection, the desire to lock away the threatening and even dangerous aspects of 'the other' who is also, somewhere, myself.

Final thoughts

The archetypal world is multiple: in Jung's understanding, psychic energy is fuelled by a continual interplay of opposites. Alongside the archetypal urge to come to together in the harmony of 'right order', there is its counterpart: the urge to differentiate, to separate, and to break apart. The constant interplay between these patterns seems to be basic to human beings and social process. Cells come together, they separate, they come together in a new complexity; families form and separate to come together in another, wider way; nations are formed, they separate, they reconfigure. So both adversarial and restorative approaches to justice can be seen as equally necessary expressions of fundamental psychological patterns. The best we can do, perhaps, is to try to become more aware of the 'right order' which lies in bringing the two to balance on Justice's scales.

A greater awareness of how psychological forces may be at work within and between participants in restorative process may help to foster sturdier positive effects. This applies not just to designated antagonists, but to practitioners and facilitators as well. Their neutrality and impartiality have long been seen as twin pillars of conflict resolution, written into codes of practice and highly valued by participants. But the nature, possibility and even desirability of these virtues are also keenly debated. Is it time that that practitioners more critically explore the unconscious cultural biases and shadow-projections which they may be contributing to the psychological field in which a restorative encounter takes place (Shearer, n.d)? As Jung once said, 'there is no cure and no improving of the world that does not begin with the individual' (1945, para 373). In the end, our own self is all that we can reliably work with.

This emphasis on internal psychological processes may seem an unrealistically long way from the realities of a necessarily brief, even prescribed restorative encounter. But Jungian theory offers the hope that if we become more aware of these processes, and so more responsible for them, we may contribute to helping others to do the same and even to a shift in the collective consciousness of our day. This may not always be possible. Participants in restorative process may be too rigid in their defence of their own self-perception to be able to see aspects of the other in themselves. The outer social and economic circumstances to which offenders return, often with inadequate support, may overwhelm the best of intentions. But at the very least, a greater awareness among practitioners of underlying psychological process may keep alive the idea and even glimpse the reality of that archetypal 'right order' to which restorative process aspires.

References

Donleavy, P. and Shearer, A. (2008) *From Ancient Myth to Modern Healing: Themis, Goddess of Heart-Soul, Justice and Reconciliation*. London: Routledge.

Iacoboni, M. (2009) *Mirroring People*. New York, NY: Picador.

Johnstone, G. (ed) (2002) *A Restorative Justice Reader*. Cullompton, Devon: Willan.

Johnstone, G. (ed) (2003) *Restorative Justice: Ideas, Values, Debates*. Cullompton, Devon: Willan.

Jung, C. G. (1945) 'The Relations Between the Ego and the Unconsciousness.' In *The Collected Works, Vol. 7*, Reed, H., Fordham, M. and Adler, G. (eds), R. F. C. Hull (trans.). London: Routledge and Kegan Paul.

Morris, N. and Usborne, D. (2008) 'Meet your victim – can criminals ever be shocked out of a life of law-breaking?' *The Independent*, 15 July.

Shapland, J., Atkinson, A., Atkinson, H., Chapman, B., Dignan, J., Howes, M., Johnstone, J., Robinson, G. and Sorsby, A. (2007) *Restorative Justice: The Views of Victims and Offenders*. Ministry of Justice Research Series 3/07. London: Ministry of Justice.

Shearer, A. (n.d.) 'Conflict Resolution: the myth of impartiality'. Paper originally written for the Birkbeck Graduate Certificate in Conflict Resolution and Mediation Studies, 2010. Available from the author.

Shearer, A. (2012) 'Restorative Justice: Some Archetypal Roots'. In D. J. Christie (ed) *The Encyclopaedia of Peace Psychology*. Oxford: Blackwell Publishing.

Sherman, L. and Strang, H. (2007) *Restorative Justice: The Evidence*. London: Smith Institute.

Stevens, A. (2001) *Jung: A Very Short Introduction*. Oxford: Oxford University Press.
Storr, A. (2001) *Freud: A Very Short Introduction*. Oxford: Oxford University Press.
Tutu, D. (1999) *No Future Without Forgiveness*. London: Rider.
Zehr, H. and Toews, B. (eds) (2004) *Critical Issues in Restorative Justice*. Mousey, NJ: Criminal Justice Press.

CHAPTER 5

Nonviolent Communication

SHONA CAMERON

Introduction

The work of clinical psychologist Dr Marshall Rosenberg and his model of Nonviolent Communication (NVC) (Rosenberg 2003a) has been the bedrock of my practise as an educational psychologist for over ten years. I chose to practise the model of NVC as I speak with, listen to and support all the people I come into contact with. Learning about and exploring restorative practises aligns with NVC's aims of finding solutions that work for everyone. Hopkins (2004, 2009) also cites Dr Rosenberg as heavily influencing the development of her restorative work in schools and elsewhere. This chapter will explore and share my use of NVC in schools as I meet young people, parents and educators who are often in difficult places in their lives and who are all trying to do their best.

All encounters are viewed as a chance to be restorative, which is the chance to build on the social connections between people. This includes interviews with young people, within meetings with parents and whether or not conflict has arisen. Nonviolent communication has practical applications for anybody working in education and moves restorative approaches into every interaction. It is an ethos and a way of being rather than a process or a model to learn. However, NVC can also be used when conflict has arisen and indeed it has proven to be highly effective in heated meetings and in mediation between pupils and schools and parents and schools.

Nonviolent communication is used by educators (Hart and Kindle-Hodson 2004; Rosenberg 2003b), in prisons, in business (Lasater 2010), in coaching (Cox and Dannahy 2005) and within families (Hart and Kindle-Hodson 2006). Its use has been documented in, among other contexts, the favelas of Brazil (Barter 2012), with 'at risk' teenagers in Canada (Little 2008) and in schools around the world.

History and development of Nonviolent Communication

The NVC model was developed over many years by Rosenberg (Rosenberg 2003a) and in a similar way to the development of restorative approaches around the world, NVC has been shared globally by a mainly grassroots movement. As Rosenberg was not involved in academia, he did not seek publication or research, preferring instead to develop the work of NVC in practical situations and working with groups around the world to share the model. He initially developed NVC as a model to use to mediate between gangs and groups during the civil rights movement and was influenced by the work of Carl Rogers in the 1960s.

Little (2008) discusses the history of the development of the NVC model in some detail and she notes that Rogers' 1964 lecture at the California Institute of Technology is frequently referenced by Rosenberg as a central inspiration. In that lecture, Rogers concluded that what he was espousing was a 'growth-promoting interpersonal communication' that was

> A sensitive ability to hear, a deep satisfaction in being heard; an ability to be more real, which in turn brings forth more realness from others; and consequently a greater freedom to give and receive love – these, in my experience, are the elements that make interpersonal communication enriching and enhancing. (Rogers 1980, p.26)

Rogers had been exploring what works within the therapeutic relationship (Rogers 1961) and went on to identify and write about three characteristics, or attributes, of the therapist – congruence, unconditional positive regard (UPR) and accurate empathic understanding. That is: Are you authentic and real? Do you care, and are you present in this moment and able to listen deeply? (Rogers 1980)

When we seek to 'be' restorative we are seeking to offer a space that is rich and encouraging. We are seeking an interaction where we are working together to find a way forward and where there is growth for all those involved. We ask others to look into themselves and explore thoughts, feelings, motivations and actions and the implications this has socially. An understanding of how to create an environment where others feel free to explore and are willing to be honest is essential.

Siegel (2007) suggests that in our selves

> with mindful awareness, we can propose the mind enters a state of being in which one's here and now experiences are sensed directly, accepted for what they are and acknowledged with kindness and respect. (p.16)

Rogers (1983) hypothesises, from his experience of work as a therapist, what happens when a person is in a trusted therapeutic relationship.

> When she senses and realises that she is prized as a person then she can slowly begin to value the different aspects of herself, more importantly she can begin with much difficulty at first to sense and to feel what is going on within herself, what she is feeling what she is experiencing, how she is reacting. (p.262)

Restorative approaches do not offer therapy and need to be seen as distinct from the therapeutic relationship. However, key characteristics of this therapeutic relationship include authenticity, caring, empathy, compassion and mindfulness. These characteristics are also key to the relationship building and trust essential for conversations within a restorative relationship, and can contribute to a culture where restorative interactions are the norm.

Learning NVC has given me the tools to 'do' all these things by 'being' them. I practise mindful awareness in the moment and try to be congruent and authentic. I care about the other, accepting that every human being is trying to meet their own needs (Rosenberg 2003a). I have learnt how to show I am listening deeply by offering guesses about what I think is going on for the other person. As a consequence people talk to me openly, and I have the privilege of hearing what really matters to young people and their parents and the schools in the community I work in. It does not look or sound like therapy, and there is a lot of internal work going on in me that others do not see.[1]

NVC is often called 'compassionate communication' and the acceptance and kindness needed in a restorative encounter in order for people to feel that they are cared about cannot be understated. As Hart and Kindle-Hudson (2004) note

> Compassion is not a static state, nor is it a destination to be reached. Compassion is not a subject to be taught. Compassion is a way of being in a relationship – a way of acting and interacting. At the same time, certain practices can help cultivate this way of being. In our experience Nonviolent Communication is the most practical and powerful of these practices. (p.5)

For me NVC is about an active compassion, a living compassion in interactions. Recent advances in neurobiology have led many researchers to share Rogers' hypothesis about what is happening between people as we communicate. Siegel (2007) suggests that

> our human mind is embodied – it involves a flow of information that occurs within the body, including the brain – and it is relational, the dimension of the mind that involves the flow of energy and information between people. (p.5)

When we can do this with empathy and show this in our tone of voice and in our questions people respond because they trust and feel safe that they are accepted and are heard.

The words 'Nonviolent Communication' imply the opposite to violence and many people resist exploring the process because they do not consider themselves to be violent in the first place. The concept of NVC comes from ideal of *ahimsa*, a Sanskrit word used by Gandhi, which means to be free of the intention to do harm. Rosenberg suggests that when we are choosing to judge or analyse we are creating or emphasising barriers between people rather than building bridges or connections between people (Rosenberg 2003a). When a mother is attuned (in Siegel's work he is referring to parent–child attachment)

---

1   The internal inner sensing is further explored in 'Focusing' as outlined by Gendlin (2003).

...(the child) is able to feel they are felt by the caregiver and has a sense of stability in the present moment. During the here and now interaction the child feels good, connected and loved. The child's internal world is seen with clarity by the parent and the parent comes to resonate with the child's state. (p.27)

This is what I propose is happening within a restorative encounter using NVC as a way to build empathy and trust, and to show kindness and a sense of equality. In this way all views are equally valued and people feel they matter and that they belong. Then we have a mindful attunement as Daniel Siegel describes, and within this people flourish.

An outline of the Nonviolent Communication model

NVC proposes that as we speak, we can choose to take care of our language and the *intention* behind our communication. At the heart of the practice of NVC lies the intention to 'make a connection' with the other by putting empathy first. This means putting aside other reasons to communicate with someone, such as getting someone to do something; teaching someone something; telling someone off; or giving advice or information. All of these other ways to communicate have their place, and I use them when the time is right. For example there may be times when giving people information may be the most connecting thing to do – 'You're coffee is spilling!' or giving someone some advice is vital 'Stop... there's a car coming'. Choosing to use NVC involves seeking connection and empathy first, as a rule of thumb and we may do this silently (see Figure 5.1). First we attune to ourselves to ensure congruence. Then we *do* one of two things. We listen to what is going on in the other person or we express ourselves honesty and with care.

Central to Rosenberg's work is the development of questions that support empathy between people. I know of no other model that explores the 'how to' of empathy, and that expands this practice beyond the therapeutic relationship and offering its practical usage in daily interactions.

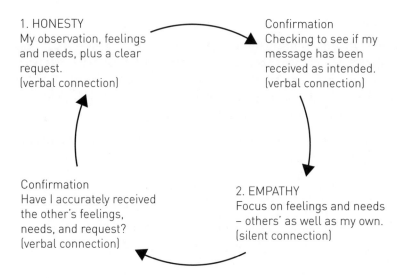

1. HONESTY
My observation, feelings and needs, plus a clear request.
(verbal connection)

Confirmation
Checking to see if my message has been received as intended.
(verbal connection)

Confirmation
Have I accurately received the other's feelings, needs, and request?
(verbal connection)

2. EMPATHY
Focus on feelings and needs – others' as well as my own.
(silent connection)

Figure 5.1: An outline of The Nonviolent Communication Model: A dynamic interplay between honesty and empathy
From Little (2008, p.58), reproduced here with permission of the author.

Listening and the four step model of NVC

The NVC model offers a unique way to frame interaction and active listening skills based on four key ingredients – *Observations, Feelings, Needs and Requests.* It continues to astonish me how quickly a trusting relationship is established within which problems can be solved and conflicts resolved. I have learnt to listen when someone is speaking, not just to the words, but also to the deeper meanings. I listen to the reason why someone is spending time and energy telling me something, the 'why' this matters to them on the deepest level to them as a human being. This *paying attention* at a needs or values level I do with mindfulness to the present moment and this *coming alongside another person* I view as empathy. I then follow a four-step process described below with an example from a school setting involving listening to a teacher who appears angry at the behaviour of a student.

Observations

First I seek confirmation from the speaker about what has happened, their *observation*. By 'observation' I mean what has been seen and heard, or what is being remembered or imagined. Without reference to any analysis or evaluation. I then check in with the speaker that I have understood their world.

> *'So you've noticed that Neil has been coming to lessons 10 minutes after the bell has gone?'*

Feelings

I then pay attention to the *feelings* being expressed or displayed, and by 'feelings' I mean the bodily sensations being felt in response to the observation. And again I check with the speaker.

> *'Are you feeling annoyed?'*

Needs

Next I pay attention to the *needs* expressed or implied and by 'needs' I mean the values we hold dear as human beings and that sustain us, and again I check with the speaker that I have understood. I want to link the feelings to the need... with the understanding that our feelings arise as a result of our needs, whether these are met or unmet.

> *'Do you need respect for your time and the energy you have put into planning your lessons?'*

I am wondering if this is at the heart of why the situation is bothering this teacher. My experience is that if I can guess the need (here the need for respect) then the person feels heard. If I am not accurate in my guess then at least the other person will trust me and feel able to give me more information. People tend to relax and I can keep guessing based on the information articulated and from the body language. I verbalise my guess in order to convey my presence and evidence that I have listened with empathy. Rosenberg (2003a) notes that 'we know the speaker has received adequate empathy when a) we sense a release of tension, or b) the flow of words comes to a halt' (p.102).

I do not ask people directly what their needs are, since in my experience people do not have a vocabulary for their needs, and tend to tell you want they want to have happen, or what they want the other person to do. *For example: 'I need him to stop shouting at me'.* Working at the 'needs level' means to work at the level of deeply held values. As the facilitator or mediator I offer the vocabulary and the presence to support someone so they can trust me and can communicate with me at this level.

Requests

The final step of this four step process is to check if I have understood what *strategies* the speaker has in mind and what *requests* they may want to make. By *strategies and requests* I mean the steps to take to move forward, keeping in mind everyone's needs. I make a guess what these may be for the speaker:

> *'Would you like him to know how important arriving on time to lessons is to you and the school?'*

At this point we can start to explore, and perhaps solve, the problem. Learning to apply the model of NVC to interactions involves, among other things, learning the vocabulary of feelings and needs, listening beyond the story to what is important to the person, and seeking to make a connection with the other person above anything else. When things are heated and relationships are at stake NVC practitioners may use the formal four-step model illustrated above. However, a more natural style suitable to the situation is recommended to keep the connection and this takes practice to develop. Like learning scales and arpeggios when learning music the four ingredients offer a scaffold, but are not the tune.

Therefore, although NVC at first glance appears to be a script, those of us who have practised over time begin to appreciate the subtle and vital aspects of the model. This model needs to be experienced in order to fully understand the power bought to interactions. In this sense NVC is both a science and an art, there is a script or a formula *and* there is an understanding of the intention and the idea of letting go of any outcome for the interaction.

Preparing for a restorative encounter

An essential part of preparing for a restorative encounter involves using an inner process called self-empathy to transform what are referred to in NVC as 'enemy images'. I want to approach the dialogue open and ready to listen. As soon as I am judging another person, labelling another or wishing they were different, albeit in my head, then the relationship between us will start to attenuate and may also be broken before I have said a word. Young people who are used to violence and abuse at home have had to learn pretty quickly to be ready for anything, and are especially adept at reading people. They have become adept also at spotting people who are saying one thing but meaning another. Sticking to a script as a facilitator is not going to be effective if internally one's intention is at odds with one's words.

In the culture I have been raised in and live in we do not usually tell another person our negative judgements about them, so tend to feel that we are non-judgemental. However, I suggest that internal negative judgements will leak out non-verbally anyway, however good at acting a person might be. Using the NVC model it is possible to transform my 'enemy images'. My judgements are thoughts which can be transformed by reflecting what needs of mine are being unmet in the situation. For example if I judge someone to be 'difficult' I can chose to check in with myself, using a private reflection tool developed by Kashtan and Kashtan.[2] I may notice, for example, that I am feeling concern, and that this feeling is coming from my need for ease and safety in this meeting. It is helpful to feel connected with my own feelings and needs at this point. If I then think about what feelings and needs the other person may be having in the situation I am able to feel empathy and compassion for them. By taking time for this reflection I may find that my initial judgemental thoughts have changed and I no longer hold 'enemy images'. If my judgements persist then I may need to explore what needs of mine are being met by holding onto this negative judgement and what feelings remain? The advice is to keep showing oneself empathy to understand what may be happening.

---

2   Kashtan, I. and Kashtan, M. *Unpublished training materials*. Used with permission. Contact Miki Kashtan via www.baynvc.org.

During a restorative encounter

I continue to stay mindfully attuned to my internal world and keep coming back into the present moment. I use the four-step model to check my feelings and needs. I use this internal process in every meeting I have in school. What follows is an example from my own experience. It is a description of a meeting between myself and Mr G, the parent of Paul, a student, in preparation for a larger meeting involving all parties. I often offer this opportunity as parents can find it daunting to come straight into a meeting in school.

My thoughts start the moment the parent walks in the room.

'Eeeek, Paul's dad has turned up, he's a nightmare to work with, he never listens... last time he came to a meeting he shouted at the head teacher.'

I first notice I am getting lost in these thoughts, memories and judgements and bring myself back into my body – sometimes by just feeling my feet on the floor or checking the temperature of my feet or the air. I drop into my feelings and internally check the sensations in my body.

'Oh, I'm feeling tense, my shoulders have tensed up, my stomach has started to churn, I feel anxious...? yes that's it I feel anxious because I'm needing to feel safe – what happens if he shouts at me? I feel scared by this thought...I get curious...what need of mine is this thought trying to bring to my attention? ...I need to have a sense that I am safe, and I need support for this meeting to go well for Paul. I'm really wanting us to make some progress here...'

I link the feeling with the underlying need of mine that is not met as I see that Paul's Dad has turned up. I relax as I identify the need. As I've practised linking my feelings to my needs for many years I can do this more quickly now – connecting with my needs in the situation supports me to be open and ready to listen to the other person. I am no longer anxious or operating from the position of being worried about this father. The process of doing this brings me to be present to myself, which supports the dialogue I am having. I can therefore offer this presence to Paul's father rather than feeling anxious and creating barriers between us by labelling him, (albeit silently). It also means my day to day job is less stressful as I am not living with the anxiety of these kinds of meetings.

I can now turn my attention to guessing what the father's feelings and needs are, and I can do this because I have done the internal work needed. I want to understand him. I am not willing myself to hear him, nor preparing for the worst. I want to engage with him at the level of his needs, so he has a sense that he is heard.

Mr G begins by saying:

'This school is terrible, they've never done anything to support Paul, he's missing too much of school, what are you going to do about it?'

I respond: *'I am guessing you are really annoyed and wanting progress here?'* (noting to myself that we share the same need for progress).

He replies *'Yes bloody right, it's been a disgrace how little this school have done.'*

His body language shifts a bit as he looks at me. I have shown that I have heard some of what he wants heard. However, I know that there are more needs he wants me to be aware of because he has repeated his thoughts about the school. I can empathise some more. I do not have to agree with him – I just show him I have heard him.

I say: *'Are you feeling really annoyed and wanting me to hear how fed up you are with the school and what you feel has been done to support Paul?'*

He replies *'Yes, they've not done a single thing.'*

I make a shift to connect with him via expressing my feelings and needs by saying:

'I'm feeling confused, Mr G, we met last month to plan how to support Paul and I know his form teacher has been meeting with him every day? Is there more you would like to have happened?'

To which he replies: *'Well yes they've done that but it's done no good and he's really falling behind.'*

So now, by choosing to listen for what is behind these words I can hear another need he is expressing. Mr G needs progress and he has just mentioned his need for the safety and security in knowing that his son is going to achieve in school. I cannot know what his needs are. I can only guess until I ask him, and wait for his confirmation or for some more information. My own needs are for progress, to contribute to this situation and to get some sense of professional safety. I am continually checking that I am still in contact with myself.

I say: *'So it sounds like you do recognise that the school are trying to support Paul and that people are putting time and effort into finding a way forward and yet you are really worried still that Paul may be falling behind and you really want him to do well in school? Is that it?'*

Mr G replies *'Yes, what are you going to do about it?'*

I am now in internal panic at the idea that suddenly I have to be the person to fix all of this, so I tune into this. My internal monologue goes:

'I am feeling panic inside me because I really worry about being seen as 'the expert' in these situations. I really want to find way to support people to find their own solutions and not get pulled into fixing people, which I know does not work in the long run.'

As I find the space in me open up as I tune into my needs I realise we do not have Paul's needs 'on the table'. I take a deep breath. I choose to try and pull things together.

I say: *'I'm really wanting us to work together to find a way to make some progress, I understand, Mr G, that you are really wanting progress, and some sense of reassurance that Paul is going to keep up with school work. I guess the school is really wanting to ensure that progress is made too, and that they support Paul to manage to stay in lessons without storming out. Do you agree that this is where we are at?'*

I notice that Mr G is much more relaxed than when he came in. I guess he has a sense that he has been heard and he confirms that he does agree with my assessment of the situation. So I can now suggest that no-one has 'the answer', but that we need to find a way to problem solve together.

Now Mr G is in a more relaxed state he will be much more likely to be able to join in with a meeting involving all parties without getting defensive or criticising the school, a stance which would in turn make the teachers defensive. This could still happen, in my experience is less likely to after this preparatory meeting. As we move into the larger meeting I will continue to remain in touch with myself and be attentive for any signs of criticism from Mr G that could upset the teachers. If this does happen I can translate what I am hearing into what needs Mr G is trying to express. When there are more people in the room the process remains the same. I check in with myself – Am I tired ? Am I needing a break? Am I feeling stuck or needing inspiration? I can choose whether or not to express these needs and feelings. I check with the people in the room and guess their feelings and needs as we go through the stages of the meeting. Sometimes I do this silently, sometimes I check by asking questions. All in all I want to create a sense that the meeting is a place to be heard, that it is safe for everyone to express themselves, and I model how to be restorative no matter what a parent or young person is saying. I make sure there is empathy before moving to problem solving and planning.

Reflections

After practising NVC within education settings for over ten years it is a challenge to write about what happens, and to illustrate such a multidimensional practice within the limitations of text. Those that work alongside me notice that something is going on, and appreciate the calming effect my questions can have during meetings. Siegel (2007) has come the closest to describing what I experience when I am mindfully attuned to myself using NVC and more exploration is needed to uncover more as to what is working here.

I encourage as many people as possible to do more than simply imagine a world where all our interactions are mindful, open, trusting, respectful and empathic: I encourage them to start to create such a world by learning the skills of NVC, and by joining the growing community of practitioners around the world.

References

Barter, D. (2012) 'Walking towards Conflict'. *Tikkun Magazine, Winter Volume 17.* Available at www.tikkun.org/nextgen/walking-toward-conflict, accessed on 29th August 2014.

Cox, E. and P. Dannahy (2005) 'The value of openness in e-relationships: Using nonviolent communication to guide online coaching and mentoring.' *International Journal of Evidence Based Coaching and Mentoring 3,* 1, 39–51.

Gendlin, E. T. (2003) *Focusing: How to Gain Direct Access to Your Body's Knowledge. How to Open Up Your Deeper Feelings and Intuition.* (Revised and updated anniversary edition) London: Rider.

Hart, S. and Kindle-Hodson, V. (2004) *The Compassionate Classroom: Relationship Based Teaching and Learning.* Encinitas, CA: Puddledancer Press.

Hart, S. and Kindle-Hodson, V. (2006) *Respectful Parents Respectful Kids: Seven Keys To Turn Family Conflict into Co-operation.* Encinitas, CA: Puddledancer Press.

Hopkins, B. (2004) *Just Schools: A Whole School Approach to Restorative Justice.* London: Jessica Kingsley Publishers.

Hopkins, B. (2009) *Just Care: Restorative Justice Approaches to Working with Children in Public Care.* London: Jessica Kingsley Publishers.

Lasater, I. (2010) *Words That Work in Business: A Practical Guide to Effective Communication in the Workplace.* Encinitas, CA: Puddledancer Press.

Little, M. C. (2008) Total Honesty/ Total Heart: Fostering Empathy Development and Conflict Resolution Skills. A Violence Prevention Strategy. (Unpublished Master's Thesis, University of Victoria.)

Rogers, C. (1961) *On Becoming a Person: A Therapist's View of Psychotherapy.* London: Constable.

Rogers, C. (1980) *A Way of Being.* New York, NY: Houghton Mifflin.

Rogers, C. (1983) *Freedom to Learn for the 80s, 2nd revised edition.* New York, NY: Merrill.

Rosenberg, M. B. (2003a) *Nonviolent Communication: A Language of Life.* (2nd Edition) Encinitas, CA: Puddledancer Press.

Rosenberg, M. B. (2003b) *Life-Enriching Education: Nonviolent Communication Helps Schools Improve Performance, Reduce Conflict, and Enhance Relationships.* Encinitas, CA: Puddledancer Press.

Siegel, D. J. (2007) *The Mindful Brain:Refection and Attunement in the Cultivation of Well-Being.* New York, NY: Norton Publishers.

CHAPTER 6

Personal Construct Approaches

PAM DENICOLO

Introduction

Most, if not all, theories within interpretative paradigms could claim to be some form of 'just theories', since they recognise that individual worldviews are idiosyncratic and truths difficult or impossible to discern. However, few apart from Personal Construct Theory (PCT) and Social Constructionism have both a philosophical basis (ontology and epistemology) and a set of tools within a practice framework that so well fits them to such a description. As its name suggests, PCT focuses on the individual's viewpoint, being essentially a psychological theory, whereas social constructionism is a sociological theory that takes a societal perspective (Berger and Luckmann 1967; Burr 1995). These two theories are congruent and have much in common, including some main tenets, techniques and instruments, but it is PCT that is addressed in detail in this chapter to demonstrate its potential within restorative encounters as well as in clinical, research and educative settings.

In the following section the origins of PCT are addressed, since they demonstrate its philosophical foundations, and its main tenets are described, with some brief examples provided of the diversity of its application. The ways in which it has been, and can be, deployed to resolve conflict and encourage productive dialogue, form the substance of the section which follows. Included are examples, with references, of such situations in which it has been effectively used, followed by a more detailed illustration of the processes that draws on examples from actual case studies.

The final section acts as both a summary and an encouragement to explore further the theory and its potential applications, with caveats and reminders of its incisive power.

The development and scope of the theory of personal constructs

Dissatisfaction with the prevailing psychological approaches of his era both within his own North American environment and in Europe led George Kelly to explore other ways to address clinical and educational issues (Fransella and Neimayer 2005). He reasoned, for instance, that a patient's diagnosis and subsequent treatment was dependent on the theoretical framework of the clinician, rather than being determined in an unbiased way from the symptoms. As an example, the behaviourist and Freudian therapists would differ in the rationale given for a person being an addicted tobacco smoker and each would suggest different 'cures' for the problem. Neither would be likely to respect the patient by asking his/her reasons for smoking originally and subsequently, nor would they afford the patient the dignity of exploring for him/herself alternative visions of self as a non-smoker and potential means to attain that state. He also found frustrating the way that psychology, and thereby understanding of human beings, was carved up into theories about perception, about learning, about memory, about emotion and about behaviour as if they were not inextricably linked.

Such ruminations led him to propose a complex and wide-ranging theory about how people construe their worlds, how such construing develops and how more personally effective re-construing can be stimulated and supported (Kelly 1991). This personal construct theory has guided my own research, teaching (and personal learning) and psychological practice, that of my close colleague, Maureen Pope, as well as that of the multitude of doctoral researchers, working in diverse disciplines, whom we have supervised. Like Kelly, we agree that there may well be a reality out there but humans cannot access it directly; instead we can only view it through the lenses constructed from our previous experience and understanding of the world. Again like Kelly, before becoming psychologists Pope and I were scientists so for us his description of people is apposite: all are personal scientists who build up hypotheses about what is going on and what thinks are like and then test them out, changing them if they are repeatedly challenged or if a personally more useful hypothesis emerges (Denicolo and Pope 2001).

For us, PCT is appealing because we interpret its core assumptions thus: people are responsible agents (not totally subject to external reinforcement or internal, unknowable forces such as the id and ego, nor driven only by instinct); all kinds of psychological growth (cognitive and emotional) can take place at any time in life through reflection on and in action; understanding the viewpoint of others requires conversation and negotiation since it derives from different prior experiences from our own. Thus people are creatures that actively seek meaning, have the potential for lifelong learning, are capable of self-direction and can engage in cooperative enquiry to gain empathy and understanding of alternative constructions of reality, while not necessarily agreeing with them.

Kelly set out his theory as a formal fundamental postulate with eleven corollaries.[1] For our purposes here the following premises may suffice:

1.   In order to live in the world, physical and social, people erect representational models of it and hypothesise about what leads to what within it; that is, they make predictions about what the world is like and what their future experiences will be.

2.   These hypotheses, or *constructs*, are continually tested and may be revised if frequently challenged, though some core constructs that have served well for interacting in the world in the past may be resilient to change. More peripheral constructs have had less survival value and so are less resistant. As an example, for me a core construct is about the kindness of people – checking out my hypothesis, and consequent expectations about how a degree of kindness influences other behaviour, has served me well for a lifetime. More peripheral constructs concern individuals' age, gender, and how they prefer to dress. I am happy to be challenged and change my views/constructs about what I consider to be relatively trivial aspects of how people are.

1   For an accessible digest of these as well as insights into Kelly, the man, see Fransella 2005.

3.   Constructs link together in a complex, idiosyncratic construct system. Individuals have different experiences and opportunities both to develop their constructs and to challenge them. For this reason they differ in the number and kind of constructs they have about any event, situation, person or object and the way in which these constructs are organised, their own construct system, is unique. For example, I have few constructs about cars or varieties of pasta, while my daughter and husband have many and varied. Neither of them have my range of constructs about detective novels or shoes.

4.   Since constructs emerge and are tested in different situations this leads to complexity in the system but also to an individual's ability to retain apparently contradictory constructs in different parts of the system. For example a deeply religious person might well also be convinced by the arguments of nuclear physics. Someone with 'green' views may nevertheless drive to work in a petrol-fuelled car to earn a living.

5.   Constructs tend to encompass cognitive, emotional and action elements although each will have different proportions of these elements. Some elements may be very logical, with little emotional content or vice versa. However, each will influence action in some way since constructs inform our predictions about our experiences, and those predictions are manifest in behaviour. For example I happily eat any shape and colour of pasta and, though I love new shoes, I would wear some pairs until they disintegrate because of the meaning they have for me.

6.   Sometimes different people construe things in a similar way; that is, they use similar constructs in the same way to differentiate things. For example, my daughter, husband and I all use a construct about the reliability of cars in a similar way, and so agree about which models we would rate as likely to be reliable. This is termed the *commonality* of construing in the formal theory.

7.   It is possible to understand another's constructs in the sense of being able to view a person, thing or event (any aspect of their world) through the lens of their constructs, without necessarily sharing them or even agreeing with them. For example, I am able to differentiate cars by looking to see if they have alloy wheels or other appurtenances but I do not rate these as important in any way. I can understand why the road-holding ability of a car in difficult terrain is critical for my daughter who lives in a mountainous area. However, for me in my environment this feature is fairly irrelevant. This ability is known as *sociality* in the formal theory and this, with *commonality*, is an important concept for both restorative encounters and research on human endeavours. It is an important part of accepting that there are reasons why others do things, or not do them, that may or may not have relevance or rationality to us or be deemed appropriate by us.

The process of *differentiation* is central to the concept of constructs. Constructs are personal creations that allow us to discriminate between things, seeing similarities and differences. Thus, in PCT, constructs are considered to be bi-polar dimensions along which things can be arranged according to how well they match the descriptions of each pole. The notion of contrast in descriptions is important because it allows us to better understand the meaning embedded in a construct. For instance, we can better understand one person's description of another as being 'generous' when we learn that the contrast pole for them is 'never has time for me'. For another person, although they might describe some acquaintances as 'generous', their contrast might be 'is mean with money'. This example also alerts us to the challenges posed by using a common language and assuming that we mean the same thing by the words used to describe people, things or situations. Commonality of construing cannot be assumed because we use the same words – an important caveat also recognised by social constructionists. We need to be conscious that words are merely symbols or notations of meaning, not the meaning itself, so if we share descriptions of our worlds in an attempt to gain sociality then we need also to explore how words in descriptions are being used. PCT provides a range of techniques to help us do so.

One such technique used in interview situations of various kinds is to explore the meaning epitomised by particular constructs through questions about what contrasts apply, and through follow-up exploration of how different attributes can be recognised, and so on. For the 'generous' example above, we might ask for a particularly generous person to be identified along with a person who could not be considered as fitting that description – whether this is someone who 'never has time' or who is 'mean with money' (depending on the appropriate contrast description). In this way, fuller descriptions of each, particularly how generosity or lack of it plays out in behaviour, can be elicited. This would give us some further information beyond the verbal label about that construct. This can then be elaborated further by exploring preferences (in this example, generosity or meanness with time or money) and why that attribute is important. This can lead to the revelation of core constructs, so 'why' questions should be used with care and sensitivity. Using myself as an example, I prefer generous people because they are likely to be kind; Why? I prefer kind people because I will feel valued; Why is it important to feel valued? I want to feel valued because I need to be loved.

Another technique, the *repertory grid* (rep grid) – an example is provided later of the grid format and procedure – can help a person explore the range of constructs they use about, or within, an identified domain of experience, such as the roles they play, the people they work or play with, or the activities they engage in. The rep grid employs similar questioning techniques but in a more structured way. The degree of structure depends upon what purpose the grid is intended to serve. Some have rating scales and produce data that can be analysed statistically, while others simply provide an informal way for eliciting constructs, with other variations between. They can be compiled using relaxed, conversational approaches or through very formal, structured elicitation of constructs. Grids can be used with the same person and topic over time to identify changes in construing due to experience, and what has been learnt. Grids can also be used with different people exploring the same topic to discern similarities and differences in construing. Constructs can be elicited using pictures or drawings or a number of other devices. Any of the many methods used in PCT can be used as clinical or educational instruments, or in research. They can be used as restorative, conflict resolution techniques to alert people to their own way of viewing the world and compare that to alternative perspectives, those of other people or their own potential future ones (Denicolo 2005). This plethora of potential techniques, as Kelly noted as being subject only to the limits of our imaginations, provides access to a wide range of individual's and groups' constructs, whatever their abilities and contexts.

A further tenet of PCT is that, though we can never be sure that our understanding of the world embodied in our constructs matches correctly the reality of it, some constructions of it are more accurate than others and thus may well serve to help us make more useful predictions (constructive alternatives). This theory, then, is optimistic in recognising the lifelong potential for change, as described by Kelly himself:

> No-one need paint himself [sic] into a corner; no-one needs to be completely hemmed in by circumstances; no-one needs to be a victim of his biography. (Kelly 1991, p.11)

PCT in restorative encounters – A range of illustrations

My own experience of restorative encounters has been with individuals and groups of people investigating their own current constructs about particular issues in order to discover if alternative ways of construing might be more productive in some way, particularly in relation to how they interact with others. An example would be when interpersonal conflicts within working groups in a multi- or inter-professional work domain have been submerged for all sorts of good reasons, such as professional etiquette and the need to get the job done. However, that has not rendered them less destructive.

An example of such a situation arose when I worked with academic colleagues (who had previously worked in different health and social care backgrounds) on the shared task of designing and running higher degree programmes for professionals from that diverse range of backgrounds. The explicit logic for such multi-professional courses was that, since most work in that field required input from a range of professional perspectives, it would be beneficial if those professionals could learn together, as well as work together. Each academic overtly subscribed to this rationale, had a vested interest in developing successful programmes and behaved in a professionally well-mannered way during meetings.

However it was clear to me as a mentor from a different disciplinary background that undercurrents were arising derived from their previous occupations, each of which was considered more special in some way than the others.

Within each professional group prejudices were expressed through the language used in asides and, for instance, 'jokes' about the potential value of the courses to each of the other target professional groups. These biases I suggest derive from years of experience of in-group loyalty, specialist training and defending and promoting professional interests in a competitive career environment. This had led to misconceptions being built up about other professions related to such things as ability to communicate, and to empathise with, or gain the respect of, clients and other professionals. Fortunately, the academics concerned in the course development had all expressed an interest in learning about PCT approaches to research. I therefore suggested that, if they were brave enough to be open to constructive challenge, we could 'learn through practice' by exploring through the rep grid method how students from the diverse professional groups might interact with the course.

They correctly recognised that some potentially embarrassing, if not controversial, prejudices would be revealed. However, they agreed that a spirit of cooperative enquiry, well laced with good humour, might serve them and their students well for the future. This is in fact what happened, as myths and misunderstandings were dispelled and new respect established. So much so that it stimulated one of them, Ashwell, previously a youth worker, to undertake research under my supervision using rep grids. His research focused on multi-agency groups in the community that did not seem to be achieving their potential impact in joint endeavours such as reducing teenage pregnancies and drug abuse. As he noted in his thesis (Ashwell 2003), inter-agency collaboration was often seen as collaboration with the enemy rather than an opportunity to make the best of different skills and knowledge. The views of police representatives differed from, and clashed with, those of the youth workers, while there was a sense from the representatives from community nursing and from the teachers that, as a group, each was more effective than all the others.

The grids produced in both of these research examples revealed much to the participants about the others' perspectives on the professional world of work. For instance, a construct 'wears a uniform…works in mufti' might be linked closely with 'clients are reluctant to engage with them…clients perceive them as accessible' for one group of professionals and with 'looks professional…looks like any member of the public' to another group. Thus the noticing of someone wearing of a uniform might produce a bias about accessibility and/or professionalism.

The decision about which version of construct elicitation procedure to use depends on the purpose of the exercise, so that defining that purpose is the first task when developing any form of constructivist encounter. This should also take account of the participants' style, their preferences and their abilities so that the method produces the best outcome for all. What follows are two examples of when construct elicitation procedures were used to help resolve a conflict, one formal and the other informal. The first more formal procedure is based on the professional development example above. The informal version involves family members and uses drawings as the basis for discussion. It is important to note that any elicitation process and subsequent discussion should be led by a facilitator with the skills and sensitivity to help mediate difficult situations and that the participants should engage voluntarily having been alerted to the challenges within the situation (see the final section of this chapter).

Formal, structured elicitation and sharing of constructs

When a group of people, in this example all health-focused professionals, want to gain an enriched understanding of others' roles, and their own in relation to those others, a starting point for discussion can be the way each deals with a situation in which many of them are involved. The next step is to identify a representative range of people who would be involved in that situation and these people are known as the *element set*. This selection could well include: the general practitioner (GP), the community nurse, a pharmacist, a physiotherapist and a social worker. Another important 'helper' in any health situation is the prime carer. This person might be included in the element set even if he or she is not a member of the grid participant group. Their inclusion in the element set provides a source of contrast. The inclusion of the patient as an element to elucidate different professional's views on the role required of patients in aiding their own recovery would also add an extra dimension. Each participant could then draw up, in private, a grid with the seven 'roles' heading the columns. The constructs would then form the rows of the grid, as in Table 6.1.

The process of eliciting the constructs can be helped by using what is termed the *triadic elicitation method*. This involves asking each participant to first consider three of the helpers, a *triad*, in terms of how two are similar and different to the third. When individuals are simply being helped to recognise their own constructs then each would generate their own individual constructs. However, in a group process, as in this example, the constructs used could be suggested by individuals, then negotiated with the others to ensure a shared understanding of what each means and an agreement as to its relevance to the topic. Negotiating the constructs in this way begins the process of developing mutual understanding.

Table 6.1: Preparing the grid by identifying the elements

Similarity Pole 1	GP	Community Nurse	Pharmacist	Physiotherapist	Social Worker	Prime Carer	Patient	Difference Pole 3

For a triad of prime carer, community nurse and social worker a construct of 'has much contact with patient' as opposed to 'limited contact' might emerge. Each participant could then use a 3-point scale to rate themselves and others on this construct. Number 1 would represent very frequent contact and 3 very limited contact, 2 being some notional midpoint (five or even seven point scales can be used, depending on the degree of discrimination required). I have chosen this construct as one that could be deemed relatively objective, since number of visits per week might be used as a yardstick, even though length of visit may differ. However, from experience I suggest that there might be differences of opinion among the professionals about how they view the degree of contact of provided by themselves and by others. All of the professional groups could well be surprised by the ratings given to them by the patient.

Another triad, say general practioner (GP), physiotherapist and social worker, might elicit a construct: 'has a limited focus within the situation' in contrast to 'has a holistic view of the patient and the situation' – with similar differences in ratings from each participant in the process. A potentially even more subjective construct such as 'rehabilitation of the patient is a heart-felt concern' / 'this is only a job' might emerge from a triad of prime carer, patient and pharmacist, for instance. Again, how each professional person rates the others could thus uncover several misconceptions. The triadic elicitation can continue until no new ones emerge about how different helpers contribute to patient care.

Table 6.2: A section of an unrated grid with some constructs agreed

Similarity Pole 1	GP	Community Nurse	Pharmacist	Physiotherapist	Social Worker	Prime Carer	Patient	Difference Pole 3
Much contact								Limited contact
Limited Focus								Holistic view
Heart felt concern								Only a job
etc.								etc.

The rep grid process recognises that each person can and will interpret idiosyncratically the meaning of the words used in the construct, and will apply their interpretation in a unique way to the elements in the grid, in this case the roles held. In order to determine where *commonality* occurs and then to gain some *sociality* when it does not, a sharing process is called for. In this example the process could be carried out relatively safely by the production of an unrated communal, large-scale grid for public viewing. Each participant could then be asked to add the rating scores that they would allocate to their own role column, thus allowing the others to compare those ratings with the ones they had each allocated to others' roles, and then reflect on the differences.

For a more in-depth exploration of understandings the facilitator could orchestrate a discussion of those differences by encouraging such questions as 'Can those in role X please elaborate more on why they gave their role that score on that particular construct?' They could also be asked to share which constructs they deemed the most important in their jobs and why, to gain an understanding of differences in priorities as well as constructs.

Informal elicitation and sharing of constructs

For this illustration, let us consider a family situation in which parents and a teenage daughter each have different perspectives on the daughter's social habits and activities and that these differing perspectives are causing conflicts. Initial preparation would include establishing a shared sense of purpose, namely to gain some insight into, and understanding of, each other's perspectives. This initial preparation would not involve everyone committing to agreeing with these differing perspectives. The participants are then encouraged to draw two sketches in private: the first sketch is to depict what each considers to be a very happy social scene including the daughter, and the second is to depict a social scene, also including the daughter, that is viewed with some dismay. When the drawings are complete the facilitator asks each person to write down at the side of their drawings words that express the positive or negative aspects they were trying to convey by the contrasting scenes.

The daughter's positive drawing shows her in trendy casual clothes, the centre of attention of similarly attired youngsters in a crowded pub, with musical notes and lots of speech bubbles, while her negative drawing depicts her alone and droopy, watching television with her much younger brother. Her accompanying words included respectively: (a) fun, accepted, comfortable and (b) bored, left out, childish.

The mother's positive picture is similar, and shows the daughter at the centre of attention but in trendy, more upmarket clothes, in a more sophisticated restaurant, with smart youngsters. Her negative one shows her daughter in a gloomy street looking through a bright window at others enjoying themselves. Her words included: (a) enjoying herself, suitable company, making contacts for the future and (b) lonely, left out, no prospects.

The father's positive picture shows a demure young lady at the cinema with a friend eating ice cream, while his negative one shows her scantily clad surrounded by wolves in youths' clothing. His words included: (a) having fun, safe, age-appropriate and (b) at risk, asking for trouble, scares me.

The facilitator then encourages them each to identify areas were there might be common ground noting words and ideas that suggest that they recognise similarity of interest. A positive example would be that each shows the daughter having fun outside the home with other people. All three are also encouraged to note areas of concern, in general if not in detail. In this example these might be who the other people are, and the nature of the venue. This provides a basis for exploring further the points of difference (style of dress, focus on the here and now or on the risks in the future) to consider why some things might be more important to one person and not to another, and where compromise in behaviour or acceptance of difference might be possible.

Making sketches of scenes that please or worry us can often unlock our sub-conscious concerns and help us to articulate them to others. They then enable exploration of similarity and difference with less challenge, and often with more humour, than a confrontation of words alone. Once some understanding of other's viewpoints, and what they consider important and why, has been reached then a will to find practical ways forward that cause less conflict can be nurtured.

In other situations in which there is a need to understand potentially conflicting perspectives of other people, artefacts such as pictures selected by the participants can be used. These might include postcards, pictures cut from magazines or photographs taken by participants. Such artefacts can be used as conduits to help them articulate what they think and feel about a situation. Using artefacts such as this responds to the different ways in which people feel comfortable to express themselves and allows the focus to be less personally invasive. The focus is on the artefact rather than the individual.

Advantages of the theory and caveats about its use

The rep grid, in all its variations, along with the many other construct elicitation techniques allows for a rich, in-depth exploration of portions of a person's views on, and understanding of, the world they uniquely inhabit. One benefit of all the possible techniques is that, unlike many other techniques that yield qualitative data, they allow participants to indicate issues of personal relevance and describe them using their own media and then words. This can avoid 'interviewer or counsellor' bias, thus helping to avoid misunderstanding in the discourse. Further, each technique provides for the making of a public record as personal meaning is explored in relatively systematic ways. The range of techniques available has the additional benefits of providing flexibility so that the exercise can be tailored to suit participants' predispositions, facilitators' skills and situational constraints. This applies also to the analysis of the information produced (or data in a research context) since this information or data can be open to a range of explorations from simple 'eyeballing' to statistical analysis, each with discussion.

On the other hand each technique only provides a partial insight (albeit a rich one) since we do not have unlimited time and capacity. Further, while they provide information about how we think and feel and how situations arose, they do not provide solutions to problems. The solutions lie in the hands of those who are prepared to work with that information. It is one thing to know that others' perspectives are different from your own, but another to recognise them as authentic outcomes of their lived experience and therefore valid for them. Similarly, we may be personally confronted by our own biases but that may not prevent us from applying them thoughtlessly or unconsciously time and again.

This brings us to ethical and safety issues. This is a powerful, incisive methodology that is best applied by those willing first to practice on themselves and to understand its power. Second, practitioners using this methodology must practice sufficiently to be skilled enough to recognise and deal with any potential discomfort experienced by other participants as they realise and confront the constructs that guide their own behaviour and that of others. Even the sharing of grids on apparently innocuous topics like holiday destinations with a partner can bring forth previously unknown and unexpected revelations about worldviews. The influence of our upbringing, and what was considered polite or rude by our parents, can affect the way we view and treat people with a different cultural, including generational, background.

It is important that, when participants are invited to engage in such explorations, the usual agreements are reached about confidentiality of information revealed in the process and freedom to withdraw at any time. Revealing even to oneself the details of one's construing can be challenging. Nevertheless, participants in clinical encounters, and research projects as well as restorative encounters, generally find the results of personal construct elicitation techniques fascinating and informative. They recognise why they have embraced some perspectives and discarded others, why they have found certain situations conducive and others repellent, and why they do not always agree with close family, never mind others with whom they come into contact through work or in social situations.

References

Ashwell, N. (2003) *Perceptions of Inter-Agency Collaboration: Youth and Health.* Unpublished PhD thesis: University of Reading.

Berger, P. L. and Luckmann, T. (1967) *The Social Construction of Reality.* London: Allen Lane.

Burr, V. (1995) *An Introduction to Social Constructionism.* London: Routledge.

Denicolo, P. M. (2005) 'A Range of Elicitation Methods to Suit Client and Purpose' in F. Fransella (ed.) (2005) *The Essential Practitioner's Handbook of Personal Construct Psychology.* Chichester: John Wiley and Sons.

Denicolo, P. M. and Pope, M. L. (2001) *Transformative Professional Practice: Personal Construct Approaches to Education and Research.* London: Whurr Publishers.

Fransella, F. and Neimeyer, R. A. (2005) 'George Alexander Kelly: The Man and his Theory' in F. Fransella (ed.) *The Essential Practitioner's Handbook of Personal Construct Psychology.* Chichester: John Wiley and Sons.

Kelly, G. A. (1991) *The Psychology of Personal Constructs (2 volumes).* London: Routledge (Original work published 1955).

CHAPTER 7

Towards a Relational Theory of Restorative Justice

MARK VANDER VENNEN

Introduction

For the past ten years I have been privileged to work simultaneously in two distinct areas: psychotherapy with children and youth who have significant attachment disorders, and restorative justice facilitation in a wide variety of community contexts. I am both a trained psychotherapist and a certified restorative justice trainer.

The psychotherapy work takes the form of dyadic developmental psychotherapy, developed especially by psychologist Daniel Hughes. The restorative justice work has focused especially on schools, faith communities, and workplaces. My restorative approach has been generously shaped by a rich vein of leaders in the field.

What has been the impact of this deliberate, simultaneous engagement in these two areas? The sensation is something like living in an echo chamber. Key themes from each field, all having to do with the fundamental dynamics of human relationship, have been reverberating, even ricocheting off one another. In this chapter I make sense of some the more pronounced echoes.

Let me begin with one observation. In my experience, psychotherapy is not a form of restorative practice, nor is restorative practice a type of psychotherapy. A restorative encounter (which I define below) can have even more profound therapeutic effects than what may happen in a psychotherapy office, while movement in psychotherapy can take a restorative direction. But when I facilitate a restorative encounter I explicitly do not assume the role of a psychotherapist, even if sometimes a therapeutic sensibility may be apparent. This is not compartmentalisation on my part. Rather, I have learned that the therapeutic impacts of a restorative encounter diminish if, in the encounter, I begin to do psychotherapy with participants, no matter how insightful or clinically sound my psychotherapy approach may be.

How then does the attachment model inform my engagement in a restorative encounter, if it does not prescribe my actual restorative practice? What attachment offers me is a theoretical construct for understanding what is happening in a restorative encounter, and why an encounter is effective or ineffective. Attachment provides me with the outlines of a theoretical compass for restorative justice. It is often said that restorative justice is, at bottom, about the 'repair of harm done to relationships'. I believe that an attachment lens, supported by recent developments in neuroscience, can strengthen restorative practice by grounding it in a comprehensive theory of human relationship (Llewellyn 2011, 2012).

In this chapter I first outline the theory of attachment and attachment psychotherapy. I then describe my restorative encounter practice. As I do so, I overlay themes from the attachment model to help understand what makes the restorative encounter effective. Finally, I reference how each field understands the role of shame and propose a differential understanding of shame that seeks to be more comprehensive than each field's individual understanding.

Attachment

Attachment has emerged in the last fifteen years as the 'central organising theory' of human development and human relationship (Hughes 2013, p.2; Cozolino 2006; Johnson 2013; Siegel 2013). The dynamics of attachment are seen as the driving force behind our ability or inability to connect with others. Attachment theory's basic hypothesis is that our interactions with our primary caregivers (attachment figures) from birth onwards create an attachment style that serves as the blueprint or template by which we 'do' relationships with others, from cradle to grave (Cozolino 2006; Golding 2014; Hughes 2013; Siegel 2013, 2010). This style serves as our 'internal working model' for understanding relationships and the world. I will provide just enough description to set the stage for a conversation about restorative practice.

The early work of Mary Ainsworth *et al.* (1978) following the footsteps of attachment pioneer John Bowlby (1969, 1973, 1980, 1988), led to the identification of four basic attachment styles (Cozolino 2006). These styles are relatively stable through time, though they are malleable and can change as a result of experience. Neurological research has identified the brain processes operative in each style and has found that they are plastic well into our nineties (Siegel 2010).

The four styles are divided into *secure* attachment and three types of *insecure* attachment. The insecure attachments are called avoidant, ambivalent and disorganised (Golding 2014; Hughes 2013; Siegel 2013). In a secure attachment, the primary caregivers provide both a safe haven and a launching pad for exploration of the world. When the baby or child is distressed or anxious and cries out, she is soothed and comforted. As she soothes the child, the parent will mimic or match the baby's affect, a process by which she regulates the child's affect. After a time, with her sense of safety in the attachment relationship restored, the baby or child ventures out, able to again dedicate her boundless curiosity to exploring the world. This pattern repeats itself in different forms countless times. It is crucial to recognise that the child experiences herself and the world through her parent's eyes:

> What is the infant most interested in exploring? Mozart, mobiles, *Sesame Street*? Not so much. Infants and young children are most interested in exploring the world of their parents' experience. They are fascinated by what their parents are fascinated by. And their parents are fascinated by *their child!* When parents experience and express joy, delight, love and interest when they are engaged with their child, the child in turn experiences him- or herself as being joyful, delightful, lovable and interesting. (Hughes 2013, p.5)

This experience of oneself through the eyes of one's attachment figure – a process called *intersubjectivity* – becomes crucial in the treatment of children and adolescents with significant attachment disorders.

Key in secure attachment is the practice of relationship repair. A toddler may do something to hurt himself or may transgress a parental limit, and when redirected may dissolve into tears, distress, anger, frustration or shame. But the parent steps in, matches the intensity of the affect, offers empathy, explains why the limit is there and reassures the child that she loves him, that this does not alter their relationship. Once the relationship is repaired, the child can venture forth again.

Adults who have been securely attached as children are confident, rely on both others and themselves, can access painful experiences without becoming dysregulated, have a coherent personal narrative (without the repression of aspects of memory or experience), and have abilities to repair relationship when conflict and harm occur. Their brain processes are integrated, allowing equally for felt experiences of emotion and for reflection on those experiences.

Children who have an avoidant attachment style have experienced parents who may typically respond in anger or neglect when the child is in distress and reaches out to be soothed and comforted. The child then develops a pattern of not making his needs known, of minimisation and avoidance. The child learns to rely on himself instead, since voicing his need does not result in the need being met. As he grows into an adult, he tends to dismiss emotion and miss emotional cues in others, including his partner's. He tends to be rational and linear and to value personal accomplishments over relationships.

Children who have an ambivalent attachment style often receive unpredictable and intrusive responses from their parent when in distress. The parent may give an 'over-the-top' emotional response, one which exaggerates the child's affect rather than matches it, or the parent may under-respond. The response is more about meeting the parent's need than the child's. Children with this style tend to be clingy, uncertain that her parent will meet her need, even when she does. The parent's feelings flood the child's inner world. The child's mirror neurons (more on those below) soak up the parent's anxiety and fear and make them her own, to the point where it becomes difficult to identify which feelings are whose. They become enmeshed. Someone entering adulthood with an ambivalent attachment profile will emphasise the importance of relationship with others over their own emotional independence. He or she may seek security and happiness in others rather than themselves, even as their relationships tend to be insecure and unsatisfying. They may emphasise emotion over reason in making life decisions and managing stress, even as they may find it difficult to identify their emotions.

A child or youth with a disorganised attachment style has experienced significant early trauma or neglect. For whatever reasons, the parental environment is terrifying to the child. In response, two opposing, irreconcilable systems are activated simultaneously: 'flee!' (to get safe) and 'attach!' (to get safe) (Siegel 2013, p.154). In a desperate strategy, the child simultaneously approaches and avoids the same person, his attachment figure. This repeated pattern leads to dissociation, to a fragmented, chaotic self, where memories are compartmentalised from feelings and thoughts from actions.

Such children and youth experience almost every situation as unsafe. They will often quickly try to gain control over each new situation they enter, as a way of becoming at least less unsafe. So fundamental is the need for safety that they may engage in increasingly high-risk, self-undermining behaviour until they escalate into a container that will hold them, such as jail. They are immersed in a pool of shame and self-loathing, blaming themselves for their abuse or neglect. They cannot use relationship to get their needs met. Most important, because they cannot engage in meaningful relationships, their personal autobiographical narrative, critical for mental health, is largely incoherent and inaccessible to them.

But processes like dyadic developmental psychotherapy can bring about significant change. The goal is to facilitate attachment to the child's current primary attachment figure – foster, adoptive or biological parents. Attachment figures are thus critical participants in the therapy itself (hence the term 'dyadic'). Hughes (2007) sums up the psychotherapeutic interventions with the phrase PACE (Playful, Accepting, Curious and Empathic). Through affective attunement and matching, co-regulation of the child's affect by the parent and therapist, and non-judgemental acceptance and empathy for his story, slowly the child or youth starts to experience himself as his current parent and the therapist do – as a delightful, lovable person. In other words, the child is provided with an experience of the reciprocal intersubjective attachment interactions that he missed in his early life. A rhythm of affective/reflective dialogue – storytelling – takes place. From that foundation, he is helped to connect the dots of his life story and to build a more coherent autobiographical narrative.

Key concepts

Let me now briefly summarise and then add a dimension: the neurological understanding of attachment. People with a secure attachment style are connected to both self and others. People with an avoidant attachment style (called 'dismissive' in adulthood) tend to be focused on themselves, but disconnected from others. People with an ambivalent attachment style (called 'pre-occupied' in adulthood) tend to be focused on others but disconnected from themselves. People with a disorganised attachment style (called 'unresolved' in adulthood) tend to be focused on neither themselves nor others; they are disconnected from both. As adults they are vulnerable to mental illness (Hughes 2013).

Each attachment style has its own brain signature (Hughes and Baylin 2012). All attachment styles are developed as strategies for responding to our fundamental human need for safety and security (Hughes 2013). Avoidant and ambivalent styles, no doubt adaptive at the time they were developed, are, like secure attachment, 'organised' styles: that is, they are relatively coherent, enacted in relatively predictable patterns throughout a person's life (Golding 2014). They may, however, evolve or change, even dramatically, through relationships with later significant attachment figures (such as spouses or partners), as couples psychotherapist Sue Johnson has shown (Johnson 2008, 2013). Partners serve as 'emotional safe havens' (Johnson 2013, p.26) for each other, rewiring and sculpting each other's brain patterns in new ways.

Indeed, the new field of 'interpersonal neurobiology', with sophisticated ways of understanding brain processes (due to new MRI technologies) figures prominently in attachment theory (Siegel 2012; Hughes 2013). While all areas of the brain are engaged in attachment, key areas include the amygdala, the hippocampus and the anterior cingulate cortex (which connects to both the limbic system and the pre-frontal cortex). The amygdala, located near the brain stem, is the centre of our threat-response system, which quickly tells us to fight, flee or freeze. Near the amygdala is the hippocampus, essential for autobiographical memory, context and learning. In order to function effectively in a time of threat, the amygdala, mobilised by the stress hormone cortisol, shuts down our social engagement system. But cortisol is toxic to the hippocampus. When as children we live in a continual or repeated state of threat (leading to avoidant, ambivalent or disorganised attachment), cortisol floods and damages the hippocampus, thus impeding our ability to have a coherent narrative, to make sense of events. When, however, our amygdala is tamed – our safe haven has been restored and the threat has diminished – then our social engagement system is turned on. Our hippocampus thrives, serving as the bridge to the anterior cingulate cortex, which in turn brings together emotional regulation and cognitive processes, creating an affective/reflective, integrated brain dance. Our social engagement system is open and engaged, with priority given to picking up sensory cues from the voice and the face, and ready to learn (Hughes and Baylin 2012). Mirror neurons – the mechanism by which we attune and feel empathy – are ready to fire in support of our relational health. When we watch someone engage in a purposeful action, mirror neurons cause us unconsciously to internally 'mirror' the action of the other, triggering the same motor system within ourselves that the other person is activating. Because this happens quickly, this process 'trumps' verbal communication, putting us affectively 'in tune' with the other. Mirror neurons are the brain process by which we have empathy for someone, and they lie behind Stern's statement that the brain is so relational that our nervous system is

> constructed to be captured by the nervous system of others, so that we can experience others as if from within their own skin, as well as from within our own. (Quoted in Johnson 2013, p.86)

Our defence system is given to black-and-white, survival-oriented responses that require the shutting down of reflective processes. Our social engagement system, activated because safety is in place, is oriented to affective attunement and co-regulation, empathy, learning, intersubjectivity, the integration of brain functions and the ability to hold differences, even opposing viewpoints, together.

But now the echo chamber is reverberating, because that sounds remarkably like what happens in a successful restorative encounter.

The restorative encounter

In my practice, the overarching goal is to help move a setting from perhaps an adversarial or blaming, rule-based culture to one where the primary focus is on building healthy relationships and stronger, more connected communities, grounded in an internally rigorous explicit restorative relational practice framework as a way of thinking and being.

Within that more fundamental pro-active framework, a restorative encounter is a dialogue with three or more people whose purpose is to name harm and its relational impacts and to repair relationships to the degree possible. In most situations in which I work the harm has occurred because of interpersonal conflict, sometimes deep, long-standing and highly painful for the people involved.

The restorative encounter work has three phases: preparation, circle facilitation and follow-up. In none of these phases am I looking for themes of attachment, trying to discern attachment styles, or doing some form of attachment psychotherapy. Rather, attachment helps me to understand why I have been drawn to certain restorative processes. I will focus my discussion on three areas in the restorative encounter where the theoretical links to attachment seem especially prominent.

Preparation

Prior to the restorative encounter, I individually interview each participant. The purpose is to hear their story (using the same questions that will be asked of them in the circle), explain the process of the circle and ascertain their willingness and readiness to participate.

Often in a pre-conference interview, particularly with a workplace manager, the Chair of Church Council dealing with a polarising conflict in a congregation, or a teacher struggling with classroom management manifested by an enduring conflict between a couple of students, I will show them the 'practice domains window' developed by IIRP – Canada and REAL Justice Australia[1] and articulated by Vaandering (2013) as a 'Relationship Window'. I ask them to identify which relationship domain they typically find themselves in:

---

1   This model has not been published but is used widely in training by the Canadian branch of the International Institute of Restorative Practices (IIRP Canada).

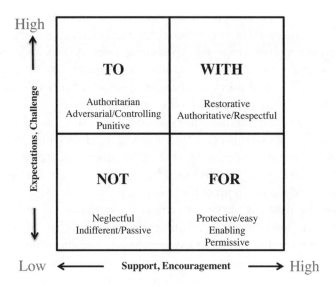

Figure 7.1: Practice Domains Window
Adapted from Costello et al. (2009, p.50) by O'Connell, T. and
Schenk, B. (Unpublished, reproduced here with permission)

The notion is that with high expectations and high levels of support to reach those expectations, we tend to do things 'with' people. With high expectations but low levels of emotional support, we tend to do things 'to' people. With high levels of emotional support but low expectations of people, we tend to do things 'for' people. And with low expectations and low levels of support, we are neglectful, 'not' doing anything.

I am struck by how quickly almost everyone understands this window, readily places themselves within it, understands the consequences, and even begins to change their behaviour because of it. Even young primary-age school children get it. They quickly and accurately recognise teachers who operate from the different domains and the impact that those teachers have on them and their classrooms.

I have often wondered: Why is this simple window so effective? What explains its revelatory power? I now understand that this is in fact a window onto attachment styles, which is where all of us already live, usually implicitly. The window engages our 'internal working model' for understanding relationships and moves it towards becoming explicit. And once explicit, our way of being in relationship with others can change.

The restorative domain is a description of secure attachment: it is both a safe haven (high emotional support) and a launching pad for exploration (high expectations and high degrees of challenge), the domain most amenable to learning. Hughes notes (2009, p.158), 'many parents and children tend to avoid possible breaks [in their relationship] by trying to overlook them or through compliance or permissiveness'. But relationship repair does not hinder attachment security: 'the relationship actually deepens as the child knows that in spite of separations or differences the relationship always continues' (Hughes 2009, p.157). Note that Hughes has here landed on all four of the relationship practice domains.

The avoidant/dismissive attachment style lines up precisely with the authoritarian or controlling domain, while the anxious/pre-occupied style belongs to the permissive, enabling, enmeshed quadrant. The springboard to disorganised attachment can occur from within any of the relationship domains, including neglect (Hughes 2013; Siegel 2013).

The restorative encounter

In the restorative circle itself, I emphasise in the preamble that participation is voluntary and that we are not here to judge anyone. I then ask everyone consistent, pre-determined questions, the same questions each participant has already begun to engage with individually prior to the circle.

In other words, I use what is sometimes referred to as a 'scripted' approach, though a term like 'consistently structured' may be more apt. I am drawn to the question framework used by Costello, Wachtel and Wachtel (2009, p.16) with such questions as:

- What happened?
- What did you think when you first realised what had happened?
- What have you thought about since?
- Who has been affected by what happened? In what way?
- What is the hardest thing for you?
- What needs to happen to make things right?
- What are you prepared to do to help make things right?'

Though these and similar questions appear simple, psychologically they are sophisticated. They create an open space inviting each person to tell their story while others in the circle listen. Participants are invited, in other words, to develop more coherence in their personal narrative about the event. This engages their social approach system and sets the stage for integrating their highest brain functions. The 'impact' question is empathy-activating, while the 'hardest thing' question, prepared for by the excursion into empathy, provides space for people to dare to share their vulnerability. Finally, the 'make things right' questions address repair, a fundamental feature of secure attachment – and restorative practice. The questions sponsor an affective/reflective dialogue and dance.

We know from attachment how critical safety is. I am increasingly convinced that the consistency, reliability and predictability of the questions in a consistently structured circle is a primary factor in the creation of safety for participants. The safety created serves as a secure base from which to do the hard emotional work. Any number of participants have said after conferences that knowing that everyone would be asked and would answer the same questions, themselves included, was critical in helping them to stay in the conference and participate successfully. It is my experience that the consistency of questions creates a safe container, vessel or scaffold within which participants feel comfortable enough to express intense emotion. The repeated questions, sometimes used with a talking piece, start to take on a ritual quality. And as Hughes notes (2009, p.21), 'predictability, with structure, routines, and rituals, creates a general sense of safety'.

In most situations, if I vary the structure – if, in other words, I begin to engage in psychotherapy in a circle – I interrupt the circle's safety and become dangerous to the participants.

Shame

Throughout the restorative encounter I am keenly aware of the presence of shame. At no time, in my view, is the purpose of a restorative encounter to cause or create shame. But it is clear to me that people coming into the circle are carrying some level of shame, and that the circle is a vehicle for helping participants to process their shame and move beyond it.

I have found the topic of shame to be a stumbling block in almost all contexts. One possible reason is that attachment theory and at least some streams within the field of restorative justice understand shame differently. Attachment theory distinguishes clearly between shame and guilt. Consider the definition from renowned shame researcher Brené Brown (2010):

> The majority of shame researchers and clinicians agree that the difference between shame and guilt is best understood as the differences between 'I am bad' and 'I did something bad'. *Guilt = I did something bad. Shame = I am bad.*

> Shame is about who we are, and guilt is about our behaviors... Guilt is just as powerful as shame, but its effect is positive while shame often is destructive. When we see people apologize, make amends, or replace negative behaviors with more positive ones, guilt is often the motivator, not shame. In fact, in my research, I found that shame corrodes the part of us that believes we can change and do better. (2010, p.41, emphasis hers)

Along the lines of Brown, within the attachment framework, shame is only corrosive, paralysing. The goal working with children and youth with disorganised attachment is to move them from shame to guilt. Guilt brings with it a motivation to repair, whereas shame carries no such motivation. The presence of guilt means that enough of a sense of self has now been created that one is able to contemplate the possibility of repair.

Restorative justice theory has taken a different approach. Criminologist John Braithwaite proposed the distinction between 'reintegrative shaming' and 'stigmatising, outcasting shaming', with reintegrative shaming having a positive effect. Braithwaite is clear that the aim of a restorative conference is never to shame (Harris, Walgrave and Braithwaite 2004). Costello, Wachtel and Wachtel (2009), building on the work of affect theorist Sylvan Tomkins (2008) and psychologist Donald Nathanson (1992), have argued that shame is both corrosive and motivational. Shame goads us to seek repair. In Tomkins' view, shame is an auxiliary affect; it requires first the presence of positive affects which shame interrupts (Nathanson 1992, p.138). Built into the experience of shame, therefore, is a desire to return to positive affect.

Living as I do in both the attachment and restorative practice worlds, and experiencing simultaneously the discordant sounds of these two incompatible notions of shame, I have struggled to find a resolution that will adequately comprehend the encounters with shame that I experience in both worlds. To that end, I propose, in the context of Nathanson's larger view (1992) that shame is a fundamental regulator of human interaction, a differential understanding of shame that neither approach currently entertains or accepts.

Each definition of shame has helpful explanatory power within its own sphere. What is problematic is when each field takes what it has learned about shame and universalises it, applying it to all people in every situation. The attachment definition of shame takes what has been learned about shame from disorganised attachment and applies it to people with all attachment styles. To my mind, its understanding of shame is too black-and-white and fits too neatly into a scheme. Often it strikes me that participants in a restorative encounter are motivated to participate because the event or conflict has caused them shame – they are 'ashamed'. This has corroded their understanding of who they are, and they want to restore their sense of self by way of repairing the harm that they have done or experienced. From a strictly anecdotal perspective, I am more aware of shame than guilt as a motivator to make amends in a restorative encounter. The attachment definition of shame cannot contemplate this.

Meanwhile, the restorative practice understanding of shame fundamentally assumes a pre-existing organised sense of self, an ego structure which is strong enough to contemplate repair and to tolerate a temporary expanded experience of shame to accomplish it. But for children and youth who have disorganised attachment, it simply cannot be said, in their context, that shame is an interruption of positive affect, or an auxiliary affect, or that it has any positive internal motivational qualities. Their experience of shame may motivate caregivers to help them move to relational connection (which is Nathanson's understanding of shame as a social regulator in action). But for they themselves shame is only powerfully disconnecting and paralysing. Like the attachment understanding of shame, the restorative practice understanding of shame cannot be universally applied to each person.

My proposed nuance is therefore this. I believe that the attachment understanding of shame is accurate and necessary in relation to disorganised/unresolved attachment, but not accurate enough when applied to all attachment styles. People with disorganised attachment cannot use relationship to meet their needs until they have had a consistent, primary attachment experience. They must first experience intersubjectivity and reciprocity, through, for example, dyadic developmental psychotherapy, before they can derive benefits from a restorative encounter.

I believe that the restorative practice understanding of shame can be applicable to people who have organised attachment profiles, whether secure, avoidant/dismissive or anxious/pre-occupied, but cannot be applied to people who struggle with disorganised/ unresolved attachment. In other words, somewhere in the vicinity of shame, whether it is shame itself or a positive affect, there does lie a healthy internal motivation to repair, but only where a person has a strong enough sense of self, a basic ego structure which makes the contemplation of restoration possible.

In short, the understanding that shame is only corrosive applies solely to disorganised attachment; the notion that shame is both corrosive and constructive applies only in relation to organised attachment, whether of a participant or a caregiver. Currently, neither view of shame permits this differential understanding. But neuroscience may in fact support it. Cozolino (2006, p.235) writes:

> Shame is represented physiologically in a rapid transition from a positive to negative affective state and from sympathetic to parasympathetic dominance. This shift is triggered by the expectation of attunement in a positive state, only to find disapproval and misattunement in the face of the caretaker (Schore 1994)... Because shame is neurobiologically toxic for older infants, these early preverbal experiences can have lifelong effects. Prolonged shame states early in life can result in permanently dysregulated autonomic functioning and a heightened sense of vulnerability to others.

Regardless, I have found that stumbling blocks about shame fall away when we move from abstract discussions to an operational understanding of how we experience and express shame as human beings. To that end, I find Nathanson's 'Compass of Shame' highly effective (Nathanson 1992). I often use it in pre-conference interviews. I am impressed by how quickly people understand their own actions within it and speculate about the actions of others, also in a cross-cultural context. The compass is a powerful tool for stimulating understanding and empathy.

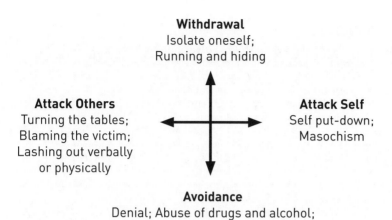

Withdrawal
Isolate oneself;
Running and hiding

Attack Others
Turning the tables;
Blaming the victim;
Lashing out verbally
or physically

Attack Self
Self put-down;
Masochism

Avoidance
Denial; Abuse of drugs and alcohol;
Distraction through thrill seeking

Figure 7.2: The Compass of Shame
Adapted from Nathanson 1992

Conclusion

What then is happening in a successful restorative encounter? People may enter the room defensive and sit with arms folded, legs crossed and head down (a physiological indication of shame). But as a relatively safe haven is established, through predictability and consistency, the amygdala calms, and the launching pad of the social engagement system is activated. Affective attunement and the co-regulation of affect begins, mirror neurons initiate empathy, people dare to share their vulnerabilities and an affective/reflective dialogue begins. New, enlarged, deepened and more coherent narratives are formed which hold differing experiences and emotions. People's postures change as shame is processed. This is a description of relationship repair, of engagement 'with' one another in the restorative domain of the Relationship Window. It is the heart of both restorative justice and attachment. At the end we may not all hold hands and sing songs, but we will have moved enough from a self-protecting, defensive, either/or, dysregulated, fight or flight state to have engaged in the intersubjective social brain activity needed to help us integrate, enlarge our perspectives and move forward.

References

Ainsworth, M. D. S., Blehar, M. C., Waters, E., and Wall, S. (1978) *Patterns of Attachment: A Psychological Study of the Strange Situation.* Hillsdale, NJ: Erlbaum.

Bowlby, J. (1969) *Attachment: Attachment and Loss (volume 1)(2nd edition).* New York, NY: Basic Books. (Original work published in 1969)

Bowlby, J. (1973) 'Separation: Anxiety and Anger.' In *Attachment and Loss (Volume 2); International psycho-analytical library no.95.* London: Hogarth Press.

Bowlby, J. (1980) 'Loss: Sadness and Depression.' *Attachment and Loss (Volume 3); International psycho-analytical library no.109.* London: Hogarth Press.

Bowlby, J. (1988) *A Secure Base: Clinical Applications of Attachment Theory.* London: Routledge.

Brown, B. (2010) *The Gifts of Imperfection: Your Guide to a Wholehearted Life.* Center City, Minnesota, MN: Hazeldon.

Costello, B., Wachtel, J. and Wachtel, T. (2009) *The Restorative Practices Handbook for Teachers, Disciplinarians and Administrators: Building a Culture of Community in Schools.* Bethlehem, PA: International Institute for Restorative Practices.

Cozolino, L. (2006) *The Neuroscience of Human Relationships: Attachment and the Developing Social Brain.* New York, NY: W.W. Norton and Company, Inc.

Golding, K. (2014) *Nurturing Attachments Training Resource: Running Parenting Groups for Adoptive Parents and Foster or Kinship Carers.* London: Jessica Kingsley Publishers.

Harris, N., Walgrave. L., Braithwaite, J. (2004) 'Emotional dynamics in restorative conferences.' *Theoretical Criminology 8*, 2, 191–210.

Hughes, D. (2007) *Attachment Focused Family Therapy.* New York, NY: W.W. Norton and Company, Inc.

Hughes, D. (2009) *Attachment Focused Parenting.* New York, NY: W.W. Norton and Company, Inc.

Hughes, D. (2013) *8 Keys to Building Your Best Relationships.* New York, NY: W.W. Norton and Company, Inc.

Hughes, D. and Baylin, J. (2012) *Brain-Based Parenting: The Neuroscience of Caregiving for Healthy Attachment.* New York: W.W. Norton and Company, Inc.

Johnson, S. (2008) *Hold Me Tight: Seven Conversations for a Lifetime of Love.* New York: Little, Brown and Company.

Johnson, S. (2013) *Love Sense: The Revolutionary New Science of Romantic Relationships.* New York: Little, Brown and Company.

Llewellyn, J. (2011) *A Relational Vision of Justice.* Prison Fellowship International: Restorative Justice Online. Available at www.restorativejustice.org/RJOB/a-relational-vision-of-justice, accessed on 28th January 2014.

Llewellyn, J. (2012) 'Restorative Justice: Thinking Relationally About Justice.' In J. Downie and J. Llewellyn (eds) *Being Relational: Reflections on Relational Theory and Health Law.* Vancouver: UBC Press.

Nathanson, D. (1992) *Shame and Pride: Affect, Sex, and the Birth of the Self.* New York: W.W. Norton and Company, Inc.

Schore, A.N. (1994) Affect Regulation and the Origin of the Self: the Neurobiology of Emotional Development. Hillsdale, NJ: Erlbaum.

Siegel, D. (2010) *Mindsight: The New Science of Personal Transformation.* New York: Bantam Books.

Siegel, D. (2012) *Pocket Guide to Interpersonal Neurobiology: An Integrative Handbook of the Mind.* New York: W.W. Norton and Company, Inc.

Siegel, D. (2013) *Brainstorm: The Power and Purpose of the Teenage Brain.* New York: Jeremy P. Archer/Penguin.

Tomkins, S. (2008, first published 1962, 1963) *Affect Imagery Consciousness: The Complete Edition: Two Volumes.* New York: Springer Publishing Company.

Vaandering, D. (2013) 'A window on relationships: Reflecting critically on a current restorative justice theory.' *Restorative Justice: An International Journal* 1, 3, 311–333.

CHAPTER 8

Resonant Empathy[1]

PETE WALLIS

Introduction

There are three interesting features of restorative justice meetings, in my experience. The first is that they almost always go better than anticipated. The second is that the more anxious the practitioner feels in advance, the better the meeting is likely to turn out. The third is that where harm runs deep and emotions are strong restorative meetings are more powerful and lead to better outcomes as a result.

A restorative justice meeting where the perpetrator is deeply remorseful from the outset and the person they harmed has already forgiven them will probably go as well as expected, feel helpful all round and be relaxing and rewarding for the practitioner. The restorative encounter that feels truly transformative is the one that could go either way; hopefully make things better but potentially make them worse, where the practitioner is on high alert, using all of their craft and experience to keep things safe. Participants are typically anxious and defensive, and some feel aggrieved and even antagonistic towards the other party as they arrive at a restorative meeting. Frequently by the end of the meeting everyone is leaving on the best of terms. Witnessing the 'movement' that occurs during a restorative meeting is humbling for the practitioner, who may wonder how such a seismic shift in attitudes can come about in such a short time.

---

1   This chapter, including the notion of 'resonant empathy' and the diagrams in Chapter 11, is a development of themes first introduced in Pete Wallis' book: Wallis, P. (2014) *Understanding Restorative Justice: How Empathy can Close the Gap caused by Crime*. Bristol: The Policy Press.

One thing explains all of these features, and it is the magic ingredient that makes restorative justice work. Baron-Cohen (2012, p.130) calls it 'one of the most precious resources in our world' and without it restorative justice would not rise above shaming the perpetrators and vindicating those they harmed. The element that gives restorative justice its transformative and healing power is, of course, empathy.

This chapter will explore some of the features of empathy and how it relates to the restorative process, starting with the offence, where empathy was absent and progressing through to the extraordinary moment when people who have been locked in conflict may suddenly express the deepest empathy for one another. It will consider how the restorative practitioner can enhance the conditions for empathy to develop during a restorative meeting, and the potential for victim empathy and protective behaviours interventions to encourage empathy in the preparation stages. Finally it will introduce the notion of 'resonant empathy' to describe the dynamic unfolding of empathy that can occur between people who are often meeting for the first time since the day of the crime. Although this chapter is written from a criminal justice perspective, resonant empathy may occur in other settings and be relevant to other restorative models and approaches. While no expert in the neuroscience of empathy, as a practitioner I find it helpful to consider the role empathy plays in the restorative process and believe that restorative justice can be a crucial opportunity for this precious resource to be developed and nurtured.

Empathy

Empathy (the Greek means 'in-passion' or 'in-suffering') is 'the capacity to think and feel oneself into the inner life of another person' (Kohut in Stepansky and Goldberg 1984, p.82). Because it is not an intellectual quality it is difficult to define empathy precisely, but for the sake of this discussion there are three features of empathy that can be related to the restorative encounter. The first is an unconscious reaction that can occur spontaneously when we recognise the emotions of another person, eliciting a similar emotional response in ourselves. Neuroscientific research has identified 'mirror neurons' in the brain and found that 'the perception of another person activates similar neurons in the subject and the target' (Stueber 2013). Just seeing someone and picking up non-verbal cues on their state of mind can trigger empathy. Following the initial empathy response, if we are prepared to listen to someone talking about their thoughts and feelings on a particular subject we may develop 'cognitive' empathy for them, as we think and feel ourselves into that person's lived experience and identify with their story. Finally we may be moved to do something to express our empathy, through an offer of help if the person is struggling or simply with a smile or kind touch to communicate our shared understanding and compassion. De Waal (2009) likens these nested three elements to a Russian doll. The automatic empathy response (which de Waal believes is shared with other mammals) is at the core, and evolution has added the capacities of perspective taking and consolation in ever more sophisticated layers to the point where 'our ancestors not only felt what others felt, but understood what others might want or need' (De Waal 2009, p.209).

Empathy is precious because it could be argued that a lack or loss of empathy is at the root of all conflict. Looking back to the crime that led to any restorative process, it is a safe bet that while the incident was unfolding empathy was totally absent between the person responsible and those they targeted. To deliberately cause harm we have to shut out any thought for the pain and upset that will result from our behaviour, simply because if we had empathy our actions would hurt us as much as they hurt the person we are harming. Treating someone as an object that we can use or abuse for our own ends we must first dehumanise them.

Lack of empathy can be long- or short-term; a stable trait enabling the perpetrator to commit acts of cruelty without remorse, or a brief lapse brought on by circumstances. In his research into empathy Baron-Cohen (2012) developed an 'Empathy Quotient' or EQ test to determine how well people attune to, and are affected by, others' feelings. Most people have some capacity for empathy, but Baron-Cohen identified specific personality disorders in which empathy appears to be completely absent. Genetic, psychological and social factors, often including childhood experiences of neglect and abuse, may affect the empathy circuitry in the brain which is found in healthy individuals. This may cause an individual to exhibit a long-term empathy deficit, leaving them with 'zero degrees of empathy'. A small number may even derive pleasure from harming others, fully aware of the impact of their actions. Fortunately these cases are rare, and the large majority of the population have at least some capacity for empathy.[2]

Many factors can cause empathy to drop temporarily. Our natural empathy will be suppressed when we experience shame and humiliation, believe that we have been unjustly treated, are threatened, feel irritated or become enraged over a perceived wrong. Alcohol, physical pain, stress and lack of sleep can also contribute. When sharing their story with the restorative practitioner people who have offended are often able to identify specific factors or experiences preceding their offence which are likely to have reduced their capacity for empathy, such as an experience of victimisation or abuse, an unresolved bereavement, a break-up with their partner or other significant loss. Without excusing harmful behavior this 'back story' to the crime may provide an explanation for their actions.

Thinking about those who have been victimised, there is likely to be little empathy for the person who deliberately chose to cause them harm. Many offences are fairly trivial, experienced as a 'survivable nuisance', although for some even a minor crime can come as a shock. Those harmed may need to protect themselves externally, through locks, alarms and increased vigilance. If the hurt runs deep they may change their behaviour, avoid the area where the crime occurred and drop out of work, college or school. Internally they may withdraw and separate themselves from others as protection from further attacks, and be left feeling angry, upset, hostile and defensive. Meanwhile the person who caused them harm will typically create an array of excuses and justifications to minimise their actions and deflect blame from themselves, using 'defensive thinking' to bolster their self-worth and to avoid letting in the shameful consequences of their actions.

After the crime both parties are likely to be in defensive mode, building internal walls against the other party, which can solidify into fixed positions, creating an empathy divide or 'gap' between them. In terms of empathy for one another both share the same starting point on the restorative journey. Each holds an equally poor view of the other, and neither has an insight into the experience and the inner world of the other person.

---

2   McGregor and McGregor (2013) use the term 'sociopath' to describe people with low or zero empathy, and in reviewing a number of studies conclude that 'estimates of sociopathy in the general population vary from less than 1 person in 100 to 1 in 25' (p.2).

Few people hand themselves in following a crime, and if the perpetrator gets away with it the gap will remain. The perpetrator will come to believe that there are no consequences for harmful actions if he or she is not found out and apprehended. The person harmed will be denied an understanding of the circumstances that led to the offence, and will suffer a knock to their sense of a benign, safe and orderly world. For younger people there is strong evidence that those who externalise their feelings of anger and rage are at risk of going on to commit offences themselves (McAra and McVie 2007; Owen and Sweeting 2007). For all, a valuable opportunity for developing empathy and connection is lost.

When someone who has committed a crime is caught they enter the criminal justice system. Although it has its flaws, without the actions of the police, crown prosecution service and courts there would be very little restorative justice. Once in the system, most perpetrators admit their guilt, but even if they accept responsibility for their part in the offence, they may have no empathy for those they harmed. People who commit crime often have little knowledge of the impact of their actions, and if they hear about it from reports, for example when a victim personal statement is read out in court, they are likely to remain in defensive mode and continue to justify and neutralise what they have done.

In the days and weeks after the crime, the empathy divide is often accompanied by a physical gap. The two parties may be complete strangers and unknown to one another, or if they are known they may be avoiding one another, or at least avoiding a conversation about the offence. Some are ordered by the police or the court to have no contact due to safety concerns, and if the perpetrator is in prison their separation from the community will affect every relationship they have. If there is no opportunity for restorative justice, the person harmed may get some satisfaction from the criminal justice outcome and the perpetrator may gain benefit from the support and any courses they may be offered as part of their programme or sentence, but the gap will remain, the parties will always perceive one another in terms of 'us' and 'them' and the world will remain that much less connected and more fractured.

As a stand-alone intervention or the first step in preparation for a potential restorative process, many probation, prison and youth offending services in the UK have developed victim empathy courses, working with people who offend to challenge their excuses and encourage them to reflect on the impact of their offences (Wallis, Aldington and Liebmann 2010). These courses are founded on the faith that empathy is a skill that can be learnt, whether the crime was committed during a brief lapse in empathy, where the perpetrator is young and their capacity for empathy hasn't fully developed, and even in those cases Baron-Cohen describes where 'zero empathy' has become a stable personality trait. Whatever we do shapes our neural circuits and we never stop learning, our brain continually developing in response to what we experience. There is a strong argument that, since crime is a product of a lack of empathy, victim empathy work should be compulsory for everyone who offends.

Victim empathy courses often start by asking participants to consider a time when they themselves were victimised. This can encourage empathy to develop within the group, enable individuals to become more compassionate towards their own suffering, and help them make connections between their own experience and the harm they have caused to others. Some courses use case studies, or introduce someone who has experienced a crime as a 'surrogate victim' who shares their story with the group, both of which can foster empathy. The perpetrator will also be asked to talk about their own offence, which may be done as a narrative, or through creative methods such as cartoon strips, video work or drama. Often the most powerful elements of victim empathy courses are those where the perpetrator focuses directly on the harm their behaviour has caused. With luck there will be information about the impact of their crime, perhaps from court paperwork, a victim personal statement or directly from those harmed, who may offer permission for their story to be shared for this purpose. The perpetrator can be asked to imagine themselves as the person they harmed in a role play, speaking for them, describing their thoughts and feelings about the offence, and thinking about what they may need to feel better. Being one step removed, a victim empathy course can't create conditions for a full empathy response in people who offend but it can encourage them to think about others rather than just themselves. If we consider a scale of empathy from low rising to high, the course may potentially lift them off the bottom rung. Some find that their victim empathy course moves them to want to make amends and leads to a request for a restorative meeting.

During a crime, the person who was targeted may have experienced anxiety and fear, which in some cases can be unbearable, and internal defences may have kicked in as an automatic and adaptive response to the traumatic event. Over time these can become rigid patterns that start to shape their personality and change their interactions with others. They may rationalise the experience, place internal defences around intense emotions to avoid feeling them, or project painful feelings onto others. The restorative practitioner can have a crucial role in helping people harmed by crime to soften their defences and become less stuck. During their individual meetings the practitioner will invite them to talk about the incident. They will help them to bring their thoughts and emotions about the experience into awareness by sharing what they were feeling and what was going through their mind at key moments in their narrative. Memories of the traumatic event and the primal feelings of fear and anger that accompanied it may have been laid down involuntarily as 'implicit' memories, which can be buried in the subconscious. The person harmed may wish to go over their story many times, recalling and venting the emotions until eventually they are no longer driven by them but are able to reflect and learn. If there is severe trauma leading to post-traumatic stress there may need to be specialist trauma counselling, and in general the deeper the harm the more preparation and time will be allowed. *Protective behaviours* is an intervention which can be particularly useful with young people at this stage, helping them regain their confidence, build resilience and work on strategies for being safe in the future (Keen, Lott and Wallis 2010).

During these preparation stages the practitioner may drip-feed information between the parties, painting a picture for each of what the other person is like and how they are faring, so that they can start to feel that person's inner world. As they gain information and insight they may begin to experience empathy. The defensive walls may start to lower, and there may come a time when each party reaches their 'threshold of confidence', the point at which they feel safe enough to take the leap of faith required for a restorative meeting.

Exactly why people opt for restorative justice can sometimes remain a mystery. There may be clear needs expressed during preparation which can only be met through a meeting, for example answers to burning questions or a strong desire to apologise. At other times it can feel to the practitioner that there is an unconscious pull at work between the two parties. The mind has a natural drive towards connection and healing, and if the practitioner can use the preparation stage to create the conditions for the parties to connect, people often grasp the opportunity, realising intuitively that it will be helpful. It is important that the practitioner allows the motivation to arise from the participants where possible rather than presenting them with a tick box of options from which to choose.

For some, indirect communication is as far as their restorative journey goes. In these cases, the practitioner must accept and honour each person's choice as the best match in their particular situation, and not force a meeting. Empathy can emerge during the preparation stages, but empathy is better with a face, and indirect communication is inevitably less powerful than a meeting. As the practitioner tries to describe the other person they often see the listener struggling, failing to experience an empathy response from second hand information.

The model for a restorative meeting that has been handed down from practitioner to practitioner since the early pioneering work in the field is tailor-made to encourage empathy. It is natural for people to arrive at their restorative meeting feeling anxious. They may have conjured up all sorts of fantasies about the other person and how they will react. Those harmed sometimes say afterwards that they expected to see a 'monster', and perpetrators often anticipate being shouted at or hit. The first major shift can happen in the first few seconds of the meeting as people finally get to see the other person, sometimes for the first time, and if not, in an entirely different context to the day of the offence (or the adversarial court setting). Seeing the other person looking fearful and uncertain, the mirror neuron system can trigger an automatic empathy response, taking everyone by surprise. In one meeting, a mother whose son had been killed had to ask for a break before the meeting had even started. In her own agony she had assumed that the man responsible was uncaring and unaffected by the offence, and needed to confirm with her supporter what her eyes were telling her but her mind was struggling to process… 'He is really suffering, isn't he…?'

Cognitive empathy, the more imaginative kind of empathy response, requires the participants to gain insight into one another's inner world, in this case their thoughts and feelings about the offence. People may arrive with the intention of strengthening their position, getting a point across, defending their actions or establishing the 'facts'. Empathy can penetrate these defences, but for empathy to develop each side will have to allow their defensive positions to drop sufficiently for them to properly hear the other person, to be open and receptive rather than entrenched and reactive.

To encourage listening, the practitioner creates an empathic space, introducing expectations to ensure that people will refrain from interrupting when someone is speaking, and asking everyone to be honest, respectful and gentle with one another. Realising that they don't feel emotionally or physically threatened, people are able to move beyond their defensive positions, their inner state shifting from a reactive 'fight and flight' response to a more open, receptive state in which they feel seen and feel safe, and become confident that they will be heard. To avoid a tit for tat argument about the details of the crime (bearing in mind that our memories are not reliable and stories shift and change over time), the practitioner places a greater focus on what people were thinking and feeling as events unfolded, rather than conducting an investigation into 'facts'. Facts can be disputed, but as people share what they were thinking and feeling at key moments during and after the crime, the participants may start to imagine what the incident was like from the other's perspective. They may even realise that they would have thought and felt the same in the same circumstances. Who wouldn't be 'terrified' at the moment they were breaking into someone's home, and who wouldn't be 'shocked' and 'angry' on realising that someone had broken into theirs? Who can't relate to someone thinking 'Oh shit!' when they sense that they are about to be robbed, and if it is the robber speaking it rings true that their first thought was 'Oh shit!' when they opened their front door to find the police had come to arrest them.

Listening to the stories awakens memories of similar situations each have experienced, and participants may sense the others' intentions behind each action and gain insight into what meaning it holds for them. If the back story comes out, the person harmed may learn about the factors that led the perpetrator to deliberately cause them harm, may even conclude that they might have done the same, given the same background history and circumstances. The practitioner also brings into awareness people's inner state in the present moment, with questions like: 'What do you think about what happened now? How do you feel?' and 'What do you need to feel better?' all of which can elicit an empathy response in the other.

We usually think of empathy in terms of one person empathising with another; a 'subject' empathising with a 'target', in which both become attuned to the thoughts and feelings of the 'subject'. A restorative meeting may be a unique situation because it involves two people in a dynamic process in which each are both the subject and target, the do-er and done to, not only responding to the inner world of the other with empathy but also to the empathy that the other is expressing for them. Calling this 'resonant empathy' is something of a misnomer since resonance is the very essence of what we understand as empathy, which Lipps (1907), the German psychologist responsible for developing the concept described as 'a psychological resonance phenomenon'. However, in a restorative meeting participants are not only resonating with one another's thoughts and feelings, they are also resonating to the empathy response of the other person.

In the initial stages there are two different stories, with empathy developing on both sides as each gains insight into the experience and inner life of the other. The feelings expressed create 'emotional contagion'[3] and empathy becomes mutually reinforcing in the room, each experiencing empathy from the other and becoming more empathic in turn. As perspectives converge it isn't uncommon for participants to start to tell the story of the crime together, each side chipping in details about what happened to create a single shared narrative. As the third element of empathy emerges, people start to express compassion for one another, often accompanied by a strong desire to help. By this stage each is hooked into the others' perspective and situation, losing any lingering desire for them to suffer because improving the other person's life resonates within them, as they draw this new individual into their 'circle of concern' (Seigal 2011). It is humbling to witness the spontaneous generosity of those who have been harmed, who frequently leave a restorative meeting wishing wellbeing for the very person who harmed them.

---

3   Emotional contagion has been described as 'the tendency to automatically mimic and synchronise facial expressions, vocalisations, postures and movements with those of another person and, consequently, to converge emotionally' (Hatfield, Cacioppo and Rapson 1994, p.5).

A helpful roadmap

Considering restorative justice from the perspective of empathy can provide a helpful roadmap for the restorative practitioner, who may wish to consider that their primary role is to create the conditions for empathy to develop between the parties involved in the crime. At the starting point of the crime and its immediate aftermath when empathy is absent, the practitioner can themselves express empathy for those they meet, helping people to feel heard and believed, to have their experience validated. They can be curious during the preparation interviews, encouraging their clients to open up and tell their story as often as they like, accepting that those stories will shift and change, helping them to bring difficult thoughts and feelings into awareness. For perpetrators of crime victim empathy work can give people a chance to practice and learn empathy, and protective behaviours work can enable those harmed to feel safe enough to 'risk for a purpose', and opt for restorative justice. When the time is right the practitioner may share information between the parties, taking care to remain neutral and non-judgemental, making it clear that they are 'on everyone's side' with their focus on repair. They will identify any barriers which may be blocking people's natural desire to connect, using skilful means to help each reach their 'threshold of confidence' where they feel safe enough to take the leap. Ideally the practitioner will allow participants to come up with the idea of restorative justice themselves, and by focusing on the conditions for empathy they will ensure that people believe that the process is for them, not one designed for the benefit of the 'system'.

As people opt into a restorative meeting, the practitioner will recognise the risk that they are taking in moving towards a challenging experience and opening themselves up to becoming vulnerable. They will ensure that everyone knows what to expect and is well supported and as comfortable as possible with the process and arrangements. The practitioner too is taking a risk, and sometimes needs the faith that comes from experience, knowing that people almost always rise to the occasion in a restorative meeting and behave better than they may have done during preparation (when they sometimes need to express things that they wouldn't say to someone's face).

As the day of the restorative meeting approaches, the practitioner will think carefully about how to create an empathic and creative space, enabling the restorative circle to be contained and as safe as possible, with enough structure for people to share while allowing participants to determine how their meeting goes. They will consider the choice of room and the layout of chairs, being mindful of arrivals (avoiding chance meetings in the car park) and placing people in an appropriate seat in the circle. As people arrive they will be nervous and defensive, and the practitioner will need to exude confidence (even if they aren't feeling it), and create a clear focus for the meeting. They will model the qualities they hope for in the participants, choosing their words carefully when negotiating expectations to promote an encounter based on honesty, respect and sincerity.

Whether the disparate people coming together in a restorative meeting are able to identify with one another's feelings and develop empathy depends largely on the quality of the story telling. The word 'emotion' means stirring or moving, and, while the practitioner can elicit people's narratives through skilful questions, they cannot create this movement. Attempts to manipulate the process with questions like: 'Are you sorry?', 'Do you want to apologise?' and 'Will you forgive him?' are unlikely to encourage empathy and may backfire. Instead the practitioner carefully allows people to share their experience, focusing on people's inner world, their thoughts and feelings as events unfolded. The practitioner may need to be aware of their own empathy response during the meeting itself – they may feel, but should not express empathy. Being seen to be neutral and non-judgemental is crucial and the practitioner must avoid bias, including condemnation or praise, and be seen to be there for everyone.

The practitioner can step back if people are speaking directly to one another, providing the contributions are leading to empathy, and step in if people are becoming defensive and reactive, if they sense that people are sliding down the empathy scale towards antipathy. Red flags to look out for include expressions of front or attitude, a tendency to minimise or shift the blame, and attempts to convince the other party to agree on a position or opinion. If empathy is draining out of a meeting the practitioner has some further tools up their sleeve. They can bring people back to the agreed expectations, remind the meeting of its original focus, and ask participants for permission to share constructive things they said during their preparation interviews. Time out can be suggested if people are moving into defensive or reactive mode, and if empathy is tumbling the meeting can be stopped.

During the restorative process the practitioner has many different roles although their overriding task is to nurture empathy (Wallis 2014). They will endeavour:

- *to listen*: hearing everyone's perspective

- *to offer*: building on people's desire to engage in a restorative process, offering to facilitate that process for them

- *to arrange*: making all the logistical arrangements for the meeting

- *to facilitate*: placing some boundaries round the process to keep it safe

- *to enable*: ensuring that everyone can speak and listen

- *to allow*: letting go of control so that the dynamic of the restorative process can take over

- *to vanish*: disappearing completely if things are going well, shifting back their chair, looking down at their feet

- *to clarify*: picking up some control again to ensure that outcome agreements are SMART[4]

- *to monitor and support:* carefully following up on the meeting so that benefits aren't lost

- *to record, reflect, evaluate.*

Empathy cannot be forced or guaranteed, and the meeting must work, even if the process of resonant empathy doesn't kick in. Providing the practitioner remains true to their restorative values and keeps to best practice there can be benefit from a meeting even when no empathy is expressed. Sometimes one side shows deep empathy for the other and a genuine desire for connection that is not reciprocated, and the practitioner has to accept this even though it can be painful to witness. The practitioner's focus will be sharpest in marginal cases where things have the potential to go wrong, and once the magic starts, as it almost invariably will, they

---

4   SMART is a widely accepted acronym for target setting – to be effective a target or outcome needs to be Smart, Measurable, Achievable, Realistic and Time-bound or limited.

can step back, get out of the way and allow the dynamic process of resonant empathy to bring people together. After the meeting the practitioner must be scrupulous in their follow-up processes, monitoring outcome agreements and arranging review meetings to ensure that any gains in empathy are not lost.

Restorative justice creates conditions for the development of empathy which can move people rapidly from defensive 'fight or flight' mode where they may feel threatened emotionally or physically, to being open to seeing, voicing, hearing, helping one another and healing. People who may start off perceiving others in the room as threatening strangers who belong to a different group, status or class can end up identifying with and even befriending them, creating community cohesion and a stronger society. A precious resource indeed!

References

Baron-Cohen, S. (2012) *Zero Degrees of Empathy*. London: Penguin.

De Waal, F. (2009) *The Age of Empathy: Nature's Lessons for a Kinder Society*. London: Souvenir Press.

Hatfield, E., Cacioppo, J. and Rapson, R. L. (1994) *Emotional Contagion*, Cambridge: Cambridge University Press.

Keen, S., Lott, T. and Wallis, P. (2010) *Why Me? A Programme for Children and Young People who have Experienced Victimization*. London: Jessica Kingsley Publishers.

Lipps, T. (1907) 'Das Wissen von Fremden Ichen.' *Psychologische Untersuchungen, 1*, 694–722.

McAra, L. and McVie, S. (2007) *Criminal Justice Transitions*. University of Edinburgh: Edinburgh Research Explorer.

McGregor, J. and McGregor, T. (2013) *The Empathy Trap: Understanding Antisocial Personalities*. London: Sheldon Press.

Owen, R. and Sweeting, A. (2007) *Hoodie or Goodie? The Link between Violent Victimisation and Offending in Young People*. Prepared for Victim Support by: BMRB Social Research. Available at: www.victimsupport.org.uk/sites/default/files/Hoodie%20or%20goodie%20report.pdf, accessed on 23 July 2015.

Siegal, D. (2010) *Mindsight: The New Science of Personal Transformation*. London: Random House Publishers.

Stepansky, P. and Goldberg, A. (eds) (1984) *Kohut's Legacy: Contributions to Self Psychology*. Hillsdale, NJ: The Analytic Press.

Stueber, K. (2013) *Empathy*. First published 2008; substantive revision February 14th, 2013. Available at http://plato.stanford.edu/entries/empathy/, accessed 14th February 2013.

Wallis, P., Aldington, C. and Liebmann, M. (2010) *What Have I Done?* London: Jessica Kingsley Publishers.

Wallis, P. (2014) *Understanding Restorative Justice: How Empathy can Close the Gap caused by Crime*. Bristol: The Policy Press.

CHAPTER 9

A Social Constructionist Approach to Restorative Conferencing

WENDY DREWERY

Introduction

In this chapter I will show how social constructionist ideas enable me to think about how the work of restoration is done in a conversation that is intended to be restorative. To that end, I will give a brief overview of the conceptual tools I am using, followed by a discussion of the process of a restorative conversation, and I will explain what I see as the key features that lead to the desired outcomes. Restorative conversations tend to be used formally after something has gone wrong, or when there is conflict. They may be about one person's behaviour, or they may be about a problem between two or more people. In addition to this formal usage, the principles of restorative conversations I shall enunciate here can be used in everyday life, to good effect. To that end, I think of these principles as useful ways of speaking, rather than simply about formal conferencing. This observation applies both to the form of the conversation and to how you say what you say within it. I will draw attention to both aspects in this chapter.

The notion of social construction has become quite popular, and thus may be familiar to many readers. However, people use the term in varied ways, and it is important to appreciate how I am using it here. In particular, I distinguish social constructionism from social constructivism. Constructivism is the idea that persons form theoretical models in their own heads, with which to understand the world, and of course they may do this drawing on the resources available within their social context. Social constructivism is thus primarily a theory about cognition, or cognitive development. It is often seen as a theory about learning. Social constructionism by contrast is a broader, more philosophically based intellectual movement which focuses on how persons and groups come to understand themselves and the world, and how such understandings develop, and are shared. This theory extends to the ontological status of objects and knowledge, and of things-in-the-world, including psychological concepts such as identity and emotion. A table comes to be known as such, it does not have an essence that makes it a table. Similarly, identity is not fixed or given; it is a concept that offers the possibility of different understandings in different contexts.

Weak social constructionism is the relatively simple idea that all meaning is made in social situations. Strong social constructionism is a discursive or meaning-making perspective on knowledge, research and practice. The practices that I am proposing in this chapter owe a huge debt to the archaeological work of Michel Foucault (1970, 1972, 1973), which argued that knowledge is not cumulative and increasing in clarity and truthfulness, but rather, what we know as truth shifts and changes over historical time. Progress and science are not continuously marching forward towards clarity. Foucault gave an account of how we come to know: what counts as knowledge changes with time. Scholars in psychology (for example Gergen 1999; Parker 1992, 2005) have continued to build these developments into a relatively new tradition of critical psychology. This new tradition enables us to think about concepts such as identity, personhood and subjectivity differently. In addition to these scholars, the work presented here owes a major debt to scholars in narrative therapy and narrative mediation (White 2007; White and Epston 1992; Winslade and Monk 2008). Throughout this broad intellectual movement there is an underlying concern with diversity, power relations and social justice. The model of practice presented here originates in work originally done by The Restorative Practices Development Team (2003), of which I am a member. That work is focused on restorative practice in schools; however, the issues around conforming behaviour and justice are held by schools on behalf of society, and there are many links with justice in schools' struggles to produce appropriate citizens.

What is social constructionism?

The point of departure for a *social constructionist* approach is that the meanings of words are not given and immutable; rather, meaning is made by people as we interact with one another (Burr 2003). So from a constructionist perspective language usage and meanings of words are constantly changing, subject to time and context. This idea is familiar, because even the dictionary, which sets out to record the meanings of words as if meanings are set in stone, provides regular updated editions, as terms come into and out of use, and usages change. If we accept the basic tenet that no meanings are fixed, and meanings are produced in interaction, then there are some important implications. For example, what we think we know, about life, the world, ourselves and others, is the product of meaning-making, subject to change over time and in different contexts. In other words, what we think of as knowledge can change over time. A second important implication is that meaning-making cannot be done by one person on their own: to make and understand a communication, all parties have to observe some conventions – which by definition, are shared. This is what it means to say we are *social* constructionists. That is to say, the rules of language use are developed and *performed* within social contexts, when people come together. Sometimes meanings can be taken for granted by different participants in a conversation, particularly if you know one another well. Other times, what some people mean by what they say may not be quite so clear to others. And the same words may not mean the same things to all persons. We all negotiate meanings in conversation frequently.

The *discursive context* is what we draw upon in trying to make ourselves understood to others. But of course, every person has both meanings in common, and meaning-making resources that we can draw upon individually, which we draw upon to communicate. Each person can only use the discursive (meaning-making) resources they have available to them. The discursive context we draw upon to make meaning together is one with which most of us are familiar (otherwise we could not communicate at all). So, we presume some shared discursive resources (words, ways of speaking, rules) when we try to talk to others, even though all communications by individuals are informed by the previous experiences and learning of each individual.

Central to my account are the concepts *discourse* and *agency*. A *discourse* is a group of statements, beliefs or ways of doing things which loosely cohere together. When you and others share in a discourse, you can make certain assumptions about how people will behave (including how they speak). For example, in some places there is a discourse of ageing which allows people to make jokes about getting older, and can lead to a range of cruel behaviours towards older people – behaviours that can be rendered unremarkable by the taken-for-granted discourse. Understanding meanings as belonging within a discourse can help us to appreciate what other meanings are taken for granted – what assumptions are being made by persons who may be in dispute with one another, or who are behaving in ways that seem odd. This process, of finding the background assumptions that enable the persons present to make meaning, is called *deconstruction*.[1] Thus the dual concepts of discourse and deconstruction can help facilitators to select the focus they take up and the questions they ask.

A constructionist approach also assumes that, at least in principle, every person is potentially able to influence meaning-making. This is what I mean by *agency*. In principle, every person has the capacity to participate in the conversations within which they perform their lives. In practice, however, this is not always the case. I refer here to the moral being or rights to recognition as a moral entity, which I believe we should accord to each person we meet, and those we may meet (Biesta 2003; Levinas 1998). I do not mean by this that if you have agency you have control over anything though. Unless we are a sovereign with ultimate power over others, the usual state of our meaning-making is a bit hit and miss: and we generally negotiate meaning when (or if) we notice that we may not be 'on the same page' as those with whom we are trying to communicate.

Power, language and knowledge

The theory of language which I have referred to above also is informed by a theory about power and power relations. The notion of power as it is used here derives from the work of Michel Foucault, whose broad influence is noted above. He traced how some psychological knowledge changed over time, arguing that these shifting meanings of knowledge reflect power relations.

---

1   See White 1991, 2007 for an account of this skill as a therapeutic practice.

So, those who have more power, prevail more often in meaning-making. (This is a very condensed version of a much broader and more complex contribution to Western thought.) In particular he offered the idea that power relations are productive, and that we cannot avoid using power. Power from this perspective is not thought about as a commodity where there is a fixed amount (so if I have more, you must have less); power operates like the capillaries in our circulatory system, at the lowest and most pervasive levels of society (like our kitchens, bedrooms, and footpaths) (Fraser 1989). And it is always there. We can see how power operates in any particular social environment when we notice what are the dominating discourses, or meanings, in that context. So, for the purposes of restorative practice, a person could look at a school culture and see the dominating values – preferably of respect and inclusion (sometimes called 'power with'), rather than 'power over'. But we could also look at a school and find what discourses (which reflect the dominating values) dominate: and to do this we could look at how people 'do' relationships in the school, and the variety of other practices that reflect the dominating understanding of the knower-to-learner power structure across the whole school. We can notice whose voices dominate, how they position themselves as powerful speakers in the school or not, what kinds of power relationships dominate, and so on. We could potentially also give an account of how some do not thrive.

Power, roles and relationships

Notwithstanding that we may deliberately choose to promote respectful relationships, different players or actors hold different positions within a discourse. So for example the discourse of learning and teaching invokes particular roles, teacher and learner, and a fundamental relationship between them. The meaning of the role 'teacher' invokes the role 'student'. So the two depend on each other, and the discourse brings that relationship into being. What kind of relationship it will be depends on how participants think about learning and teaching within their context. It is not a surprise though to notice that the role or position of teacher is usually thought of as more powerful within the discourse. So, discourses bring different power relationships into being. How these roles play out is also influenced by the particular school culture, which can be characterised by the ways the discourses of teaching and learning in schools play out in any particular school, office or classroom.

Using these background ideas, then, I will now go on to discuss how conversations can be *intentionally productive* of both subjectivities and relationships. I will show how they can be analysed using the concepts presented here; and I will discuss what this tells us about how different ways of speaking produce different kinds of relationship. I will couch these tenets as ideas that we can use to approach a restorative conversation. But they may be applied to all conversational exchanges. The sequence of what happens in conversations is something that we are all familiar with: I am now asking you to pay attention to how the steps in a conversation produce an outcome.

How does it explain what happens in a 'restorative' conversation?

My theory is that the work accomplished in a successful restorative conference is two-fold: to re-establish the moral agency of the offender, so that they are able to take up a position of responsibility in relation to the others involved; and to enable all involved to move to a position of relative generosity to the others, such that the issue is settled psychologically, cognitively, morally and socially. To do this it is important to pay attention to both the process of the conversation, and to what is actually said in each step of the process.

In the beginning

The discursive context of a conference is framed by the assumptions people bring with them. There is no guarantee that parties to a conversation will make the same assumptions, and so the terms of the formal restorative conversation must always be set out at the beginning. In a formal restorative conference, the situation which brought the parties together will already be well known. In preparing for the conference, participants will have been spoken to about their willingness to enter into a conversation about their offending. So some aspects of the conversation may already be known before anyone turns up. My work has been focused on restorative practices in schools, and so my examples come from that context. There will be some expectations in common between a justice context and a school context, however, namely, that somebody has done something they should not. The ways they are dealt with will be determined by the assumptions made beforehand by those who have the authority. What actually happens may differ according to the specific context, including the ethos or culture of the school, and/or the model of restorative conferencing that is being used. The facilitator should always introduce the conference in a way which creates an ethos of equality and respect, and sets out the ground rules for the conversation. So, behind the conference is a *discursive context*.

The conference itself sets out to examine the stories that people tell about the incident, and the positions they take up within each different account. Then, by introducing the stories of others, there is the opportunity to fill out a common story in a way that will enable all participants to take up more respectable positions in the story. This 're-storying' may also need those present to commit to actions, such as an apology. An apology is an action with words; the whole conference itself is an action-packed event.

Attending to the language in a conference

Speaking respectfully has at least the following characteristics: when you speak,

- you are not assuming ignorance on the part of the person or persons spoken to;

- you are not assuming you know all about either the person(s) spoken to, or about what happened; and

- you are inviting them into conversation with you about whatever it is.

This is what I call a 'stance of respectful inquiry'. This could be called a 'not-knowing stance', a concept from narrative therapy (Anderson and Goulishian 1992), where the speaker does not assume they know all about the student's position on whatever it is. For some persons in authority, such as teachers, parents and policemen, this stance of respect may not be congruent with their ideas about their role. These folk will generally not support the model of restorative justice as I am describing it.

Respect and a belief in the rights of all to exist and to be agents of their own lives are the baseline values of restorative justice (Zehr 1990). A constructionist approach states that meanings are produced in social situations; taken together with this RJ commitment as I understand it, this translates into a commitment that, in principle, all people have the power to effect (contribute to) meaning-making – not just about their own lives. A restorative conversation is required when someone's right to that respect has been trampled upon (either figuratively or in reality), and their ability to be an actor is denied or reduced. It will apply to both the 'perpetrator' and the 'victim', because neither would prefer to be in the position they are in. We could see a conference as the conversation we need to have when this has happened to the two parties and their social support systems.

The work of the restorative conversation

It is possible for a conversation to set out intentionally to achieve something. This can happen casually or professionally, in familiar or unfamiliar circumstances. It is perhaps more common to recognise this in relation to professional activities such as therapy. So for example a counselling conversation begins in particular ways related to the reasons the people have come together, and the 'work' of therapy gets done in a variety of steps according to the theoretical framework being followed by the counsellor. The work of narrative therapy is based on a social constructionist paradigm and my understanding of how that 'works' helps to inform my thinking about the process of restorative conferencing. The work of narrative therapy is to deconstruct the 'problem story', and to reposition persons as actors rather than acted upon in their story. I have argued elsewhere (Drewery 2005) that this work is therapeutic because it moves a person from being a colonised or passive subject who has been 'done to', to a position where they can see how they can act on their problem – they become agent or actor in that story. As a result, they know how to go on, and the psychology of it seems to work so that they feel a lot better. I think this is because they are no longer helpless – they are restored to a position of agency over their problem – and this is often through seeing it in different terms, or with expanded understanding.

I see a restorative conference as doing something very similar, only we do not usually call a conference 'therapeutic'. Of course, being able to manage this process well takes a relatively high level of skill and experience, but I do believe that the form and sequence of the questions or scripts given in restorative justice manuals are usually good guides to how to move through the different steps of the conversation. I have not examined other models sufficiently closely to know if they can be said to have the effect of re-installing the persons involved as ethical actors in the conversation about the incident – each from their different position in the story. When the agency of a person/s is restored, they are in a sense liberated, and more fully human. If the conference has done well, the relationship breakdown is understood, and superseded with a way to relate going forward. This does not mean the protagonists have to be best mates. But it does mean that each must experience the respect of the other as a result of the conversation. And this also means that they can go forward – with recognition of the right of each to peaceful co-existence in the future.

There may be a need for restitution of some kind besides this particular conversation – so the repositioning may very likely include a plan to make amends in terms understood and seen as appropriate by both/all parties. Repositioning has to be worked for, and a conference is not a magical one-off accomplishment. I believe it is the experience of respect which can give participants in a conference a heightened experience within a conference – in a psychoanalytic paradigm, this might be described as catharsis. The model that I am explaining does not work explicitly for such an experience, but it does recognise that being in different positions in understanding a situation can have very different effects. Another way of thinking about this is to say that persons can take up different subject positions, some of which enable them to go forward, and some of which do not.

In general, subject positions which are experienced as enabling are preferred. In a world where we accept that all persons have a right to be, we need to accept that at times we are going to run into situations which are understood very differently, and negotiation of meanings will be required. A restorative conference is a formal, usually officially mandated, event which is crafted so that particular forms of negotiation of meaning can go on. This is not a process that will be successful with people who are unwilling to engage in such negotiation. In a restorative conversation, all persons are accountable for their own positions, and are treated as such. Bringing very divergent stories together can be a delicate task.

Phases of the conference

Once the group has come together, the facilitator has set the tone of the conference, and the introductions of those present and their role in the conference have been completed, the facilitator, or someone representing the authority who has called the conference, will state the facts of the incident. The victim should be asked if the official account is fair. This is not a time for negotiation, so this process should be relatively brief and stick to known facts, which have usually been established prior to the conference. When agreement has been established, the perpetrator should be asked the same question. Both should be asked to state their willingness to make amends for what has happened.

Next comes a working phase, where the different perspectives of those present on what happened can be surfaced. During this phase, the main protagonist(s) in turn can be asked for more details of what happened, for example: How did this come about? Did you intend this to happen? Often during this phase it is possible to see how the incident came about, and sometimes important information which has not previously been known by all parties is revealed. For example, it may be discovered that the accused bully was retaliating for previous bullying by the victim (Holm 2014). After this we involve all the persons present, by asking them to name the problem, and these names are recorded on a whiteboard, as each person contributes from their perspective. Notice here that the language used intentionally separates the person from the problem, and the work being done in the conversation is focused on the problem rather than the person. The facilitator has a major role in this; they may pick a name for the problem from the whiteboard which seems to be reasonably readily accepted by a majority.

A facilitator working in this paradigm will not reinforce names which suggest an inherent negative quality or characteristic of the person, because such descriptions do not offer the possibility of change, and therefore are not useful as an object of therapeutic intervention. This is not to deny that reactions such as shame, doubt, humiliation or exhilaration exist, it is just that they are not the primary object of our interest. We are not attempting to diagnose what is wrong with the perpetrator, or to fix them. We are looking for a way forward that restores the 'mana' or dignity of all persons.

Mana is a Māori word which means strength, integrity, or dignity; in Māoridom every person, including criminals and miscreants, has mana. Mana can be enhanced, and it can be diminished. One's mana is enhanced by deeds which inspire admiration; a person with mana is often also humble, and they do not talk themselves up. Mana is the product of social action, bestowed within and by the social sphere, and is not an object which can be directly manipulated. I do not know an English word to describe the improved state of moral agency and integrity which is the objective of this process/model.

In one conference held in a school, with a young man whose continuous disobedience had finally sent someone over the edge, a friend of the young man offered 'No Way Out' as the name of the problem. When asked about this, he described the situation of his friend as impossible: he was trying to care for his siblings at home before school, getting their lunches and ironing their clothes; he was being picked on in the school grounds at lunchtime; and he could not do everything and had lashed out in utter frustration. No-one in the school knew these things about him prior to this disclosure.

In the next phase we ask the support groups in turn to talk about the effects of the problem on them, beginning with the victim and their supporters. The victim should speak first, and then their support people. Effects might include feelings such as anger and disappointment, physical effects such as headaches or insecurity, effects on relationships, and social confidence. Those who are present should each be invited to speak. The focus here is to get the breadth of the effects of the incident, rather than to diagnose any one particular person's reaction. This is not a time where we are inviting people to speak at length about their grievance, or a chance to shame or blame anyone. It is not an opportunity to make a victim impact statement.

By the end of these two phases we have a good idea of how all the people in the room see the story of the problem, and how they position themselves in relation to it. We have avoided implying that the perpetrator is a bad person, and we have made the problem an object that can be acted upon, separating it from the person. We have also implicitly shown the person a way forward which does not involve them accepting that they are inherently bad, and which offers them the possibility of taking agency by facing the problem (though this may not yet be obvious to them). We have also advanced the possibility of common understanding of the problem by all present, without spending time on getting exact agreement. If anyone is still talking about punishment and is still obviously hostile, it may be that they have not had sufficient opportunity to be heard. It may be necessary to go back over the steps above: at such a time it may also be useful to introduce the possibility that the perpetrator may not be a completely bad person, and to invite their supporters to speak in response about the person they know as a loved family member or friend, and to speak about the qualities they have which are obscured by the fact of their wrongdoing.

The meeting may now move to a future focus; this should take about one third of the meeting time. The victim may be asked directly what needs to happen, to make things right. Alternatively, a more general question may be addressed to the group: 'What needs to happen now, to make amends?' Again, this may take a while, and it may be useful to record some of the suggestions before settling on a specific focus. A further useful question might be 'What will a plan for the future have to include?' Some models provide for withdrawal of the two groups after this point, but I do not like this as I think it reverses the work that has been done to bring them together. As well, it is important to continue to avoid succumbing to the temptation to be vindictive.

Everyone in this meeting is accountable for the position they take in the conference, and in the resolution of the matter, and when the work is done publicly there is more chance of developing respect, and a sense of common accountability for the future and success of the conference. A plan for the future should be specific; responsibility for overseeing it should be clearly designated; times for reporting back, and to whom, should be set. The different aspects of the resolution should have clear end dates, and who will take responsibility for different aspects should also be clear. There will be some things that the offender will need to do, and there may be a range of other things that others undertake also. There should be a contingency plan in case this one proves unworkable, a date for a review, and a clear date for closure of the matter.

At the end, the facilitator will review what has happened, summarising the positive aspects of the conference and thanking

164 Restorative Theory in Practice

everyone for their participation. The decisions made about how to take the process forward will be reiterated. Participants may be asked for any final comments, offering them an opportunity for making meaning of the events of the conference. This invitation can lead to some moving expressions of reconciliation, regret, apology and forgiveness among those present.

We recommend that all present be invited to stay for a cup of tea. This provides an opportunity for those present to talk one on one with others who have made disclosures within the conference, and it can be a very powerful and emotional time.

References

Anderson, H. and Goulishian, H. (1992) 'The client is the expert: A not-knowing approach to therapy.' In S. McNamee and K. Gergen (eds) *Therapy as Social Construction*. London: Sage.

Biesta, G. (2003) 'Learning from Levinas: A response.' *Studies in Philosophy and Education, 22*, 61–68.

Burr, V. (2003) *Social Constructionism*. London: Routledge.

Drewery, W. (2005) 'Why we should watch what we say: Position calls, everyday speech and the production of relational subjectivity.' *Theory and Psychology 15*, 3, 305–324.

Foucault, M. (1970) *The Order of Things*. London: Tavistock.

Foucault, M. (1972) *The Archaeology of Knowledge*. London: Routledge.

Foucault, M. (1973) *The Birth of the Clinic*. London: Tavistock.

Fraser, N. (1989) *Unruly Practices: Power, Discourse and Gender in Contemporary Social Theory*. Minneapolis, MN: University of Minnesota Press.

Gergen, K. (1999) *An Invitation to Social Construction*. London: Sage.

Holm, R. (2014) *Constructing a successful restorative justice conference: A tentative analysis*. Unpublished thesis for Master of Education, Hamilton New Zealand: University of Waikato.

Levinas, E. (1998) *Entre-nous: On Thinking of the Other*. New York: Columbia University Press.

Parker, I. (1992) *Discourse Dynamics: Critical Analysis for Social and Individual Psychology*. London: Routledge.

Parker, I. (2005) *Qualitative Psychology: Introducing Radical Research*. Buckingham: Open University Press.

The Restorative Practices Development Team (2003) *Restorative Practices in Schools: A Resource*. Hamilton, NZ: School of Education, University of Waikato.

White, M. (1991) 'Deconstruction and therapy.' *Dulwich Centre Journal, 3*, 21–40.

White, M. (2007) *Maps of Narrative Practice*. New York, NY: W.W. Norton and Co.

White, M. and Epston, D. (1992) *Narrative Means to Therapeutic Ends*. New York, NY: Norton.

Winslade, J. and Monk, G. (2008) *Practicing Narrative Mediation: Loosening the Grip of Conflict*. San Francisco: Jossey-Bass.

Zehr, H. (1990) *Changing Lenses*. Scottdale, PA: Herald Press.

CHAPTER 10

Transactional Analysis

MO FELTON

Introduction

This chapter offers a brief account of the principles and practice of transactional analysis (TA) and how this can inform and enhance the restorative encounter with a developmental approach. It describes how to use TA in a restorative meeting, and how to enable people to manage conflict more effectively.[1]

Transactional analysis

TA is a theory and practice that incorporates several models for understanding human behaviour, communication and relationships. Originally formulated by Eric Berne in the 1950s and 1960s, it is now widely used in counselling, psychotherapy, education and organisations around the world. Berne was a survivor of the Second World War, and along with several of his peers such as Carl Rogers, Albert Ellis and Fritz Perls, was inspired to develop new ways of understanding the human dilemma. This was especially pertinent in the 1950s for those returning from battle suffering from shell shock and post-traumatic stress. Berne was a prolific writer, and since the publication of *Games People Play* (Berne 1964) TA has developed, and some would say it is 'probably the most comprehensive theoretical framework currently available in the field of counselling and psychotherapy' (Mcleod 1998, p.192).

---

1   For a comprehensive introduction to the basic theories and core principles of TA see *TA Today: A New Introduction to Transactional Analysis* (Stewart and Joines 2012).

TA incorporates a theory of personality and of child development making its use with young people and for parenting highly accessible and effective. Combining this with the analysis of transactions, we have a comprehensive framework for enabling people of all ages and backgrounds to deal with difference and conflict.

TA therapy is focused on enabling individuals to change repetitive patterns of thinking, feeling and behaviour. These repetitive patterns are called *rackets*, which are an aspect of *script*, a personal narrative that we design as a result of early experiences and conditioning. The decisions we make can limit potential and strongly influence our communications and interaction, both inter- and intra-psychic. The Life Position which refers to our basic beliefs about the value and worth of self, others and life can strongly influence our relationships and choices (Berne 1962).

Along with Levin (1982) I see child development as a dynamic on-going cycle of growth throughout life. This is powerfully linked to brain development (Siegel 2007), levels of self-esteem, and autonomy. Damaging, missed or simply misunderstood stages of childhood development can cause a closed frame of reference and painful relationships. In order to maintain the frame of reference and *script* an individual will need to *discount* certain aspects of reality and options, and play psychological games that are played out of awareness. *Games* are a repetitive sequence of transactions resulting in familiar bad feelings that do nothing to solve a problem (Berne 1964). Karpman (1968) identified a closed system of transactions from a limited frame of reference, which he refers to as the *drama triangle*, which holds both the desire for change and also the potential for reinforcement of *script decisions* and life position. Berne identified three *ego states* known as *Parent, Adult* and *Child*, which are patterns of thinking, feeling and behaviour and are closely linked to stages of development.

At any one time we are thinking, feeling and behaving in one of these ego states and in interaction we invite a particular ego state in others. The *ego state model* is one of the core concepts of TA represented by three stacked circles (see Figure 10.1). Many of the models in TA are simple to understand but are rooted in a deep theoretical base.

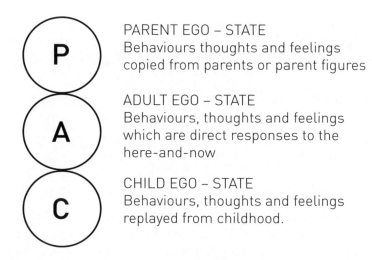

PARENT EGO – STATE
Behaviours thoughts and feelings
copied from parents or parent figures

ADULT EGO – STATE
Behaviours, thoughts and feelings
which are direct responses to the
here-and-now

CHILD EGO – STATE
Behaviours, thoughts and feelings
replayed from childhood.

Figure 10.1: First-order structural diagram; The ego–state model
Reproduced with permission from Ian Stewart, TA Today: A
New Introduction to Transactional Analysis *(2012)*

TA philosophy and values

The philosophical assumptions of TA are:

- *People are OK.* Essentially people are born OK. They have equal worth and value as human beings regardless of gender, race age or religious beliefs. I may not like or accept your behaviour, but your value as a person remains intact.

- *Everyone has the capacity to think.* We all have the capacity to think unless we have suffered severe brain damage. Each of us is responsible to decide what we want from life, and will live with the results of those decisions.

- *People decide their own destiny and these decisions can be changed.* Decisions we made in childhood may still be influencing our lives now. When we made those decisions about ourselves, others and life we were probably strongly influenced by parents and other authority figures, and we had little knowledge or understanding of the world outside our own environment. However, those decisions can be changed and we can increase our options about how we think feel and behave in the here and now. We can make real and lasting changes to our lives.

Alongside these philosophical assumptions of TA are two basic principles that inform practice, the *contractual method* and *open communication*.

The Contractual Method

You and I relate on equal terms and therefore in our professional contact responsibility for the outcome is negotiated and shared. In order to be clear about this we enter into an agreed contract.

Open communication

Berne promoted the practice of openness between practitioner and client. The language of TA is simple and easily understood, although the underpinning theory is profound and carefully reasoned. Case notes are open for inspection and the practitioner will share thinking with the use of diagrams and models. Clients are invited to share their thoughts and feelings and to have these equally valued and considered.

Developmental stages

We can think of the life energy or *physis* as the driving force for life, growth and development, moving first into 0–6 months to learn about being in the world, and if all is well experiencing a mutually validating relationship with primary carers. This experience triggers the production of oxytocin, and feelings of joy. See Figure 10.2 where *Pre birth* and *Birth* are shown at the centre of a quadrant.

At around six months a child will naturally start to explore the world. Learning how to do things such as crawling, walking, climbing and running is in the foreground. Now begins a very active stage involving risk, an awareness of dependency and therefore feeling one down or powerless. This is the time a child is more likely to experience the feeling of fear or vulnerability, and their need from primary caregivers is to experience both permission to explore, and protection from harm. The outcome of a successful experience at this stage results in the child learning his or her own limits and *introjecting* a protective and encouraging parent ego state.

Now the baby is becoming a toddler and at around 18 months will begin to explore personal power and to develop an ability to think and consider the consequences of actions. This stage incorporates the 'terrible twos' and the emotion the toddler is learning about is anger and a feeling of being powerful, and overpowering to everyone else. Successful navigation at this stage teaches the child to consider the limits of others and to begin developing a sense of empathy.

Finally, in the fourth stage at around three years old the frontal cortex will be developed and a child now moves into a period of integrating earlier experiences of being, doing and thinking into a cohesive identity. The feeling in the foreground here is sadness as the child begins to learn to come to terms with the limits of the human condition. There is realisation that there are some things that cannot be changed, either by self or others, and this leads to a feeling of futility. Once again physis, the life force, which is represented by the symbol of infinity, the figure eight at the centre of Figure 10.2, takes us back to a 'being' experience and each stage is recycled up to three times taking the child to adult at around twenty-four.

Each stage or quadrant carries opportunities, risks and the linkage of differentiated parts of the system (Siegel 2014). For example an adolescent in the third stage of taking power, 'thinking' will have had two previous opportunities to learn about and establish personal power, while also learning the rules that enable him or her to live with others.

A young person who has many deficits at previous stages of *being* and *doing* is likely to approach the *thinking stage* with whatever *script decisions* he made to manage those earlier deficits. So we have to meet the young person where they are, and having connected we can then step back into exploration to track down earlier *script decisions* and where the flow of physis is blocked. This is a little like dismantling scaffolding around a building. *Script* is the scaffolding erected at different stages to manage unmet needs.

18 months to 3 years
THINKING I+U–
Experiences personal power
Learns about anger
Power over others
Accepts the limits of others

0 to 6 months
BEING I+U+
Experience of OK-OK
Joy
Accepts good in the world
Establishes trust

3 to 6 years
IDENTITY I–U–
Experiences despair
Learns about sadness
All powerless
Accepts the limits of the
human condition

6 to 18 months
DOING I–U+
Experiences vulnerability
Learns about fear
I am powerless
Accepts own limits

*Figure 10.2: Building the Self. An integration
of developmental stages (Felton 2012)*
Adapted from Ernst 1971; Illsley Clarke 1978; Levin 1982;
Moiso 1984; Sunderland 2006

The restorative encounter

The restorative approach offers an opportunity to explore a new way forward with open communication empowering individuals to share experience and arrive at an agreed solution or closure. From my TA perspective a restorative encounter is achieved when individuals or groups who have a difference or dispute that has caused pain will come together to be open, to listen, and be willing to share vulnerability and power. This encounter may achieve a resolution or be part of a longer healing process. For the facilitator, an understanding of the analysis of transactions and the deeper processes carried by individuals will enhance the restorative encounter. When all parts of the system are heard and *accounted*, then individuals involved are aware of the reality and of the contributing factors. They may not necessarily agree with others, but in knowing the reality they are then less likely to fill their 'not knowing' with fantasies from their own *script. Accounting* for reality is part of what is known as *Adult Ego State* function. The act of inviting all to *account* for each other is, in itself, an invitation into 'Adult' that is the problem-solving state, and facilitates mutually validating relationships and restorative practice.

When the restorative encounter involves a victim and offender there is often an important developmental learning for one or both parties; an understanding of this will increase the likelihood of a successful encounter. Sometimes, on closer inspection, an apparent offender–victim conflict reveals a pattern of miscommunication and escalating harm on both or all sides, known as a *game* in TA.

For example, the offender may not have experienced a safe holding environment in childhood from which to learn about personal power and empathy. The first opportunity to learn this is around 18 months to 3 years, and is closely linked to the quality of attachment the child has had with primary caretakers. If the child does not get the necessary experiences and support to learn about the limits of others, then they may not fully understand or practice empathy.

Likewise the victim may also have missed an experience of personal power at the same stage, or may have been victimised several times through life. In these cases a restorative encounter may mean that at least each party has the opportunity to be heard and have their feelings accounted for, and that ultimately the offender is able to apologise for actions taken, and the victim is able to hear the apology and account for the offender's intentions. They may not be ready for resolution, but complete a stage in the process. Often the very experience of having another option emerge in the meeting will be healing in itself, and in TA terms may provide a step out of the *game*.

A restorative encounter in couples therapy enables both parties to account for the needs of the other and has the potential to be a central skill in a transformational journey toward mutual healing, personal growth and what Hendrix (1993) calls a 'conscious marriage'.

The restorative process

In preparation for a restorative meeting a central element will be to make good contact and invite participants to be open and willing to attend. There might be a potential parallel process of what Clarke and Dawson (1998) described as 'becoming' (the period of time *in utero*, before birth) in order to be with others. Therefore the planning and the ability to empathise with the experience of others is paramount.

Information about how people will get to the meeting is like preparing for a birth. Similarly when planning the arrival of a new young person in the residential home, or the foster home, the team would be considering the quality of preparation and invitation to be here with us. The warmth of the room and the protection we seek to provide is paralleled with the issues of comfort and privacy in a restorative encounter. The preparation can be in itself healing, when we acknowledge that not everyone has had good experiences to do with their arrival. A person who was not prepared for, nor welcomed, at birth may have had this experience repeated several times through life and has constructed a *script* in which they expect to be unwelcome at the meeting. If this is the case, a participant may appear to be guarded or defensive and distrustful of the facilitator, other participants, or the process. This may be a reason for what Hopkins (2009) describes as 'resistance to engaging'.

The structure of the seating and information about facilities again gives an opportunity to demonstrate accounting for the individual needs of participants. During the stages of preparation it is also important to be aware of any internal process. Does the facilitator notice having a particular feeling or fantasy about any one? Is there a similarity with a previous experience or person in the facilitator's life? This may be a process known as *transference* which is likely to interfere with the ability to stay focused and non-judgemental.

If the facilitator finds him or herself identifying people as *persecutor, rescuer* or *victim* this can indicate that there may be a 'game' in process, a rigid system (Siegel 2014) represented by the Drama Triangle. There is a need to be aware of, and *account*, these possibilities from the first moment of involvement in facilitating the meeting. The self-supervision map (Figure 10.3) indicates where energy is focused by identifying thinking, feeling and behaviours associated with each frame of reference.

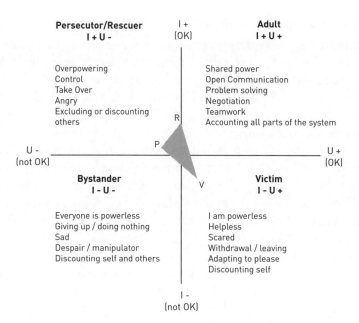

Figure 10.3: Self supervision positions (Felton 2012)[2]

For example, in a couples session, when my male client raises his voice and looks red in the face I notice a desire to 'put him in his place' by competing and speaking louder with more authority. I recognise my move to compete with him in Persecutor (see Figure 10.3) and so I deliberately change my posture, soften my voice, *account* his anger and ask him a question in Adult (I+U+). His partner responds to his anger with tears and defensiveness, withdrawing and looking helpless, and feeling like a Victim (I-U+). I notice my desire to 'stick up for her' and a leaning to having more empathy with her position. I remind myself that my success as a facilitator will depend on staying non-judgemental. I shift my energy from Rescuer (I+U-) to Adult (I+U+) and while accounting her vulnerability, also enquire as to her experience when her husband is angry.

TA theory and practice is central to my thinking at each stage of the process. Many of the models and diagrams of TA are particularly potent and blend almost seamlessly with the thinking and practice of RA.

---

2   There are four basic *Life Positions* which represent the essential value a person places on self and others: I am OK (I+); I am not OK (I-); You are OK (U+); You are not OK (U-) (Berne 1962).

The restorative meeting

As described above the welcome can be seen as being first made in preparation for the restorative meeting. Voice tone, language, body language and facial expressions would all indicate a particular ego state – Parent, Adult or Child. It is important to be aware of the non-verbal signals of all participants. The analysis of transactions is used to identify, manage and invite change. I might notice a desire to speak from my own *Parent ego* state, or perhaps from a *Child ego* state and then deliberately move my energy, voice tone, body language and facial expression to an *Adult ego* state. This in turn invites the other person to respond from their Adult ego state. The use of TA will demonstrate my *accounting* (as against discounting) of the underlying feelings that may have caused these types of transaction. Checking whether each participant is still willing to participate is a check on the contract we have and inviting a further contract to continue with the meeting. I am conscious of modelling mutual validation including a subtle expectation that a positive outcome is possible regardless of the current situation.

Introductions, clarifications, reminders of the purpose and my role are all aspects of the session contract. Explanation of the process and of my role as facilitator is again clarifying the details of the contract. I would see this stage in developmental terms as paralleling the holding environment for the new baby, the stage of being in the world (0–6 months). At this stage of development the infant needs to make a noise to get needs met. The carer, or in this case, facilitator, is responsible for being aware of environmental needs and being responsive to the participants' requests. In child development this stage requires the (M)other and baby to attune to each other and where successful, results in basic trust. As Hopkins (2009) points out if this stage is mismanaged the meeting can be doomed from the start, as is also true of the early stages of child development.

However, as a transactional analyst I am also mindful that the participants here are individuals and may respond differently. It may be possible to repair mistakes at this stage by *accounting* for them and enquiring about needs. In stage two of the restorative process, where those concerned get a chance to tell their story, it will be important to account each person's interpretation of events. Certain aspects may be amplified or minimised, sometimes people just see particular aspects as more important or holding greater significance and emotional responses. The *script* of each person may influence this.

Giving equal attention to the accounts of each participant and ensuring a non-judgemental mutual approach will generally provide enough holding in the process. The facilitator has an opportunity at this stage to model what may be a new experience for those involved. It is pointless to put on an act here, if the facilitator is biased the participants will know it in what is called their '*Little Professor*', an aspect of the Child ego state which picks up unconscious processes and messages.

Thinking and feeling can be conditional and repressed, and therefore the facilitator needs to be mindful of the connections a person may make and look out for discounts which indicate that a *game* may be in process. Knowledge of TA enables a choice of intervention, to offer understanding and potentially new options (Karpman 1971). Essentially I see a restorative intervention as an opportunity for participants to discuss their perception of who did what, and for each person to become increasingly aware of their own and the other person's vulnerability. If each person truly listens to the other's painful experience, the meeting is more likely to move on to the next stage.

There is a possible transition here, which I see as similar to stage three of the Integration Grid, *Thinking*. Between eighteen months and three years there is huge shift in the child's ability to think and reason about what they have done, and most importantly to discover empathy and the ability to recognise the limits of others. This is also the stage of learning about anger and power, and how to use anger to establish boundaries when we feel intruded upon. Many people have not learned to use anger effectively, and this stage in a restorative encounter can offer an opportunity for rebalancing this aspect of emotional development. The facilitator, by holding the space for new or emerging anger, recreates a learning space. Returning to each speaker to add or clarify aspects of their own experience, and accounting for the other's needs, may result in a meta-perspective where each person can see a bigger picture that encompasses other's needs and feelings as well as their own. At this point it is possible to consider who has been affected by what happened.

Needs

I see the restorative encounter as an opportunity to rebalance thinking, feeling and doing. The recognition that each person has needs enables a move out of the Drama Triangle, a closed system, and into problem solving. For participants to take the time to identify needs they must have reached a point of trust in the process and believe that their needs are equally important and accounted. When anger is used as a defence against vulnerability this will prevent access to feelings of scare and therefore prevent an awareness of vulnerability and needs in oneself and others.

Ownership of problem solving

When each person involved has an opportunity to bring about change, and also account for what cannot be changed, they are empowered to come to terms with the limits of the human condition (Moiso 1984). The person is able to integrate their own experience of vulnerability and power into a new identity and a way forward. Young people who have only known situations where there are winners and losers can see other options where all are equally important and damage can be repaired or reduced. Reaching a mutual agreement of the way forward and what each person is agreeing to and responsible for engages an integrated mindset where thinking, feeling and behaviour are employed to enhance and maintain relationships, connection and attachment. This agreement creates a new contract.

Closure

Endings are important. Taking the time to say goodbye is an essential step. Unfinished business takes up attention and energy, and many people have traumatic endings in their lives. Young people in care may have experienced multiple difficult and painful endings where they have been unable to come to terms with loss and make closure in order to move forward. This can result in a difficulty in letting go of the issue, even though they may have reached an agreement. Having an awareness of this will make the offer of a review date a useful check, and again demonstrate that needs are still accounted, and that others will not move to game positions of *persecutor, rescuer, victim* or *bystander* (Clarkson 1992) when agreements have been apparently reached (see Figure 10.3).

An experience of a restorative encounter may well be therapeutic in itself by offering the participants another option in contrast to their *script*, which is a closed system. As in restorative approaches there is a paradigm shift from a blaming culture to authentic relationships. Choy (1990) used a version of the Drama Triangle to demonstrate a move from a game to *autonomy*. The persecutor moves to assertive behaviour, the rescuer moves to caring, incorporating support without control, and the victim moves to acknowledging their vulnerability and accounting for needs in self and others.

Conclusion

Interpersonal communication is said to shape the growth of the integrative regulatory circuits of the brain (Siegel 2014). Transactional analysis can be applied to all forms of human communication, ranging from improving everyday personal, relational and social systems, to working with severe forms of distress and disorder in long-term psychotherapy. The core theories of TA can be combined effectively with RAs. For psychotherapists a knowledge of the restorative encounter can prove to be a valuable tool and method to use with clients, and particularly couples and family therapy. Similarly restorative practitioners may find the insights that TA provides can deepen their awareness and understanding of what is happening during a restorative encounter.

References

Berne, E. (1962) 'Classification of Positions.' *Transactional Analysis Bulletin 1,* 3, 23.

Berne, E. (1964) *Games People Play.* New York, NY: Grove Press.

Berne, E. (1966) *Principles of Group Treatment.* New York, NY: Oxford University Press

Choy, A. (1990) 'The Winners Triangle.' *Transactional Analysis Journal 20,* 1, 40–46.

Clarkson, P. (1992) *Transactional Analysis Psychotherapy: An Integrated Approach.* London: Routledge.

Ernst, F. H. (1971) 'The OK Corral: The Grid for "Get on With."' *Transactional Analysis Journal 1,* 4, 231–240.

Felton, M. (2012) 'Touchstone and Talisman.' *The Transactional Analyst 2,* 3, 12–20.

Hendrix, H. (1993) *Getting The Love You Want.* London and New York: Simon and Schuster UK Ltd. Pocket Books.

Hopkins, B. (2009) *Just Care: Restorative Justice Approaches to Working with Children in Public Care.* London: Jessica Kingsley Publishers.

Illsley Clarke, J. (1978) *Self Esteem: A Family Affair.* New York, NY: Harper and Row.

Illsley Clarke, J. and Dawson, C. (1998) *Growing up Again*. Minnesota, MN: Hazelden Publishing.

Karpman, S. (1968) 'Fairy tales and Script Drama Analysis.' *Transactional Analysis Bulletin 7*, 26, 39–43.

Karpman, S. (1971) 'Options.' *Transactional Analysis Journal, 1*, 79–87.

Levin, P. (1982) *Cycles of Power*. California. Health Communications, Inc.

Mcleod, J. (1998) *An Introduction to Counselling*. Buckingham: Open University Press.

Moiso, C. (1984) 'The Feeling Loop.' In E. Stern (ed.) *TA: The State of the Art*. Dordrecht, Holland: Foris Publications.

Siegel, D. J. (2007) *The Mindful Brain*. New York, NY: W.W. Norton.

Siegel, D. J. (2014) *Brainstorm: The Power and Purpose of the Teenage Brain*. New York, NY: Penguin Random House.

Stewart, I. and Joines, V. (2012) *TA Today: A New Introduction to Transactional Analysis. Second Edition*. Nottingham: Lifespace.

Sunderland, M. (2006) *What Every Parent Needs to Know*. London: Dorling Kindersley.

CHAPTER 11

Ten Different Ways to Approach a Restorative Encounter

Introduction

In preparation for this chapter all ten contributors were sent the same two scenarios to comment on. Both scenarios involve school-aged young people. The first describes an altercation between a student and a teacher and the second describes the theft of a mobile phone. Each scenario was presented to the contributors in the form of an initial description of the case, followed by some insights gleaned from initial private preparation with those affected. Both cases are based on real scenarios[1] and have been used in my own training organisation as the basis for skills practice.

Each contributor shares some of the thought process they might use approaching the case and elements of how they might embark on, and facilitate, the case if required to do so. A shared scenario shows how different theoretical lenses might add to the practice of facilitation. The first scenario comes from a school setting. One contributor, Pete Wallis, chose not to contribute his thoughts to this case as his area of expertise and experience is primarily in youth justice settings.

For ease of understanding and comparison each contributor's piece is presented in the same order as their initial chapters.

---

1   Thank you to Caroline Newton for providing these scenarios from her practice as restorative justice co-ordinator in the London Borough of Lewisham some years ago.

THE FIRST SCENARIO – A CONFLICT BETWEEN JAMES AND MR SCHOFIELD

James, a young teenager of about fourteen years old, has been removed from lessons for the day because of an incident in one of his lesson's classroom. He had failed to bring in his homework project. When the teacher had come over to his desk and told him off in front of the class, James had become angry and thrown his pencil case on the ground whereupon it hit the teacher's leg. The teacher sends James to the deputy head who listens to his side of the story and refers him to the pastoral team so he can explain everything that has happened.

James's story

James, a young teenager of about fourteen years old, had tried to do his science project, but it had got lost at home. He was feeling really angry with his older brother, suspecting him of having taken it. He did not feel he could talk to his mum about what had happened because she had just had a new baby. She seemed to be really tired, and also really sad at the moment because her partner, James's dad, has gone away. There are baby things all over the house and there is nowhere for James to do his homework apart from the bedroom. He shares the bedroom with his older brother. He is missing his dad too, and is not sure when he will see him again.

James wanted to explain to Mr Schofield what had happened. However, when he came round the class to collect the work and saw that James had nothing to hand in he began, in James's words, to 'have a go on at him'. Mr Schofield reminded James that he had already given him several chances to finish the task and that this was the third time his homework would be in late. James felt himself getting tearful and, not wanting to cry in front of everyone, he picked up the nearest thing to him, a pencil case, and threw it on the floor. A pencil fell out and hit Mr Schofield on the leg. At this point the teacher became very angry and sent him out of the classroom to see the deputy head teacher. James realised he was in serious trouble. He is dreading going back into the science lessons and worried about what Mr Schofield will say to him. He tells the deputy that he is not going back into his science class and is kept away from lessons for the rest of the day.

Next day, following a meeting with a member of the pastoral team, a trained restorative facilitator, the offer of a face-to-face meeting with Mr Schofield is made and the process explained. James agrees to this.

Later that day this same facilitator approaches Mr Schofield, lets him know she has spoken to James and invites him to tell her what has happened.

Mr Schofield's story

Mr Schofield explains that he has always found this particular class a bit of a handful, but had felt that he was getting to grips with them. He had been trying to encourage them to take responsibility for doing work off their own back and had designed special project books to help them do this. However, there are three or four students who regularly do not hand in their homework, and James is one of them.

He is also feeling really tired at the moment as he has taken on a new set of classes. He explains that home life is very stressful at the moment as he has a young baby at home. He acknowledges that his patience is not at its best at the moment.

Yesterday when James did not have his homework ready to hand in again, after two extensions already Mr Schofield decided he needed to make a point to both James and the rest of the class that it was unacceptable to avoid handing in homework on time. He told James that he needed to start pulling his weight if he wanted to succeed. Mr Schofield explained he felt very shocked when James reacted so violently by throwing his pencil case on the floor. He saw that the set of compasses had fallen out and was fearful that someone could have been hurt. As it was, it was just the case that hit him on the shin but even this was quite painful.

Mr Schofield sent James out of the class to the deputy head to be dealt with. He remains unsure what the boy's reaction will be when he comes back into the class the following week.

The teacher is also asked if he would be willing to meet with James. It is explained that the meeting would involve looking at what has happened and at how to reintegrate James back into class, as he has said he is now scared to come back. Mr Schofield feels a little concerned about what will happen and whether he will lose face. However, he also wants to have good relationships with his students so he agrees to attend the meeting.

The facilitator is reassuring about this meeting and encourages Mr Schofield to tell James how the whole incident has left him feeling. She leaves it up to him whether or not to share what is happening for him outside school and what is contributing to his stress levels.

1. The affect and script psychology approach – Margaret Thorsborne

James has had a series of difficult moments leading up to the incident with his teacher. Failure to find his science project has triggered shame and this has become amplified by the suspicions that his brother has taken it. The worry about turning up at school without it, not wanting to increase the load on his mother and missing his father has greatly increased his distress. So he turns up at school already in a state of arousal (angry and primed for more shame expected from the teacher). As his distress threatens to overwhelm him, he defaults to defending himself against the shame of public tears. Combined with how diminished he feels as his teacher berates him for the absence of the project, this creates a perfect storm of 'Attack Other' on the compass of shame (see Chapter 1, Figure 1.1). He throws the pencil case, which then hits the teacher. He becomes fearful of the repercussions.

Mr Schofield is very distressed – a new baby at home and, no doubt, sleep deprivation, a 'rumpety' class that has tested his sense of competence (also a source of shame and distress for him), a whole set of new classes with students yet to know … and this makes Mr Schofield easily aroused to anger. I suspect he has taken James's failure to bring his project personally, and this has triggered shame. Mr Schofield's default is the public dressing down of James – as much 'Attack Other' as James's response. In my view, he should not be surprised when James reacts – Attack Other behaviours often result in Attack Other behaviours!

The affect pattern for both parties is very similar – distress, anger, shame. The facilitated conversation between them will help them understand each other, provide relief from their difficult emotional states and with a careful plan provide a way forward to restore their relationship. The impact of the incidents on classmates needs to be addressed in some sort of carefully facilitated conversation.

2. The attribution theory approach – Juliet Starbuck

Attribution Theory helps us to understand both 'the incident', in which we can identify three causal events, and 'the restorative intervention'. Mr Schofield responded angrily when James told him that he had not got his homework. If we think of James's failure to bring in his homework as a 'causal event' then this reaction fits with Proposition 1, (see Chapter 2) which states that 'the harmed' (in this event Mr Schofield) will describe feelings of anger and thoughts of reprimand, and/or other negative reactions, following an initial causal act against them.

So, as predicted by the theory, Mr Schofield reprimanded James. He perceives the act as 'against' him because it had happened before, and because he was feeling anxious and unsure about his relationship with the class anyway. He responded by 'telling James off'.

Of course, the theory also suggests that if 'the harmed' makes 'an inference of responsibility' they will feel angry. It is noted that Mr Schofield has been trying to get the pupils to take responsibility for their work and that he thought that James needed to start 'pulling his weight' – strongly suggesting that this 'construct' was at the forefront of his mind. Mr Schofield's response was angry.

The second causal event occurred when Mr Schofield tells James off. James responded as if he had been harmed. He experienced 'feelings of anger and thoughts of reprimand' and so threw his pencil case to the ground. James interpreted Mr Schofield as responsible for the first 'causal event' because, in his mind, he certainly was not responsible for failing to hand in his homework. This failure he attributes instead to all that had been going on for him at home.

The third causal event occurred when James threw the pencil case to the ground. The pencil case hit Mr Schofield and, in the teacher's heightened state of arousal, was interpreted as a purposeful act for which James was responsible. So Mr Schofield felt further feelings of anger and reprimanded James by telling him to leave the class.

Having described how causal attribution theory would explain what has happened, I describe how the theory explains what can happen during a restorative meeting. First, if the meeting is run according to the five stages of a conference (see Chapter 2) then it will give James and Mr Schofield the chance to hear each other's story. This will give them an alternative interpretation of the other's behaviour. Both parties will feel safe enough to accept responsibility for their part in the conflict; to indicate remorse and to offer reparation. If they both (in their position as 'harmed'), listen to the other 'confess' then they will, according to Weiner's theory, perceive that the other (the wrongdoer) is not an inherently bad person. They will feel confident that the other is not likely to commit the causal act again. They will also have a more positive moral impression of each other. They will have reduced feelings of anger and increased feelings of sympathy towards each other. They will acknowledge the increased likelihood of restored interpersonal relations between each other. In addition, both James and Mr Schofield will feel better about themselves. All of this will make it less likely that a similar incident will happen again. Discussion about choices and behaviours during the storytelling and agreement phases of the meeting will also give James and Mr Schofield the opportunity to think about alternative and more pro-social constructs that could be drawn upon if there is a next time.

3. The critical relational theory approach – Dorothy Vaandering

Critical relational theory alerts one to power dynamics when situations like the one James and Mr Schofield experience occur. Engaging first with the overarching questions, 'Who is benefiting?' and 'Who is bearing the burden?' there is an immediate recognition that the adults in this situation hold power and James is expected to comply. By confronting James publicly and removing him, an immediate hierarchy is identified and reinforced. James has far less choice in the matters that led to his reaction than did Mr Schofield. If James had complied immediately, though it can be said he would have benefited, the power and authoritarian manner employed by the adults illustrates how compliance is a significant characteristic of schooling.

When conscious of this discrepancy in power, it challenges me to empathise and consider how power might be used pro-actively to turn this situation into a learning experience that will benefit James, Mr Schofield, and the institution. With this in mind, I consider the details of the situation and cast these in the context of the following question: 'How can I honour James, Mr Schofield, and any others directly or indirectly involved in my intervention so as to support them to resolve what has happened?' I also consciously consider how my interaction with them could cause them to feel further judged or measured. This internal critical reflection allows me to prevent using my power as a facilitator in a manipulative manner.

Though this may take but moments of my time, it is a crucial aspect of a restorative justice encounter if the most vulnerable are to be supported.

Mentally prepared, I would then approach James and Mr Schofield separately, as in this scenario, and invite them to share with me their stories by using a variation of the restorative justice framework questions (see Chapter 3). Then I would ask them if they are interested in a restorative justice dialogue and if there are others they feel need to be part of such a conversation. In assessing what I have heard, I reflect on the power dynamics expressed and consider if the safety of the circle space and the resolution reached are at risk.

If assured that a dialogue could occur where they both benefit and the burden of the incident would not be shuttled onto the most vulnerable present, I would approach supporters and others suggested. I would also inform both James and Mr Schofield that representatives from the class would be present as well as the deputy head, as they have all been involved indirectly. Within critical relational theory, the students as observers of the incident will fulfil a significant role in supporting both James and Mr Schofield after the circle conference in the decisions that are made. Without them present to contribute to the solution, they could incite further frustration for either or both if only told a resolution has been reached. The deputy head's presence is important for in hearing the stories as an authority she is the direct connection to the possibility of changes that may be necessary in terms of school policy and structure. If all agreed then I would follow the process described in Chapter 3 on pages 71 and 74.

Variations of the preconference and conference facilitator guidelines as described are available from a range of proponents of restorative justice and could be used. However, what critical relational theory can contribute to these is its potential for identifying power dynamics within the process that are rooted in oppressive power. For example, in various restorative justice processes, acknowledgement of responsibility is required for the conference to proceed. James would likely be the one considered to have caused harm and would be expected to acknowledge responsibility for causing the incident. In some contexts the facilitator might expect Mr Schofield to acknowledge his responsibility; however, given that he sent James to the deputy, this is unlikely.

Critical relationship theory works on the premise that identifying who has caused harm is complex. Requiring that James admit to causing harm and carry full responsibility for it is not necessary. Nor is it necessary for Mr Schofield to do so. Both are part of a systemic structure, embedded in a society comprising dominant social groupings that are hierarchical. What is necessary is for both to recognise their involvement in the situation, that those indirectly affected be involved, and those with the capacity to affect systemic change be present, such as, in this case, deputy head.

4. A Jungian approach – Ann Shearer

What strikes me first about this conflict is just how vulnerable the two protagonists appear. They are both struggling with difficult situations at home, and this lack of a sturdy base seems to have made their reactions to the conflict more painful than it might otherwise have been.

So when Mr Schofield fails to give James the chance to explain why he still hasn't done his homework, the boy becomes tearful rather than angry; he only throws the pencil case to defend himself against his tears, not with the intention of hurting anyone. As the story unfolds, he seems to feel no anger or sense of injustice; instead, he 'dreads' going back into science lessons and is 'worried' about what Mr Schofield will say to him. For his part, Mr Schofield knows that his patience is at low ebb. But more than that, he seems almost hurt by James's failure to do his homework, after all his own efforts to encourage students with his special project books. When James throws his pencil case to the floor Mr Schofield is 'shocked'; he immediately makes more of the incident than actually happened – 'someone could have been hurt'. He feels unable to deal with the situation other than by removing the boy from the class.

The second thing to strike me is how the conflict is permeated with stories of fathers. So from the perspective of Jungian theory, we could suggest that the root of the problem could lie in a father complex, which has caught both James and Mr Schofield in a shared and painful psychological field. James is effectively fatherless: his father has left; he doesn't know when he will see him again. He is left with a very frightening paternal image that he is projecting onto the school. We could imagine that what he needs most is a secure and kindly authority to help him see another side of 'father' and so gain a more secure sense of himself. Mr Schofield has not been able to provide that, seeming instead to become one more adult who does not have time for him. Mr Schofield has his own 'father work' cut out already, with a new baby to deal with. At the same time, his sense of his own authority is not secure: he does not seem able to deal with James himself but refers him up the hierarchy; he fears 'losing face' if he meets with the boy.

Based on this reading of the conflict, my sense would be that James especially would find it extremely helpful to have his story sympathetically heard by a representative of authority; this could do a lot to diffuse his complex-driven fear. My hope would be that through the restorative process, the school might find ways in which to provide the 'paternal' structure that both James and Mr Schofield seem to lack, so enabling them to find a more positive version of the father complex within themselves, and greater senses of security at home and at work.

5. The Nonviolent Communication approach – Shona Cameron

In a one to one meeting with James I would, using the skills of Nonviolent Communication (NC) described in Chapter 5, choose to turn my *attention* to how James is feeling now and what needs he has. This may be enough at this stage, although I can also explore with James how to support those needs being met. In this way I honour the *intention* to connect with him before the meeting with the teacher. As described in Chapter 5 I would get curious about what is happening for James and make an observation by saying things like: '*I wonder if* you really want us to know that you tried to do your homework?'

I would offer empathy about his feelings and needs by using phrases such: 'James. *I am wondering* if life is hectic for you right now, a bit full on?' (such a phrase is described as a colloquial feelings guess).

'And there's not much time for you in the family, and you'd like to be a bit more certain about things?' (such a phrase we describe as a colloquial needs guess – the need for security)

This may encourage James to share how he is, and to develop trust as he senses that he is being heard without judgement. I would then come to the present:

'So right now? Are you worried about talking to Mr Schofield again, and wanting to feel safe to have this conversation?'

Before bringing the two together I would also spend time with Mr Schofield and offer him a similar opportunity to develop trust and connection, using similar tentative guesses to check I have understood.

'*I wonder if* you're noting an improvement with this tricky class and you are really pleased with how you've managed this?'

'*It sounds like* you really want me to know and understand all the pressure you are under right now?'

'*So it sounds like there* are two things going on here. On the one hand are you feeling concerned because you really value respect in your classroom, and it's a bit scary having a meeting and allowing James back in given all that's happened and all that the other pupils have witnessed? And on the other hand you do want to go ahead because you value the relationships you have with the students. Have I understood accurately?'

During the face-to-face meeting, having listened to both, and given them a chance to feel heard, I would guess that they will also be able to hear each other, and will both naturally want to apologise.

6. The personal construct psychology approach – Pam Denicolo

This case illustrates the personal construct psychology (PCP) fundamental postulate that each person, because of differences in experience and opportunities to test out their intuitive theories about the world, their constructs, construes the world, and particular events in it, in a different way (see Chapter 6). Both of the participants in this case are enveloped in a complex and trying personal situation which has led to them responding to a challenging situation in a way that, in other more positive circumstances, they might not have done.

A neutral observer, having access to their stories might well have sympathy with both, recognising the embarrassment and frustrations that resulted in Mr Schofield 'telling off' James in public and James, unable to articulate his own frustrations, throwing his pencil case. That it inadvertently struck the teacher's leg heated the situation further. A PCP counsellor would aim first to give each of them an opportunity to consider an alternative perspective, that of the other participant, so that they may reach an understanding that the situation is the problem, rather than a personal threat from the other. Second, they would be encouraged to work together to explore resolutions to the situation that would satisfy the concerns of each.

Various methods exist to facilitate those discussions, depending on the preferences of the participants. These vary from writing simple lists that they exchange to line drawings with labels or speech bubbles that allow the participants to express their ideas in a comprehensive way, with no interruptions from the other, about their situation to build *sociality*. In this case, since they have been able to articulate their circumstances and how they felt to a member of the pastoral team, there may be no need for tools to facilitate that articulation. However, having them prepare something tangible to refer to would ensure that each conveys the complexity to the other. For instance, they might each draw in the centre of a sheet of paper a circle containing the word HOMEWORK with arrows to it showing the things that impinge on it. In James's case this could include the elements of the home situation that frustrate his attempts to do and bring in his homework. For Mr Schofield, the elements could include the importance of homework for students' success, the need to ensure that all students recognise its importance, and the assertion that favouritism is not part of that classroom culture.

James's diagram should provide an opportunity for the PCP counsellor to note the turbulence that a baby can bring to a household. This would provide the teacher with an opportunity to reveal that he too suffers a similar stress, and that this may have led him to be a bit less diplomatic than he might otherwise have been. This is an opportunity for the two to share an experience and build some empathy, known as *commonality* in PCP terms. This would be the prelude to working on a way forward that might salve the concerns that each has about the return to the classroom. They might be guided towards considering a solution, such as James doing his homework at lunchtime or just after school so that he has peace in which to do it. Such a solution would also save the teacher's face as it would indicate the importance of homework being completed, and that James had not been 'let off' for his misdemeanour.

7. The relational theory approach
– Mark Vander Vennen

One can sense that both James and Mr Schofield are experiencing levels of shame. James carries shame about not having his homework completed (despite his best intentions), about his home situation and perhaps about the pencil case incident. It is likely that he did not expect that the case would hurt Mr Schofield. It is also likely that James experienced the 'lecture' by Mr Schofield as a public 'shaming'. In turn, Mr Schofield may be experiencing some shame about his classroom management abilities, about his intervention with James (which did not go as expected, despite his best intentions), and about the need to engage with the deputy head teacher about it. There are also significant back stories behind the event for both James and Mr Schofield that the event itself does not reveal. For these two reasons – the need to hear the stories behind the incident, and the need to move past shame, in order to repair their relationship so they can move forward – the deputy head and the pastoral team are on the right track to encourage a meeting between both student and teacher.

From attachment theory, we know how important safety is for participants to feel able to dare to risk the hard emotional work needed, and to explore and learn. For both James and Mr Schofield the meeting will feel less safe if the meeting process itself is 'parachuted' in from the outside, rather than seen as a consistent expression of how relationships are done across the board at the school. In the first case, both would experience the meeting as an expression of a relational double-standard: a restorative expectation applying to them but not to the others in the school, including staff. The deputy would thus do well to be explicit, prior to the meeting, about her own relational practice and that of the school. Similarly the pastoral team would also be explicit during the preparation and the facilitation of the meeting itself.

The person facilitating the meeting would be clear about what James and Mr Schofield can expect from him/her in the meeting. S/he would express full confidence in both of them and would offer them both full support. S/he would ask them each consistent questions (provided to them both ahead of time) that they each know. S/he would not 'mediate' a solution between them, knowing that the expertise needed lies with the two of them, but would help to create a safe space for them to do the work needed to move forward. S/he would further explain that the school itself is committed to creating an environment where relationships matter, where there are high relational expectations of one another in an environment of support, where everyone has a voice, where listening is valued, and where there is no coercion. The meeting is one expression of a continuum of relational practice at the school.

My prediction is that the meeting will go well. As both listen to each other's stories about what happened, how they and others have been affected, what is hard for them about the event and its aftermath, and what they are each prepared to do to move forward, their mirror neurons will fire and empathy will develop. They will start to co-regulate each other's affect, which will then lead to new reflection. Co-regulation of affect is the foundation of connection and relationship, of relationship repair, of solutions for moving forward, and of a successful restorative encounter. Co-regulation, which precedes self-regulation, will allow them to move from negative to more positive affects.

The meeting will also need to lead to some way of addressing the harm done to the class by the incident, since the class was also affected. The agreement for how to move forward will almost certainly contain a nuanced, sensitive and restorative way of engaging the class so that harm is addressed, relationships are deepened, and learning is enhanced.

8. The resonant empathy approach – Pete Wallis

This is not represented here as Pete Wallis's experience has been primarily in youth justice settings.

9. The social constructionist approach – Wendy Drewery

If I were the facilitator in this scenario I would be thinking that there is a very good chance of a peaceful resolution to this problem. The pre-meeting meetings have shown that both the teacher and the student have issues that have nothing to do directly with the incident, and both need support with their issues. The young man clearly needs help to work through the issues directly with his teacher; and there are things about the student that the teacher really needs to know. The teacher has a problem with this particular class, which goes beyond, but feeds into, the incident. In the group meeting it would be helpful if the teacher were to share his situation with James about having a new baby in the house – but we cannot require this. As facilitator what I can do in the meeting is create the conditions within which this may happen, safely and professionally. In preparing myself for the meeting, the power differential between the teacher and student is also a major consideration.

Consistent with my theoretical perspective, I see as central the process or form of the conversation that I would seek to facilitate. It is important to hold to the order of the conversation, but I do not move slavishly from one question or phase to the next. It is important to create the right conditions for the restorative work to occur, and this is one of the functions of the pre-conference meetings. The 'work' includes, but is not confined to, providing opportunities for each protagonist to listen to and hear the other – the meeting is an opportunity for learning and building relationship, and hearing the other's story alongside one's own is fundamental to this development.

The attitude of the teacher in the conversation is crucial, and I am making some assumptions here. In the prior meetings with each separately I would work on explaining, in appropriate language, what I am reaching for in the group meeting. I will explain that this is not a situation where we need to determine blame, and I will encourage both to approach the conversation with an inquiring rather than a defensive mind-set. I will also explain that I will be working for an outcome where both can move forward, James with his learning in science, and Mr Schofield with teaching his class, in a way that means they do not have to dread their next class, but rather, to enjoy it and move forward with optimism. I may not use these words, which are formed specifically for you the reader, in order to give you an overview. In my conversations with James and Mr Schofield, I will model optimism and openness, in language that reflects respect for each of them.

In the actual meeting, I would welcome them both, and reiterate the 'rules' – the problem is the problem, the person is not the problem – and I will present this meeting as aiming to help them both to get a better understanding of what happened and why, and to make some agreements about what to do about it.

I would ask James to speak first. This helps to reduce the power differential. I would encourage James to explain why he did not have his homework that day, basically getting the story that I already know, but which Mr Schofield does not. I would expect that as he tells this story James may become quite emotional, because I have encouraged him to speak from within himself, how it is for him, and it would become clear that he is upset about the situation at home. He is not getting much support from anywhere, and I am expecting that this conversation might trigger further action to help him. I would expect, within this narrative, to offer him the possibility to apologise to Mr Schofield, if he does not take that up himself. It is important to notice that I am not helping James to construct his story, so much as to convey himself within his situation, which includes both classroom and home. A constructionist perspective acknowledges the 'ecology' of persons – the conversation cannot ignore that he is living within a much broader context than the school and the science classroom. Constructionists are not focused on eliciting emotion or 'affect', but acknowledge that emotion is an expression of how something matters. We are interested in the accounts people give about why things matter, and the meaning they make of situations that produce strong emotion particularly (because this is what has brought us all together here in the first place).

In response to James' story, Mr Schofield will probably have learned something that he did not know previously about James, and hopefully he is a supportive teacher who realises that he has circumstances in common with James, and that his own reaction may have brought some of those personal circumstances into the incident. He may talk about his new baby. This is an opportunity for developing common understanding. He may then go on to talk about what he could do to help James get back on track with his science. If he does not, I would work towards this. I would ask questions in a way that does not presume to know the answer: and I would keep track of the process, trying to gauge when it is possible to move to the next step in the conversation. It is important that people have time to speak, to hear themselves, to 'get it off their chest' – and that they do this in a way that speaks about themselves, and does not make assumptions about the other. When people get the idea of this manner of speaking, they can find it quite liberating. This is because the alternative, assertion of *power-over*, where one assumes they know the meanings of the life of another and imposes such meanings on them, creates a defensive sense of entitlement which works against the development of relational wellbeing. The whole idea of my approach is that we avoid such imposition, aiming instead to preserve, respect, and in this conversation hopefully restore the moral agency of the other. As I have outlined, I see this as a two-way interaction, affecting all parties to the conversation, even those not present. This attitude or moral stance of respect, made manifest in ways of speaking, can actually produce respectful relationship.

When we get to the point of asking what can we do about what has happened, I would want to discuss not only the relationship between Mr Schofield and James, but also James' progress, and we might touch on what could be changed in his situation at home. Later, after the meeting, I might invite James' mother to come in and have a chat to bring her up to date about the incident. I would tell her it is fine to bring the new baby and show it off. And within the next week I would certainly check in with Mr Schofield about how things are going with that particular class, and offer further support. In referring to issues beyond the incident, I am assuming that the school has a commitment to respectful relationships, and I am demonstrating the social constructionist position that we are all interdependent, and the quality of our relationships, including the school's and teachers' relationships with home, are crucial to the wellbeing of all involved, including success at school. Within the week too I would make a point of running into James around the school and acknowledging him.

10. The transactional analysis approach – Mo Felton

In the overall outline of the case I am first noticing that this may be what we call a 'game'. James had not produced his homework project. The teacher had come over to his desk, which sounds like he was standing over James and told him off in front of others. This looks like Mr Schofield was in the Persecutor role on the Drama Triangle and James was in the Victim role. James reacted angrily and threw his pencil case, which hurt Mr Schofield. At this point they have changed positions with James in Persecutor role and Mr Schofield in Victim role. By sending James to the deputy head Mr Schofield is possibly looking for her to rescue him from a difficult situation. In keeping James out of class the deputy head possibly moves to Persecutor, however this would depend on her attitude towards James, and her motives in keeping him from lessons for the day. I would also be thinking I need to check out established contracts and rules, including the accepted protocol for situations such as this, where there is perceived violence.

The change of roles would meet the criteria for a *game*, and would suggest that the participants would have some unmet needs that are hidden, and possibly a closed frame of reference as to the available options. Since both have agreed to a meeting then resolution may be possible, with an opportunity for both sides to be *accounted*, taken into account and acknowledged (Ed.).

In listening to James I am struck by the level of stress in his life. As suspected he is telling me of some fairly major unmet needs in his family. James is possibly being bullied by his older brother, and has lost the support of his mum due to her own stresses. He is probably *rescuing* mum in fear that she may not cope and he might lose her too. Dad is absent and so another loss for James. A new baby might also impact on James in terms of his loss of position in the family, and loss of space. When the teacher started shouting he will have momentarily felt his vulnerability and the need for support, and as a defence moved to anger. James may also experience his isolation and lack of support as dangerous to his survival in his *Child ego state*. In being unable to authentically express his fears of what was happening in his family, he would inevitably be unable to express and integrate his sadness for his losses. This creates a closed system represented by the Drama Triangle (see Chapter 10, Figure 10.3). By supporting James to acknowledge his fear of facing Mr Schofield, the facilitator has an opportunity to give James an experience of facing up to his fear with support.

Listening to Mr Schofield I am struck by the common theme of the impact of a new baby into a home that is probably already quite pressured due to the stresses that are on-going for teachers. These pressures include constant internal and external reviews of performance and the fear of losing control of the class, and of being judged as 'failing'.

Similar to James, Mr Schofield will probably have experienced a moment of vulnerability when James did not hand in his homework. He apparently moved rapidly to a position of *Control* in the Drama Triangle. When James reacted by throwing his pencil case Mr Schofield would be likely to feel attacked, and has at that point moved to a *one down* frame of reference, or the *Victim* role in the triangle. I am also aware that Mr Schofield, as a new parent may also be feeling quite isolated and coming to terms with his new identity. Also he may, like James, have lost the support of his main attachment figure due to her attention being necessarily focused on the needs of a new baby.

Overall I am seeing an opportunity for increased empathy for both parties. However as one of them is a child I would need to keep in mind his real dependency on the adults to provide appropriate boundaries. A key aspect would include *accounting* Child needs, Parent demands and Adult options through an analysis of transactions and the need for mutual respect.

THE SECOND SCENARIO – THE THEFT OF A MOBILE PHONE

Sam, who is 15, has stolen a mobile phone from another boy, Ted, also 15, grabbing it from him as he was talking on it. This happened around the school gates at the end of the day, and was captured on the CCTV cameras by the gates. This led to his arrest later that evening and a subsequent caution.[2] It is the first time that Sam has been in trouble with the police. The phone has not been recovered.

As restorative facilitator you have talked to everyone involved and they have all agreed that they would like to have a restorative meeting, particularly as the two boys attend the same school and live near to each other.

Sam's story

Sam had already fully confessed to the police officer about what had happened after being told there was CCTV coverage of the

---

2   A caution is a formal warning in the UK that is given to a person who has admitted the offence. If the person refuses the caution then they will normally be prosecuted through the normal channels for the offence. Although it is not technically classed as a conviction (as only the UK Courts can convict someone) it can be taken into consideration by the UK Courts if the person is convicted of a further offence. Cautions are covered by the Rehabilitation of Offenders Act 1974 and become spent immediately. www.askthe.police.uk/content/q562.htm, accessed February 24th, 2015.

theft. He was not initially comfortable about having a restorative meeting but his mother had insisted.

During the initial meeting he admitted that he had taken the phone to impress some of the other boys in the school, and to gain their respect, as he had difficulty making friends. He had not thought it was that serious, or would cause anyone any harm, as he knew the phone would be insured.

However, on the way home he had become scared at being found with it, and had thrown it in the bushes, but cannot remember exactly where.

Jill's story (Sam's mother)

Jill is feeling very worried about Sam, whose behaviour has been proving difficult over the last year or so. She is feeling shocked and angry about the theft, and she emphasises that she has not brought her children up to be thieves. She is hoping that the restorative meeting will make him see that what he has done is wrong since nothing she says is getting through, and she is very worried about his future.

Ted's story

Ted felt shocked and angry when Sam took his phone. He recognised who he was, as both boys are in the same year at school and live near to each other. Ted does not understand why Sam behaved the way he did. Some of his friends are encouraging him to beat Sam up. However, he just wants his phone back.

Mark's story (Ted's dad)

Mark was very angry when he first found out about what had happened. He had calmed down by the time he had the preparatory meeting, but he nonetheless wants to understand the reasons behind what happened to his son. He is very worried that since Sam and Ted know each other, something else might happen between them. He wants assurance from Sam that nothing like this will happen again.

1. The affect and script psychology approach – Margaret Thorsborne

The motivation behind the theft seems to be about the sense of isolation and of not belonging – so Sam seems to suffer from chronic shame and the distress that comes from no relief from that.

The theft of the phone will, Sam believes, elevate his status in the eyes of other students to make him more accepted. His default behaviours are most likely, with reference to Nathanson's Compass of Shame (see Chapter 1, Figure 1.1) Attack Other and possibly Avoidance.

For the primary victim, Ted, and the other 'victims'–caregivers of both boys, the incident triggers surprise, then shame, masked by anger. Worry (fear) is triggered in all parties when they contemplate the future from each of their perspectives.

The restorative conference will give Sam chance to explain himself and hear from the others about the harm, as they tell their stories and share their negative feelings about what happened. They will have most of their questions answered, hopefully. This should begin the process of empathy development in Sam and also mobilise the community of care to support him to make some new friends. The process itself follows the Blueprint (see Chapter 1) by allowing the discharge of negative affect, and the development of a sense of connectedness as plans are made for solving the problem of the phone and Sam's sense of isolation.

I would not be at all surprised if, down the track, Sam and Ted become quite good mates. This would be highly unlikely if a restorative process were not used in the wake of the caution.

2. The attribution theory approach – Juliet Starbuck

By engaging in a restorative process Sam, Ted and their parents will revisit the motivation process discussed in Chapter 2. If I were facilitating then my main aim would be to give them all a chance to have their say. They would have a chance to discuss their perceptions of intent and their thoughts about responsibility. This will help everyone to understand what happened and affect their subsequent feelings and behaviours. Most importantly, engaging in a restorative process will give Sam the opportunity to 'confess' and to show remorse. This may change the judgements made against him. However, it is my view that this will only happen if I follow all five stages of the conference (see Chapter 2).

The first, introductory, stage creates an atmosphere of safety, which will encourage honesty. This will make it possible for Sam to confess, a fundamental part of Weiner's theory. During the introduction to the conference I would emphasise that the focus is on Sam's behaviour and not on Sam's moral worth or lack of it. Sam will effectively separate his 'bad' behaviour from himself as a person and be given the opportunity to repair his social identity.

In the second, storytelling, stage stakeholders will get a chance to 'hear the evidence'. Weiner's theory is based on the assumption that the 'person is a judge' (2006, p.4). He suggests that people will 'interpret evidence and reach a decision regarding an alleged transgression of another' (2006, p.4). Ted, Mark and Jill will get a chance to hear more about what caused Sam to act as he did and what his intentions were. This will affect how angry they will feel. If he explains how he was trying to make friends then they may feel some sympathy (Ted, Mark and Jill may offer some 'better' ideas about how to achieve this). Ted and Mark are likely to feel less angry. Sam will have the opportunity to accept responsibility for his actions.

During the third stage Sam will have the chance to show remorse and to apologise. He's more likely to do this because Ted, Mark and, indeed, Jill, his own mother, will have had an opportunity to expand on the pain and upset that Sam's actions had caused.

During the fourth stage Sam will confirm that he accepts responsibility for what he has done. He will have a chance to offer compensation. Because this is offered in a safe and structured setting Ted and Mark are more likely to believe him, and are more likely to think that the act will not happen again. If he works together with Ted, Mark and Jill then it will symbolise a shift in the relationship between them and will indicate to Sam that he is not a bad person.

In the final celebration stage Sam, Ted and their parents will have a chance to demonstrate that they are now 'OK' with each other. This will again help Sam to know that he is not a 'bad person' and will help Ted and Mark believe that he won't do it again.

3. The critical relational theory approach – Dorothy Vaandering

The role of critical relational theory and the Relationship Window for this situation are very helpful for identifying the nuances of the situation (see Chapter 3). Though it may appear that there is a negligible power differential between the boys, both personal and social power dynamics play a significant role in what has led to this situation and how it might be resolved. The Relationship Window (Figure 3.1) reveals the following:

Sam has done something *to* Ted, treating him as an object to meet his inherent need to belong. Restorative justice protocol would thus expect that Sam take full responsibility for the incident. However, his inherent need to belong stems from him feeling objectified because his humanity is being ignored both by his peers and his mother. I note that Sam will need a great deal of support to accept himself as worthy and able to contribute to healthy relationships. It will be important for one or more of the peers he is hoping to impress to be present. During the preparatory phase I would ask Sam whom he would suggest and then invite this person in, considering the potential they have for engaging with Sam in authentic relationship.

In hearing Jill's story, as facilitator I am conscious of the fact that she is responsible for his wellbeing as his parent – she holds a power position that is intended to nurture his worth. I listen for details of their relationship. Does she do things *to* him? *For* him? *With* him? Or does she *ignore* him? In reading my notes later I realise though she says she is worried for Sam, her worry is always couched within her own needs. Her image as a parent is at risk, Sam has been difficult for 'her' in the past year, and she is worried about 'the' future, not Sam's future. In essence it seems their relationship is one in which Sam is primarily expected to serve his mother's needs. Thus Sam's need to belong is perhaps coming from his relationship with his mother as much as it is coming from his need for friends. She chooses to participate in the circle and expects Sam to comply. Sam is again experiencing power dynamics associated with the *to* quadrant. I become alert to the potential manipulation of the restorative justice conference process against Sam. I ponder what is best.

Meanwhile Ted has been objectified by Sam through the incident which is an example of relationship in the *to* quadrant. He is confused and angry, which immediately drives him to be conscious of what his peers expect of him – to take revenge and beat Sam up. This would require that he move directly into the *to* quadrant and exert his power and that of his peer group on Sam to control him. The peer group represents various aspects of dominant social dynamics particularly those relating to gender – the need to demonstrate masculinity. I am alert to Ted's need for support and a re-articulation of healthy social norms. Being sure that one of Ted's friends accompany him is necessary in order for him to merge both the expectations of the adults in this situation with those of his peer group.

Considering Mark's story in the context of the Relationship Window, I recognise that his initial anger has subsided and he is genuinely concerned for the wellbeing of his son in the future. Though he could easily slip into increased expectations for Sam, he identifies his need for assurance that Sam does not further exacerbate this situation. He seems aware that both boys will need support, along with clarity about what is expected if they are not to inhibit each other's wellbeing. I note that he, as an adult, is in a power position and that he is using it for the benefit of others by contemplating what would be best for both Ted and Sam. I am encouraged by this and know this will help bring to light the support Sam will need.

Though Sam is responsible for causing the incident, critical relational theory allows me to consider the event in a broader social context. Though I believe this is a situation that will be well served by a circle process, I will not proceed until:

- I meet with Sam, answer his questions, and assure him that he is not required to participate till he is ready to do so. I will engage him in further conversation, asking him what is happening that makes him not want to participate and asking him to identify what he needs in order to feel like he is safe and respected by others.

- I meet with Jill again to explain and share with her that this circle will also result in identifying Sam's needs and how they can be met. I may use the Relationship Window to explain how a *with* relationship can develop and ask her if she can think of ways to provide a high level of support and expectations for Sam during and after the circle process.

- Youth supporters for both Sam and Ted are found to participate in the circle.

- A school guidance counsellor and/or a respected teacher of both boys can attend so that support within the school structure will be available for the boys and their peers.

- ◆ I am able to review with each participant the restorative justice approach that guides relationships within the school community (as described in the Introduction) highlighting our interconnectedness and ability to nurture to each other's wellbeing even if we don't know each other well.

I would proceed as described in Chapter 3. Although I cannot fully anticipate how the circle dialogue will emerge, I can trust that there will be less emphasis on Sam's behaviour and more on the needs of each individual present and their engagement with each other within the broader social context.

4. A Jungian approach – Ann Shearer

For me, this story illustrates vividly how a single incident can escalate in the minds of those involved into a major concern. Sam's snatching of the phone seems to have been an isolated act of impulse from a lonely boy anxious to impress his peers. He didn't even keep it, and owned up straight away when challenged. Yet for his mother, this almost seems to be the first act of a life of crime that she would be helpless to deflect. Ted seems more bewildered than anything else; although he was shocked and angry at the time, he does not seem to share his friends' feeling that he should beat Sam up. But for his father there is the concern that this was only the start of 'something else' which might threaten his son, and in this he is similar to Jill, Sam's mother.

In Jungian terms, we could say that Sam has become the recipient of quite some projection of shadow from these adults. He has become their 'bad guy'. He seems to carry their fears of a world they can neither predict nor control; they want to try to reassure themselves by making sure he 'never does it again', that he behaves in future in the way they think he should. We can only guess at their own shadow aspects of which Sam has become a mirror. But I would not be surprised to learn that Jill thinks it is entirely 'his fault' that she can't get through to him, and that Mark's idea of good behaviour can be somewhat oppressive to those who have to conform to it.

The danger of labels is that people may begin to live up to them. If Sam's central concerns aren't addressed, he might well protect his vulnerabilities by adopting the persona of the 'bad guy' that people seem to think he already is. My hope for the restorative process would be three-fold. First, that it would enable others to see more generously that this is above all a young man at a difficult stage of his development, who feels himself estranged from his peers and apparently lacks a guiding adult in whom he feels he can confide. Second, that it would help Sam to see that the world is not as unsympathetic as he perhaps thought – perhaps making possible a withdrawal of some of his own shadow projections as a precursor to discovering better ways of making friends than snatching their phones. And third, that the school might see some ways in which is could encourage Sam's greater integration – including, perhaps, offering him the chance of talking to a male teacher to whom he feels he can 'get through'.

5. The Nonviolent Communication approach – Shona Cameron

Speaking to everyone individually I would guess their feelings and needs and then check these guesses by asking the people involved using language like 'It sounds as if...' 'I am wondering if...' (see Chapter 5). My guess is that Sam is feeling anxious and needs to have a sense he belongs. Ted could reject Sam even more and has the power to ensure he is rejected from his peer group if a restorative conversation is not held. I would also note that Sam is feeling regretful and would like the opportunity to mend relationships. Jill, I would guess, is feeling worried and panicking because she needs to sense she can protect her son. Ted, I would guess, is feeling baffled and a bit conflicted and wants to understand what has happened and why. He is also a bit anxious and needs to have a sense of belonging to his peer group. My guess for Mark would be that he is feeling concerned and anxious and wants reassurance.

During a restorative meeting I would ensure that everyone present has a sense that I care about their needs, I may mention their needs as soon as I can or reflect back as they are speaking. I would see my job as the 'translator' of judgements or criticisms of anybody, so that if someone says something that I think will inflame the situation I will intervene. For example if Mark says something like:

'He shouldn't be allowed back into school. He's a thief. It's not safe around him!' I would step in quickly and say 'Are you feeling really worried, and wanting reassurance that your son Ted will be safe, and that his things are safe?'

If Mark were then to respond saying something like 'Yes, I know we're here to sort it out, but it's not been easy on my boy.'
I would respond by acknowledging his need for safety, and also how challenging and worrying the situation has been for everyone, including Jill. I am guessing that Jill will want to step in and protect her son from any attack from Mark, so bring her in to the conversation at this stage.

During the meeting I share my skills in empathy and support listening and reframing. I would also expect the boys to be feeling embarrassed by the meeting and wanting to move on fairly quickly. I can imagine spending more time with the parents and maybe offering the reassurance that any resolution is sustained.

6. The personal construct psychology approach – Pam Denicolo

This case provides an illustration of another of personal construct psychology's important tenets in action: that people, as informal scientists, generate hypotheses about what will happen in the world and then proceed to test them out in action. In this instance, both of the boys have hypotheses that are guiding their actions, as do the parents, the former based on a fairly limited lifetime's experience and the latter again on the relatively limited experience of bringing up 15-year-old boys. All are in a tense, and for some, an embarrassed, state. In reflecting on past events they are seeking explanations about causes that make sense to them. Because of the tension, in predicting future events they are casting them in terms of 'worst case' scenarios. It is the facilitator's role to calm the situation and promote understanding so that a more rational outcome can be obtained that is acceptable to all parties.

It should be noted that Sam grabbed the phone in a very public manner rather than obtaining it by stealth. The scene at the school gate is reminiscent of multitudes of others in the past, and no doubt in the future, when an article is grabbed by one student from another, often being thrown into a tree (as the number of scarves and gym shoes resting in branches around school-yards attests) as part of 'having a laugh' while showing off to peers to gain their approval for doing a daring deed. By and large these activities are opportunistic, spur of the moment silliness, usually involving a random victim and ill-thought-through 'showing off' responses within groups. The latter are frequent calls for approbation at an age when individuals tend to think that everyone is looking at them, probably critically.

It is likely that Sam's behaviour in grabbing the phone was similarly impetuous, with Ted a random victim, and only rationalised post hoc – mobile phones now being as common as the school scarves of the past. The decision to throw away the phone indicates not just fear of being found with it, but also that it was not stolen for its own intrinsic value. It is therefore unlikely that, as his mother Jill fears, this is an indicator of a criminal career ahead. On the other hand Ted feels picked on and picked out by Sam and is under a similar set of peer group pressures. Mark is concerned about potential bad feeling, perhaps with physical responses, between the boys continuing into the future.

Each of these participants needs to gain a better understanding of how the others construed the situation at the time of the snatch (the boys) and how they see it now thinking of the future (all four participants). The facilitator might think it best to leave the parents in a separate room initially, each drafting out a list of key concerns or constructs they have about the future, then working out what the contrast poles might be, for instance: getting more bad habits – learning a lesson; potential for future antagonism – potential for future friendship. This would also provide a situation in which they could find sympathy with the other's plight, the difficulty of bringing up teenage boys.

7. The relational theory approach
– Mark Vander Vennen

As I work to set up the meeting, my restorative lens tells me that the meeting needs to include not just the person harmed and the person causing harm, but also representatives from the 'arena of harm': the community that has been affected. I will thus ensure that both Ted and Sam are able to choose at least one peer support person to participate in the circle. Since Sam is highly isolated and may not have a friend, his support may be someone at the school who, depending on the outcome of the circle, could serve as a gateway for Sam to friendships or positive social networks. For Ted, the support person may be the friend that most wants Ted to beat up Sam. I also invite the police officer who dealt with the incident to attend.

I then meet individually with each participant prior to the meeting. I articulate as clearly as I can how the circle will be consistently structured and what they can expect, and ask if they are willing to participate. I ask the same questions that they and others will be asked in the circle. As I hear their stories, I pick up the intense loneliness, isolation and shame experienced by Sam. From Ted I note again the shame that an experience of violation can bring: at some level, he feels like 'damaged goods', and he desperately wants that to change.

Based on countless observations, which are supported by attachment theory, my prediction is that the biggest shifts that Sam and Ted will make in the meeting will result not necessarily from the exchange between them (though that too could be significant) but rather from witnessing the impact that the event has had on their respective parents, and observing the shifts that they make. In other words, they will be most impacted by their attachment figures. As their parents and the other adults become affectively attuned, to whatever degree, the system becomes a slightly safer, more connected community for them at the adult level. I further expect to be amazed again at the entire group's creativity during the agreement phase in helping to get Sam's need met for positive social connection and Ted's need met for the replacement of his phone, for understanding and apology, and for whatever other needs have emerged for him because of the theft.

Sam's theft was born out a profound need to belong, not a need for the phone (he immediately discarded it). He knew no way of voicing his need other than through the 'attack others' pole of Nathanson's Compass of Shame (see Chapter 1, Figure 1.1). In this case the community knew how to respond. It understood that conflict (caused by the theft) is a window onto systems issues below the conflict, an opportunity to change that system, and an invitation to deeper relationship. It grasped that there is no real relational change without the impetus or spur of conflict. It knew that when handled restoratively, conflict can lead to deeper relationship, to belonging, to attachment. That is why the school and the neighbourhood are on an explicit journey to become a conflict-friendly community, where conflict is not suppressed but embraced as an opportunity to repair and to create healthier, stronger, more connected relationships.

8. The resonant empathy approach – Pete Wallis

The process of resonant empathy is illustrated through Figures 11.1–11.6.

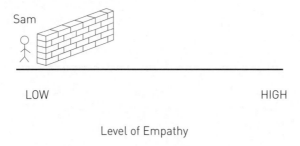

Figure 11.1: The starting point on the empathy scale for Sam

The robbery arose from Sam's unhappiness, and his unmet need for friendship and acceptance. At the time of the offence, and in its immediate aftermath, Sam's empathy for Ted is low; he doesn't see Ted as a person, merely as a means to meet his needs. After the robbery Sam either gives Ted no thought at all or perceives him as a threat, and later on he may blame Ted for the fact that he is caught. Figure 11.1 uses an empathy scale to indicate that at the time of the robbery, Sam's empathy for Ted is at rock bottom. He has built a defensive wall of thoughts and feelings to protect himself from experiencing shame.

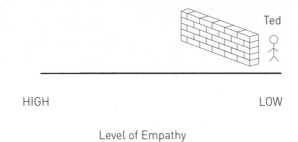

Figure 11.2: The starting point on the empathy scale for Ted

Ted experiences the robbery as a shocking moment in time, leaving him scared and angry. He has no empathy for Sam, nor any idea of the unhappiness that led to Sam's actions. Figure 11.2 shows that Ted's empathy for Sam at the time of the robbery is also low, and that his position mirrors Sam's. Ted also builds a defensive wall of thoughts and feelings to protect himself from a shameful experience.

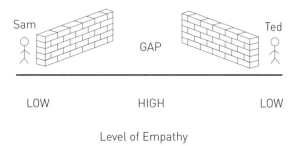

Sam   GAP   Ted

LOW   HIGH   LOW

Level of Empathy

Figure 11.3: Depicting this like a mirror, both Sam and Ted are at the bottom of the empathy scale with a large gap (empathy divide) between them

During the days following the robbery there is a gap, an empathy divide between Sam and Ted, and their positions on the empathy scale are mirrored as depicted in Figure 11.3. Neither has any idea of what the other is going through. Initially Sam tries to avoid being caught, discarding the phone. When arrested, he only admits to the crime because of the CCTV footage, and as in most offences, the criminal justice system is required to take him to the point of accepting his guilt. In the days that follow, the police are likely to tell Sam to have no contact with Ted until the caution is delivered, further reinforcing the gap. Meanwhile Ted may be fearful, avoiding Sam, walking away if he sees him at school, skirting parts of their neighbourhood to avoid a chance meeting. Both boys feel their parents' stress, and their feelings and thoughts about the other will ossify into defensive 'positions', like the walls in the diagram.

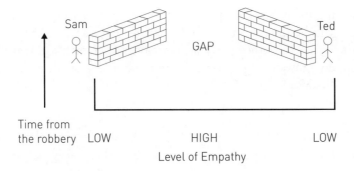

Figure 11.4: The criminal justice response may maintain or even reinforce the gap

As a voluntary condition of the caution, Sam agrees under pressure from his mother to meet Ted. The restorative justice practitioner (who may be the police officer who delivered the caution or another professional or volunteer) now meets both parties separately. They are likely to find that although Sam can't deny the offence he has no idea of its impact, and may have limited remorse. To protect his 'inner soft spot' he may employ defensive thinking including excuses ('he will have been insured'), entitlement ('everyone else has that phone – why shouldn't I have one?') and minimisation ('I didn't hurt him, so what's the problem?'). If these thoughts are entrenched the preparation phase may require victim empathy work with Sam so that he can practice and learn empathy, for example role-playing what Ted might be feeling, or using 'one step removed' to consider how he would react if it had been his younger brother whose phone was snatched.

Ted meanwhile is invited by the practitioner simply to talk about his experience and its impact. As he is encouraged to explore his needs arising from the offence; an answer to his question about why it happened; to know what became of his phone; reassurance that Sam won't target him again, he may realise that these needs can only be met through a restorative process with Sam. The practitioner may meet both sides several times during this phase, asking permission to share snippets of information between Sam and Ted in a process of indirect communication which, if both agree, is also the assessment and preparation for a face-to-face meeting. With the support of a skilled practitioner everyone's natural defensive walls will be lowered to the point where they can peek over and start to 'see' the other party as a person rather than a threat. As empathy grows though shared insight and understanding, the gap starts to close (Figure 11.5).

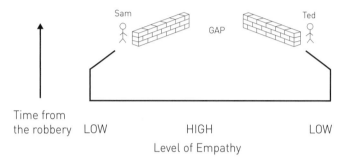

Figure 11.5: Indirect communication reduces the gap

Sam and Ted's defensive walls are lowered enough for a restorative meeting to be arranged, as each has reached their 'threshold of confidence'. The practitioner still needs to take great care, as Sam may remain reluctant and defensive, feeling that he has had to go along with a plan that wasn't of his choosing. As the day approaches, nerves and uncertainty may lead to empathy dipping again prior to the meeting. However, as they enter the room and see the anxiety in the other, and if both boys appear to be open and reflective rather than angry and belligerent, an automatic empathy response may be triggered, each properly seeing the other for the first time since the robbery.

At the start of the meeting the practitioner focuses attention on what happened, with a particular emphasis on thoughts and feelings, enabling everyone first to express what it has been like for them and then to imagine the experience of the robbery from the other's perspective. Everyone will realise that it has been an unhappy incident all round. Hopefully Sam will feel safe enough to open up about his motives for the offence; his difficult year and his feelings of isolation; and Ted will describe what it felt like to be robbed in front of his peers. These stories should help empathy to arise on both sides, as through the process of resonant empathy each shares the inner world of the other, and responds to the empathy they are receiving themselves. Underlying needs are explored, and the boys may find that they have plenty in common; a need for acceptance, support, friendship and safety. With expressions of remorse and consolation and a plan to make things better the gap may finally close completely, indicated nonverbally in the boys' body language, eye contact, perhaps a handshake – or even walking away from the meeting in conversation together. If the parents attend they may feel pride in their sons and experience empathy for the other parent(s), realising that they would have thought, felt and acted the same in the others' circumstances. Figure 11.6 sums up the process of resonant empathy from the offence to the restorative meeting.

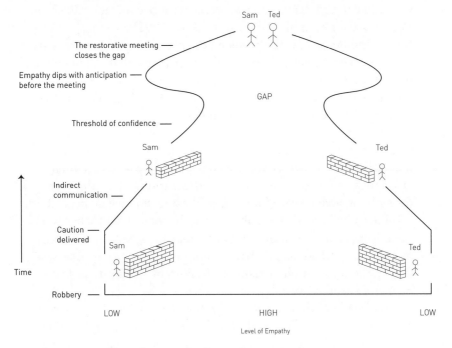

Figure 11.6: From harm to healing – how empathy has closed the gap caused by the crime

9. The social constructionist approach – Wendy Drewery

Because this matter has been referred to the police the recommendation was for a restorative justice conference facilitated by an accredited restorative justice facilitator, rather than the less formal restorative meeting at school, which would have been facilitated by a school person. Congruent with this more formal approach, and to underline the seriousness of the issue, the facilitator has invited a representative of the police youth section to the conference. Pre-conferencing meetings have established sometimes reluctant willingness to participate by Sam, Ted, Sam's mum and Ted's dad. There is a lot of tension in the accounts that have been collected. The conference is being held at the school, as they have the most suitable facilities in the neighbourhood.

Participants are sat in a circle facing the whiteboard and welcomed by the facilitator. The facilitator then outlines how he would like the conference to run: as the narrative therapist Michael White (see for example White and Epston 1992) encouraged us to think: 'The problem is the problem, the person is not the problem', is put on the whiteboard. The facilitator explains that the hope for the meeting is to give everyone a chance to hear the stories of the others involved, and as far as possible to make things right, so that people present can move forward in their lives.

The order of speaking is important, and the manner of speaking too. The facilitator asks those present to try to speak about themselves, their own actions, feelings and hopes, rather than to talk about others present. He helps them to maintain this stance throughout, giving space for emotional expression where needed.

Ted is invited to speak about what happened, and what were the effects of this on him. He talks about his shock because they had previously had an OK friendship, though not close. Ted says that the loss of his phone is more important to him than loss of Sam as a friend however.

Ted's father, Mark, is then invited to speak about the effects on him and the whole family. Mark tells the group how angry he was about this whole incident, how annoyed he is about having to buy another phone, and his fears for the future of Sam, and of Sam and Ted's relationship – not to mention the problems this has caused among their friendship group.

Sam is then invited to speak about what he did and the effects of this since on him, his friendships, and his family. Sam is on the verge of tears a lot of the time as he tries to respond. When asked why he did it, it becomes obvious that he is feeling very remorseful about doing something that he himself cannot quite explain.

The facilitator invites Sam's mother, Jill, to speak about the effects of the incident on her and her family. She too is upset, and expresses fears for Sam's future if this is the kind of person he was growing up to be. Mark nods his head at this.

The facilitator allows the impact of these stories to sink in; he asks Sam, 'So how can things be put right here?' Jill reaches out to her son and suggests to him quietly that perhaps he should offer to buy a replacement phone for Ted, they could take it out of his pocket money. Sam looks doubtful. His mother goes on, 'And what about apologising too?' This is quite a load for a young person to take, and understanding this, the facilitator might also quietly contribute something supportive and helpful. At this point Ted's father sees the young person struggling and might suggest that this would be a good start. Sam, slightly reluctant, agrees. He sits up straight, looks at Ted and his father, and says he is sorry for doing what he did. He is not sure about buying another phone though, as he does not have any money. His mother says she will help him.

Ted's father asks Ted to respond to Sam. When Ted looks reluctant he tells Ted that Sam is trying to make things right here, and Ted should recognise that. Ted speaks directly to Sam, saying he only wants his phone back.

The facilitator notes that the parent of each of the boys is working to support their young one, and remarks that he is sure that everyone present would want to express their support too. The policeman makes a supportive comment, and suggests that maybe the boys need to think about how they would behave towards each other when they meet in the playground tomorrow, and what they would say to their friends about what has happened. Ted's dad agrees, and also wants to know if they can be sure this kind of thing will not happen again.

The facilitator asks Ted if he feels he can meet Sam tomorrow and be civil to him. Ted mutters 's'pose so'. The facilitator turns to Sam and asks the same question. He gets the same answer. The policeman reminds the boys that ganging up on one another is not acceptable behaviour, and asks if they can behave like friends, even if they don't quite feel like it at the moment. They both agree they could. The policeman reminds them again that this might not be easy, especially if other friends are spoiling for a fight. Ted's father says he thinks that Ted is enough of a leader to be able to make sure nothing bad happens. Ted is not sure. The facilitator asks the boys if they can shake hands. They do this, a little sheepishly. Mark offers his hand to Jill, and offers his support if she needs it. Jill asks for his phone number so they can arrange for the new phone. The facilitator states that he will report on this meeting to the school. He thanks the folks for the spirit of their engagement in the conference, and congratulates the boys on their strength of character shown in the meeting.

Everyone is invited to stay and have a drink and a biscuit. The boys discuss what kind of phone Ted is going to get.

In this account I have described interactions which are seen many times over in restorative meetings. The central theoretical features of the process were the order or process of the conversation, which allowed witnesses to experience and learn about the positions and character of others present; and the spirit in which it was held, which was not blaming or retaliatory. No-one was out to 'get' anyone; the question was not 'who is to blame' and the objective was not to 'make them pay'. Witnessing the contributions of others changes everyone in their own way. Respectful speaking enabled all present to be and feel included in the conversation. The order of proceedings enabled everyone to hear what they needed to hear, and to process it and to respond. Over the process of the conference everyone, including the perpetrator and the victim, was called into a position of moral responsibility. Young people sometimes need help with this kind of challenge. The semi-public nature of the conversation means that witnesses will be able to help them to ensure that the plan does 'stick'.

10. Transactional analysis approach – Mo Felton

Although this is essentially classed as a theft, I am curious as to the possible undercurrents. The boys know each other, and Sam will know he will be caught for this. We could think of charting what has happened on the Drama Triangle. Sam took an aggressive position in snatching Ted's phone while he was using it, which places Ted in *Victim*. Then Sam moved to Victim position when he is arrested and cautioned. However Ted has not recovered his phone, so he is still the loser. This would certainly fit the criteria for a *game*, but I would be very interested to hear the accounts of each boy. I expect there will be more.

Sam is clearly having some difficulties with self-esteem. He is having some problems with relationships at school and also lately with his mum, Jill. I am noticing there is no mention of his father or siblings, so I am thinking of the possibility that Sam's mum may be a single parent. This would cause me to question the content of Sam's Ego States (Chapter 10, Figure 10.1). There may be gaps in his *Parent Ego State*, which might also account for his lack of self-regulation around the idea of stealing. Also stealing could be an expression of unmet *Child Ego State* needs. Sam's desire to impress other boys might also lead to the possibility that he is missing a male role model, and is seeking that in other boys, although peer pressure at this age is powerful.

Sam may need to identify and express emotions including some shame for his actions and fear about other possible consequences such as getting beaten up. If Sam has been unable to express these emotions he is likely to stay in an 'I'm not OK' frame of reference which will cause him to withdraw further and continue in the *game* to get contact.

Jill is apparently having concerns about Sam's behaviour over the last year, which might also indicate that she is without support. Sam is adolescent and will naturally distance from parents in this stage. I am interested to hear how she thinks and feels about these problems. How much is she able to let Sam take full responsibility for his actions? What is her style of parenting with Sam? Is she able to see the underlying needs for Sam, and for herself?

As the identified Victim in this scenario Ted will need an opportunity to express his anger to Sam. As facilitator I would be mindful of enabling Ted to move from I-U+ (I'm not OK, You're OK) Victim to I+ U-(I'm OK, You're not OK) to express authentic anger for being victimised by Sam, and possibly sadness for his lost phone, taking him to I-U-(I'm not OK, You're not OK) in the grid (see Chapter 10, Figure 10.3). It will be important to provide a safe container for expression of these emotions, and also to watch out that Ted does not simply make a move on the Drama Triangle to Persecutor (Chapter 10, Figure 10.3). Expression of authentic anger will include a clear request for a change of behaviour in order for there to be a resolution. What does Ted want or need from Sam for there to be closure? That may be an apology, or compensation, or both, or maybe even eventually lead to an alliance or friendship between the boys and/or the families.

Again there is no mention of another parent, and I now begin to question if there are possibly some shared concerns in these two families. This might offer an opportunity for an increase in empathy for each other. Mark's anger seems to be authentic in that he is clear about wanting an assurance from Sam that this will not happen again. Mark is looking for understanding and this approach indicates a desire for problem solving which is an I+U+ (I'm OK, You're OK) outcome for all concerned.

By monitoring the transactions between the participants I would be looking out for ulterior communications, which would reinforce the *game* positions. I would consistently invite open communication and a mutually OK relationship while we explore the underlying dynamics of the situation.

I would be looking to help Ted to increase his options other than beating up Sam. I would be also focused on enabling Sam to increase his options for building new relationships.

Check-out

All the contributors of the book were invited to Check-out by sharing their responses to the following questions:

- Having read everyone's chapter what may influence your practice in the future?

- Has anything struck you as especially interesting in relation to your own approach/theory?

- Can you see connections across chapters?

- What have you learnt?

The Check-out is again an opportunity for each person in turn to hold the talking piece, metaphorically speaking, passing it around so that people can speak in the same order as they have done in the previous go-rounds. The only difference is that, as the editor, I will come last. This is not so as to have the last word – far from it – but to close proceedings, pay final homage to all the hard work that has gone into this project and look to the future and to our next circle.

Margaret Thorsborne

While I read through each of the chapters submitted by the other authors, I have marveled at the variety in ways in which we make meaning of our lives and experiences, the ways in which we interpret the world and others' behaviours – and of course the similarities that connect each of us. I have to admit that I have been more drawn and felt more connected to any chapter that refers to our increasing understanding of how the brain works, our biology and the critical survival need we have to relate to others.

My own background in high school teaching (biology) and counseling means that I come to this work and the chapters with my biology/therapy hats on, and therefore I was looking for some indication in what I was reading that might allow me to align my knowledge and beliefs with others – to say to myself 'yes, I agree', or 'that's an interesting take on what I think' – and I dare say that the other authors may well have done the same. I'd like to focus my comments on what I see as the common themes that have emerged as I have read the chapters:

- Links between cognition, emotion and behaviour – these have been explained through the lens of a particular theory, and further, show how and why restorative problem-solving works (the whole point of this book!).

- Change is possible in cognitions, emotion and behaviour – advances in neuroscience are helping us better understand the concept of plasticity and how the changes are brought about during the phases of restorative encounter (I love this stuff!).

- These changes include perceptions about self and other(s), the wider world and our relationships within these.

- Restorative work might be regarded as therapeutic, but is NOT therapy nor a substitute for therapy.

- The skill, mindset, values and beliefs of the facilitator are critical elements in successful encounters where participants can feel safe to express vulnerability.

- The universal concept of harm (in all its versions – psychological, emotional, spiritual etc) involves punishing negative affects of distress, shame, fear, anger, disgust, contempt – healing is made possible *within* as well as *between* individuals.

- The development of empathy, compassion, kindness and generosity through the restorative process – and I especially like that most authors have been able to tie this to our better understanding of how brains work.

- The universal yearning for justice – to be heard and understood, to be acknowledged, to *matter.*

- And finally, *the recognition that we are biological beings,* social animals, driven by this biology to connect with each other, that *relationships matter* – when they are at their best *and* their worst – and that the need to restore and strengthen these connections is written into our DNA, if only we could pay attention to the information that our social antennae (our brains) have provided, and learn to act in ways that honour our biology.

Juliet Starbuck

When I sit down with my fresh faced thesis students at the start of the academic year to talk about their thesis proposal I tend to ask them just one question – 'So what?' And sometimes they look at me quizzically. Quite often they've spent so long thinking about what type of research they're going to do, how many participants they're going to need and what sort of analysis they're going to use that they have forgotten the purpose of their investigation. They have forgotten to think about *why* they are going to spend their time, and my time, examining their chosen topic area. They cannot tell me what the actual point of their study is going to be. I ask them 'So what?' because I'm only interested in doing things that make a difference.

So, when I sat down to write my thesis (from which my chapter for this book is drawn) I had in my mind the 'So what?' question. I wondered why 'my theory' of restorative justice mattered, and I became aware that it was because I want to give 'my passion' credibility. Like many of us I passionately believe in the value of restorative practices and can never really understand why everybody does not use them: I wanted to formulate a theory that could be used to direct 'good practice'.

I am a scientist and I wanted 'my theory' to do what a theory should do. I wanted 'my theory' to guide and give meaning to what we see in a restorative encounter, and I wanted to develop an orderly, integrated set of statements that describes, explains and predicts behaviour. I wanted to use 'my theory' to show how restorative justice works and which 'phases' are needed, and why. I wanted to use my findings to draw up a tool to evaluate it. I wanted to contribute to the evidence base. I am also a commissioner. Commissioners need to know 'what works'.

So, when I read my fellow contributors' chapters I similarly asked, 'So what?' and I was impressed and stimulated by the way that my colleagues had addressed that question. I note that Ann Shearer wanted to consider what makes a restorative encounter successful and why it might fail. Mark Vander Vennen tells us that attachment offers him 'a theoretical construct for understanding what is happening in a restorative encounter, and why an encounter is effective or ineffective'. He also writes 'attachment provides me with the outlines of a theoretical compass for restorative justice'.

Interestingly, Marg (Margaret) Thorsborne invites the reader to adopt a biological perspective. This seems timely when technological advances mean that an interest in cognitive neuroscience is growing. My 'So what?' question leads me to wonder whether we will soon be able to 'wire an offender up' and see if the restorative encounter has 'made a difference'!

In contrast, because it encourages the reader to maintain a focus on 'the human', Dorothy Vaandering introduces a powerful framework or matrix, the Relationship Window, which she says can be used to 'challenge restorative justice proponents to critically reflect on their use of language'. The Relationship Window leads Dorothy to challenge herself and ask, 'will all participants be honoured in the process?' and 'will the wellbeing of all be nurtured?'. She uses this as a 'self-check' but it seems to me that there is potential to develop the Relationship Window to produce a 'measure of effectiveness' for all to use. This would, of course, require the field to 'operationalise' terms such as 'honoured' and 'nurtured', assuming that we can reconcile our 'potentially conflicting perspectives' (Denicolo – Chapter 6). Perhaps we could follow the approaches that Pam outlines in her chapter on personal construct theory. Indeed, the 'so what' that emerges for me from Pam's chapter is that 'we' (the contributors and the readers of this book) are all trying to understand the world around us (in this case the world of restorative justice) and that while for some this is for intellectual curiosity, for others it is, surely, part of ensuring that effective (and in some cases cost-effective), ethical practice is carried out. After all, we are involving ourselves in other people's lives.

So, I was captivated by Pete Wallis's bold introductory statement. He says that there are three interesting features of a restorative meeting. Each is, perhaps, a warning to the ill-prepared or naïve practitioner: if we're interfering in people's lives we don't want to make things worse. Pete asserts that restorative meetings almost always go better than anticipated. (I ask myself on reading this – what happens when they don't?). Pete also writes that the more anxious the practitioner feels in advance, the better the meeting is likely to turn out. I wonder what a practitioner is likely to feel anxious about? Pete states that where harm runs deep, and emotions are strong, restorative meetings are more powerful and lead to better outcomes as a result. I ask myself what are 'worse outcomes'. My focus was immediately directed toward the question, 'So what do we have to do to get it right?' Pete suggests that we have to work with the 'magic ingredient', empathy. He goes on to explain what the facilitator has to do to make things work. He draws on his experience and a range of theories to make his argument, and it is compelling. However, and I think again of my fresh faced students – how do we know this? How can we prove that this would not or could not happen a different or better way? Wouldn't it be great if we could take some of Pete's ideas and test them out and use them to give our work more credibility?

Finally, I note that Shona Cameron tells us in Chapter 5 that, 'as Rosenberg was not involved in academia, he did not seek publication or research, preferring instead to develop the work of non-violent communication in practical situations and working with groups around the world to share the model'. But from my perspective proponents of restorative justice do not have to be in academia to contribute in a meaningful way to the evidence base or, as I put, to face up to the challenge of the 'So what?' question. They just have to be willing to ask the question.

Dorothy Vaandering

An interesting thing happened during the period when I was reading the chapters of this book. I was a participant in a formal facilitated dialogue circle with my six siblings and our spouses in an effort to address our fragmented interpersonal relationships and the impact this was having on addressing the needs and wellbeing of my ageing parents. Like bell hooks (1994, p.59) I have said of my entry into academia, and in donning the role of theorist, that:

> I came to theory young, when I was still a child. I came to theory because I was hurting... I came to theory desperate, wanting to comprehend – to grasp what was happening around and within me. Most importantly, I wanted to make the hurt go away. I saw in theory then a location for healing.

Sitting in a room with *all* of my siblings for the first time in many, many years I saw the hurt of our youth written indelibly in each of our postures and facial expressions, and heard it in our voices when we each held the talking stone labeled 'hope' and shared our confusion, our concerns, our numbness, our needs. I had often facilitated circles, both informally and formally, but never had I been a participant. Yet just as I embraced the talking stone that afternoon, I know I have embraced restorative justice as the focus of my work because of my deep yearning for an opportunity to sit with my family, a deep yearning to find a better way to be together as human beings.

As I re-read my own chapter in this book, I hear my desire to find ways to make 'hurt go away', the longing to comprehend and grasp what is happening 'around and within'. This is what a theorist does; it is what I read in each of the chapters – our collective craving to be healed.

This book sets up an 'echo chamber' (Vander Vennen, Chapter 7) that allows the reader to hear how their understanding or practice of restorative justice reverberates within a broader context. In hearing the resonance and dissonance I become aware of the complexity of restorative justice, of how its values and principles are embedded in our individual psyches, in the ways we are interconnected with others, and in myriad points in between. I marvel at the sound and come to realise that restorative justice makes so much sense regardless of one's entry point into, or explanation of, the field. Alone my stance provides some insight, but together with the perspective of others, a richness emerges that serves both as a celebration of a collective deep knowing as well as a caution for living it.

Theories, being what they are, cannot be all comprehensive. Like the encounters of the proverbial blind men with the elephant we only come to know the whole when we are exposed to all the parts. The parts explored in this volume remind us clearly that a restorative justice conference is but a microcosm of living restorative justice daily (Starbuck, Chapter 2). We are reminded that those causing harm, those experiencing harm, and their supporters experienced similar things (biological responses; natural or interrupted developmental stages; empathy or lack of it; affect; emotions; etc) revealing that regardless of our involvement what we share is a common humanity that is at once broken and sacred. And what I hear most eloquently, yet severely in this collection, is how this paradox consistently uncovers the responsibility of those who would take up the mantle of facilitator. In facilitation there is danger and hope (Felton, Chapter 10), a great risk that, like fire, can warm or destroy. The theories put forward allow for more accurate accountability and support for those of us privileged to be providing direction in the field.

In reading through the various theories of restorative justice I also notice how understanding restorative justice can be expressed along a continuum that focuses on the individual (psychology, biology) or their communal interconnectedness (sociology). I am tempted to take a definitive stand with theories that resonate with my own. And then I hear the words of Parker Palmer (0:51–1:52) speaking of the myth of the individual:

> Real life involves live encounters with other people… We emerge from community, we are dependent on community and we return to community, there is no way that we aren't communal creatures. At the same time what is critical to those live encounters is that each of us show up as our fullest self. We can't have relationships if people aren't showing up as themselves. At the level of profound truth, you often have to say 'both/and'. Is relationship the unit of reality? Yes. Is individuation the unit of reality? Yes. [We need to] hold that paradox as richly as we know how.

I would like to report that the circle I sat in with my siblings resulted in restored relationships, and that soon we will meet together again celebrating the wonder of family and our care for each other. After all my life's work is embedded in the hope that restorative justice provides such healing. Instead I reflect on what I have read and know more profoundly that what happened that day percolates within each of us. The transformation is only a tiny seed right now that requires nurturing if 'mana' (Drewery Chapter 9) is to be embodied fully.

Ann Shearer

As I've read through the chapters, I've been reminded again how compelling we humans are to ourselves, how hard we work to make sense of our motives and actions, both as individuals and as a species. And what a variety of theories we come up with! Of course

I've been more easily engaged by those which can leave an opening for the power of the irrational and imaginal in human interactions: I'm just not persuaded that we're entirely rational creatures. But I've been struck too by how many of us are essentially engaged in helping people clear the clutter of 'old stories' from past experience, near or far, that may be preventing them from living their lives more positively now. And in each chapter there is something to catch me up, and to puzzle over. Most especially, I've been drawn again to think about the attribution bias (Starbuck, Chapter 2), personal constructs (Denicolo, Chapter 6), scripts and rackets (Felton, Chapter 10), failures in empathy (Wallis, Chapter 8) and in communication (Cameron, Chapter 5) that I may be bringing to the potentially restorative encounters of everyday life.

The old alchemists, in whose arcane experiments Jung found such a powerful metaphor for psychological process, often saw their work as a ceaseless alternation between 'the volatile' and 'the 'fixed'. Theories are our fixatives, attempts to bring order and control into an ever-changing world; if they're good ones, they become volatile too, constantly reformulated in the light of actual experience. One thing that stands out for me about the theories described in these chapters is that they all take human mutability as their starting point. Whether this is expressed as a re-balancing of the biological central blueprint (Thorsborne, Chapter 1), a shift of attachment style (Vander Vennen, Chapter 7) or a belief that no meanings are fixed (Drewery, Chapter 9), or in some other way again, the message is fundamentally the same: human beings can change, to find more positive relationships with themselves and others.

This may seem as obvious as to be hardly worth saying. But aren't there theories and practices enough in the world that say the other? This is where the insistence on separating the deed from the doer, severing the link between act and disposition, often mentioned in these chapters, seems so essential to restorative process. Yet as the world tells us daily, not everyone thinks to make this leap. And there's nothing obvious either about the careful and subtle work these pages describes, from the preparation of a restorative session (starting with the facilitator's preparation of themselves) to the exact questions with which participations are asked to engage. I was taken time and again by how much seems achievable in such a short time, if the facilitator is truly fitted to and experienced in their own theoretical approach. This is a real impetus to look again at my own psychotherapeutic ways, and some of my theoretical assumptions too. I was particularly interested, for instance, in the debate on 'shame' that runs through the chapters. I've long had trouble with Braithwaite's formulations; my own bias is nearer that of Vander Vennen's social workers, who 'blanch' at a positive assessment of shame. For me, there is a world of difference between its corrosively crippling effects and the spur to reparative action that can be encoded in guilt. There is little positive about how people try to deal with shame, as several people point out (Nathanson's compass). So it's been helpful to me to read different ideas about shame and how others work with it.

Different though these pages show us to be, it seems we are united by one essential starting point: a fundamental optimism about the nature of human beings. I do not mean just an assertion that we all can change – for if positive change is possible then so is its dark opposite. The optimism may start with deceptive simplicity: think of the implications of 'all people, including myself, are worthy and honourable' (Vaandering, Chapter 3). But more than this, as she goes on to say, 'our wellbeing is nurtured through relationship'. I have been very touched by the descriptions of how different approaches work towards fostering empathy, until the virtuous spiral of reinforcement, which people call 'affective resonance' or 'emotional contagion', leads to what seems to be real transformation in individuals and their relationships with those who may have provoked their anger, fear, disgust and shame. Several contributors mention the ability to express vulnerability as a crucial turning point in this transformative process. I recognise this entirely through my own practice, and am glad for the reminder that against all expectation, we grow psychologically not through what we perceive as our 'strength' but through our 'weakness'.

What, finally, do I take away from these different theories and practices? I'm certainly left with some questions. If a restorative process 'fails', why do people think this is? How lasting are its 'transformations'? (This is certainly a question for depth psychologists, too: long-term follow-up has simply not been part of our tradition.) What, in short, happens to the shadow? But that's for another book. For now, and most of all, I take courage from the different expressions of one theme, whether this is posited as a belief, a working hypothesis or even a 'scientific' finding. This says that the overwhelming majority of human beings are disposed, our brains even hard-wired and attuned, towards connecting positively with others: the capacity for empathy is part of our nature. This may have its roots in Darwinian biology, it may be expressed in terms of an archetypal energy, or as anything in between. But whatever we call it, it does seem that there is an inherent urge to come together in 'right order' with ourselves and each other. We see and hear enough about the equal and opposite urge to split apart in anger and fear, and to reject 'the other' within and without. So it's good to be in the company of people whose theories and practices are dedicated to restoring and reinforcing 'right order' and to bringing Themis's scales to proper balance.

Shona Cameron

Reading through everyone else's contribution has increased the level of hope I have that there will be a different way to deal with conflict in my lifetime. Every chapter has contributed to my practice as a psychologist by informing me and broadening my awareness.

One of the connections I see across chapters is something about a faith in human beings. In our capacity to learn and grow, be moved by those around us and that something magic can happen between us that is healing, transformative and inspiring. That it is possible to really 'see' each other as human beings. To see past the labels of victim and offender of good and bad person and the attunement and resonance that can happen given the right facilitation.

I learnt from Marg (Margaret) Thorsborne that 'our biology is always at work', a reminder that has really stayed with me. Also the clarity in which she writes about the distinction between how we feel and how we react really resonated for me in my work with Nonviolent Communication. In particular I can hear Marshall Rosenberg's words in my head on reading the quote from Kelly at the end of Marg's chapter 'human beings care'. Marshall taught me that human beings have a need to contribute to the lives of others and that this need motivates us. That at our heart we are compassionate towards others and want to give.

Critical theory felt both new to me, and also a reminder. This chapter has already been important to me to take care about the power I wield in any encounter. I have a powerful label – 'educational psychologist', I am an educated, white, middle-class woman, I know the language to speak which gets me the results

I want in our culture. I've been made more alert to this and am grateful to Dorothy Vaandering for this life lesson. I'm noting how glad I feel to live and work in Scotland where we have guidance from our government about working within relationships as the first step to educate (The Scottish Government 2013).

I am also grateful for the learning from Pete Wallis in Chapter 8 and an increased clarity in me about what is occurring as I am 'in empathy' with another. For me this chapter points to the infinite nature of the flow of empathy between people and how it is my role as a facilitator to be in it, as much to do with me and my internal state as with the other. It happens if I am able to get out of the way, to stay present, and to be in the flow myself.

Mark Vander Vennen, in Chapter 7, talked about being in an echo chamber as he sees his two worlds as a psychotherapist and restorative practitioner come together. This is a neat summary of what reading these chapters has done for me. I've felt resonance in others' work, even those writing from a seemingly different perspective. I come away from this experience of contributing and reading with much more confidence that this is a way forward that has a solid grounding, which can suit any practitioner. Just as I have found the theories which work for me as a psychologist this collection will support restorative practitioners to find the theories that ground their practice.

The importance of endings was bought home to me by Mo Felton in Chapter 10. In all the aspects of my life and work and again I have begun to really check how I am ending conversations as a simple first step.

I end here by bringing to mind the thirteenth century Persian poet and mystic Rumi, the unofficial poet for Nonviolent Communication. He reminds us that is possible to go beyond seeing the world in terms of right or wrong. As we work restoratively it is possible to enter this place and to work together to repair relationships, perhaps for some this is a new place, one they have never been to before, and it's a place worth exploring.

Pam Denicolo

One of the constructivist tools I, and my colleague researchers, have used to explore how we or others have come to construe a particular domain is the 'river of experience' or 'snake' technique.

This involves the person in privately reflecting back over her/his life or a particular period of it, picking out a strand by noting down significant incidents that led to a change in direction or decision that had consequence for the development of that strand. These are registered as annotations at bends in the river or snake. Later these are shared with the researcher or clinician to help reconstruct the meaning that the incidents had, and the constructs that evolved for them, about the topic. Seldom does the listener need to ask a question as the person verbally re-lives the time and their thoughts, feelings and actions the incidents evoked (Denicolo 2003).

I found myself, when charged with the task of writing this section, thinking back over my 'river' and how I came to write the chapter and my experiences while doing so. In brief the story goes:

As a science teacher I wanted to fascinate students with science; I studied psychology and became entranced with the learning process. I briefly met personal construct psychology (PCP) which 'makes more sense' than stage theories; I was selected for a doctorate about understanding concepts in science and used PCP to explore others' understanding of science and philosophies of learning and teaching; I became a chartered psychologist and was recruited to an academic post focusing on postgraduate education; I used PCP in practice and in research across a broad spectrum with mature doctoral researchers from many fields; my daughter studied Law and wrote a dissertation on restorative justice (RJ) that fascinated me through its alternative conception of the world; Belinda Hopkins (this book's editor) registered for a doctorate and re-introduced me to RJ. Together we explored how constructivist approaches might be useful in exploring her topic; we became friends and shared our writing; the process of writing for this book has added to my learning more about RJ and related areas, but has also reinforced for me that there are ways of seeing and being in the world that 'make more sense' than others.

Although each author in this book aligns themselves, at least for the purposes of the discussion about restorative encounters, with particular named theories, I have found much in common with them and feel reassured by that. I will note here a few commonalties from my reading with what I understand of personal construct psychology, knowing that readers will see many more.

Juliet Starbuck in Chapter 2 writes about humans being conscious, rational decision makers, responsible for their own actions and developing coping strategies in response to how they see their world – like Kelly in his PC theory, recognising them as naïve scientists. Mo Felton in Chapter 10 and Marg (Margaret) Thorsborne in Chapter 1 reinforce that theme of responsible agents whose past experiences influence behaviour. In Chapter 9 Wendy Drewery engages the philosophical stance, also recognised in PCT, of the nature of truth changing over time as understanding develops. She also emphasises that the meaning of words change with context so they mean different things to different people. Hence PCT's emphasis on eliciting contrast poles and the importance of recognising that PCT techniques are merely conversation aids to elaborating on the meaning of construct labels. Dorothy Vaandering in Chapter 3 also uses a metaphor common in PCT of donning different lenses and adjusting to new lenses as different views of the world emerge. She too rejects responding only to people's behaviour rather than recognising context, social and temporal. A central tenet of PCT is that people continuously check out their constructs and can change the way they perceive the world. This possibility of change is echoed in Marg Thorsborne's chapter.

Our ways of working with people also demonstrate striking similarities. When Kelly's theory emerged it was suggested that it was Jungian in that it sought, as described by Ann Shearer in Chapter 4, to help people make the unconscious conscious. By helping them to understand their own constructs better, they would be aided in understanding how others might have come to see the world differently. Each in our own way, when working to explore the meanings others give to the world, strive to create an environment, as ably described by Shona Cameron in Chapter 5, in which they will feel comfortable and safe enough to share honestly how they think and feel and why they act in particular ways. Like Pete Wallis in Chapter 8, many of us have recognised the prime importance of empathy (cf the commonality and sociality corollaries of PCT) and the need to support people in 'loosening their constructs' about others. Similarly, several of us, including Mo Felton, have noted the importance of establishing explicit contracts with our clients/participants that enable us to use our skills as listeners while not engaging in therapy per se – a point also emphasised by Mark Vander Vennen in Chapter 7.

Thus the labels we use for our theories are similar to the verbal labels by which we denote our constructs – they are merely the best symbols we can find at present to convey a complexity of philosophy, cognition, feeling and stimuli to act in certain ways. It makes sense that those who are interested in treating people sensitively, preserving their dignity, should share other understandings in common, no matter how they are labelled and no matter what varied life experiences have led them to these current views on RJ.

Mark Vander Vennen

I have an image of sitting around a campfire, listening intently to each of the contributors to this book tell the story of their practice, their theoretical influences and where they intend to go next. For me, the circle has been an indelibly rich listening experience, and it has led to a deepening of insight.

I am struck by the broad diversity of psychotherapeutic influences and theories that undergird the restorative justice practices described here. To me, this is not surprising or distressing but rather affirming. As Vaandering notes (Chapter 3), restorative justice is about *what it is to be human*. And the question of who we are as human beings, as fundamentally relational creatures, seems inexhaustible, and inexhaustibly interesting, full of mysteries that have never been wholly explained or revealed. So it is not surprising that the multifarious nature of what it is to be human would generate a wide variety of perspectives and theories seeking to provide insight into that mystery and to support strong relational practice. Each perspective serves as a unique entry point into what it is to be human and offers, like a sliver of light onto a shadowy scene, new clarity.

I am further struck that each of the various psychotherapeutic and theoretical orientations pours into a description of restorative justice practice. This then seems to affirm that what it is to be 'restorative' touches something at a deep level about what it is to be human.

What has been reinforced for me through this exercise, both in the writing and the listening, is the importance of articulating theoretical influences and becoming more explicit about the theoretical perspectives and orientations that guide my restorative justice practice. Unexamined assumptions and biases can lead to unintended but real harm in practice. That includes matters of 'social location', as critical theory (Vaandering, Chapter 3) highlights.

Becoming explicit helps to minimise the possibility of causing harm. I also find myself wondering about the optimum positioning of a facilitator's 'psychotherapeutic expertise' in a restorative encounter. It may be that the role of the facilitator in this respect is one of the central themes for further discussion coming out of this circle, a potentially rich discussion.

I am most grateful for this opportunity to listen and learn from each of the contributors, become more explicit, and deepen my practice.

Pete Wallis

Here is my reflection on the experience of writing my chapter and of reading the chapters written by my fellow contributors.

Marg (Margaret) Thorsborne in Chapter 1 introduces two key themes, of vulnerability and connection, stressing that re-connection relies on expressions of vulnerability, while vulnerability enhances connection. A restorative encounter is an important personal task, a healing project, for those involved, but when we invite people into a restorative meeting, they are undoubtedly taking a risk, making themselves vulnerable, and they are likely to feel uncertain, anxious and exposed. Not unlike how I felt myself when I facilitated my first few restorative meetings, although hopefully it didn't show. Perhaps there is a parallel with writing for a public audience. I was struck by an interview that I heard some time ago with Sting, in which he was responding to a commentator who called him 'pretentious'. He reflected that when he was starting out on his career he had to pretend to be a musician. This pretence applies to us all when we try something new, when we give it a go, particularly if it involves an element of performing. In reaching out and connecting with people, we deliberately make ourselves vulnerable and open to criticism. My own writing often feels naïve and pretentious, and when I send it out into the world I brace myself, waiting for an anticipated knock back. Mark Vander Vennen in Chapter 7 quotes from Brené Brown, whose book *Daring Greatly* is a wonderful call for us all to engage with our vulnerability, take a risk and have faith in our own gifts and worthiness.

I feel passionately about restorative justice, and believe it can make for a more peaceful and connected world. The experience of reading the other chapters has been one of looking deeply at something very familiar, studying it from different angles and discovering fresh perspectives. Mark Vander Vennen talks about themes reverberating in an 'echo chamber', and ideas about attribution, confession, social identity and collective inventory are echoing round for me. Marg (Margaret) Thorsborne says that in restorative meetings there are remarkably consistent sequences of emotions, which explains why the experience of restorative justice feels universal. And yet every restorative encounter is unique, and I've rejoiced at the use of language, where situations I have witnessed so many times have been beautifully expressed. For example in Chapter 1 a participant states that they 'felt like a new person... that a cloud had been taken away'. This phrase reminded me of an elderly client who, every time I met her, spoke in graphic detail about the attack she had suffered in her own home. Visiting her again after she attended her restorative meeting she chatted for over an hour about completely unrelated family matters as if I was simply a friend or neighbour, before suddenly looking up and remembering why I was there. Her restorative encounter released her from constantly ruminating; it lifted a cloud. She described the transformation as 'like night and day...'

Practitioners reading these chapters will be helped in developing their practice. Mark Vander Vennen in Chapter 7 expresses how a successful restorative encounter can support people in developing 'new, enlarged, deepened and more coherent narratives'. I was struck by a speech at a Restorative Justice Council conference on January 20th, 2015 by Tim Chapman, who is a lecturer in restorative practices at University of Ulster. He uses the terms 'thick' and 'thin' in relation to a restorative process, distinguishing between a thick and thin story, thick and thin dialogue, thick and thin understanding, a thick or thin apology, and a thick or thin outcome agreement. In a restorative meeting, people talk about pain they have suffered and/or inflicted on others, and facilitating the sharing of pain is a delicate task. 'Thick' restorative justice requires subtle facilitators, who, as Shona Cameron describes in Chapter 5, practise with mindful awareness, presence, calmness, subtlety and skill. Like Wendy Drewery (Chapter 9) they 'pay attention' to what people bring to the restorative encounter, embody rather than remain rigidly fixed to a script, and aren't in the business of shame making, confession drawing, forced apologies or indeed, as Dorothy Vaandering reminds us in Chapter 3, any of their own outcomes.

In my own area of youth justice, with caseloads falling, most youth offending teams are finding that the majority of young people going through the courts have multiple issues, frequently arising from poor attachment and early childhood trauma. Cases involving child on parent violence, partner abuse and sexual offences all appear to be rising. No case is ever straightforward, and practitioners holding challenging and complex cases will be helped through an understanding of neuroscience, construct systems, attachment issues and meaning-making provided in these chapters. There has also been a useful emphasis on the vital importance of preparation and aftercare in 'thick' restorative practice, and Mo Felton stresses in Chapter 10 that both require care and both can be healing.

I love the challenge from Dorothy Vaandering to 'honour the inherent worth of all', to take restorative justice beyond being a simple response to behaviour and conflict where it is 'just a practice' to a place where the embodiment of a restorative ethos can become the 'fundamental principles of living in community'. In my own workplace we are exploring what it might mean to become a restorative organisation, and I am delighted for all the people in contact with each of my fellow contributors, who are also carrying this flame. As I work in youth justice, it is particularly heartening to read about quality restorative justice in schools.

I also love that my co-authors have experienced, and try to express, the inexpressible at the heart of restorative justice. Juliet Starbuck in Chapter 2 stresses the elements of surprise and mystery. Echoing the themes in my chapter, Ann Shearer in Chapter 4 describes the deep psychological urge that draws people who are 'yearning for justice' to come together to seek 'right order', and this whole book is infused with the energy that is unleashed through that encounter. In Chapter 7 we hear about 'dance' and 'ritual', and in Chapter 9 Wendy Drewery offers a wonderful description of 'mana', reminding us of our ancient lineage in this field.

Finally I would like to thank Belinda for inviting me to write a chapter for this exciting book, and express deep gratitude for her own contribution to the field, which has had an immense influence on my practice.

Wendy Drewery

On reading and reflecting on the contributions in this collection, I have been struck by a lot of challenging questions. I find the breadth of theory and explanatory power here, and the sheer variety, almost overwhelming. And I got to wondering about what kind of theory would I find satisfying: what are the elements or requirements of a theory that could explain the success (frequently) of restorative justice practice? And why am I not satisfied, even with my own?

So, prompted by reading this amazing collection, I will take this opportunity to share some random wonderings about what elements might be required for a comprehensive theory of restorative justice practice (RJP). First of all, it will be interdisciplinary, in the strongest sense of the word. I want a social theory of action that can address how the inherent moral positioning of persons can be intentionally brought forth. RJP has within it the power to move a person from a place of not being such a participant, to becoming more able to access their own moral stature. I want an account that recognises the persons as potential participants in their own life. But there has to be more to this, because justice is about how we can all live together without oppressing one another. So I want an account that embraces inclusiveness.

This in turn requires that our theory must be founded on what I would term 'human good'. I believe that most people who work to produce RJP are basically working from a sense of this possibility. And although it may be going a bit far, given that we are theorising practice here, I would suggest that we have to somehow bear in mind that what is the human good is a matter of constant discussion, disagreements, and new understandings. I think RJP is one such conversation, an intentional conversation about what is just in a particular time, with particular protagonists, in a particular situation or context.

One of the things that challenged me the most in my reading was the frequent sense of correction which seemed to dominate or underpin some of the theoretical approaches. Am I too sensitive? Years ago, in the face of critiques of psychology from Māori, I learned that the basis of Western psychology, the individual, was not necessarily the way all cultures see themselves. Māori culture, for example, tells us that *whakawhanaungatanga*, the practice of relationship, is a fundamental value. And certainly, Māori clearly foreground the practice of being in family-like relationships throughout their social structures, historical narratives, and everyday lives, considering these relationships as part of what some might call their personal identity. That experience of encounter with critique of my then humanist, individualist, psychological paradigm brought me to see much psychological practice as based in diagnosis and deficit. I do recognise that psychology can offer useful insights, and this collection demonstrates this. However I also came to realise back then that some mechanisms typical of Western approaches to social life are inherently colonising. Their underpinning assumptions are not necessarily those of every other. We cannot assume that a Western cultural perspective is the correct one. I began to understand that Western approaches to the organisation of social life in New Zealand often exclude the relational ways of being that Māori find more comfortable. Such intimations of the practice of colonising have forced me to look at psychology differently. I was convinced by authors such as Sheila McNamee and Kenneth Gergen (McNamee and Gergen 1999) and Edward Sampson (Sampson 1993, 2003) that the Western, individual self is too lonely to be an adequate account of social life, and that we are all, in fact, relational selves.

Clearly, this positioning predisposes me to find affinities with Jennifer Llewellyn's (2012) proposal that relationships are the basis of justice. The issue is, what kind of relationship is just? So it will not be surprising if I say that I found myself very attracted to Dorothy Vaandering's Relationship Window, in which the 'with' orientation is described as recognising the other as a subject, with rights. I think that what restorative conversations can do well is recognising persons as basically competent, agentic social participants, able to construct meanings in their own life. I wonder, is it too much to claim that constructing selves-in-relation is an accomplishment of a well-run restorative conversation?

I also want a theory that takes account of the locatedness of persons in their own culture. Many people in education would agree that restorative practice can become part of the whole school culture; and this ought to be a clue to the difference between seeing RJP as about justice in the sense of law, and seeing its basis of respect broadly as a disposition, or way of being and relating. Schools are more likely, at least in Aotearoa New Zealand, to embrace this latter meaning, whereas many of the practitioners writing in this book may be more familiar with the justice setting. This would possibly explain my reaction to the sense of correction noted above. And I am aware that working in education is very different from working in justice: offenders are not quite so 'hard' in schools, usually. Is it possible, I wonder, to make a distinction between justice, and Justice?

And lastly, for now at least: Is RJP practice about group belonging? Theorists such as Braithwaite would appear to claim so. It is not surprising that several of our contributors take a critical perspective on shaming and its role in RJP. For me, RJP is a way of proceeding when we do not know how to go on otherwise: when our comfort has been broken, and redress is difficult to imagine; when someone has damaged the sense of group security by breaking some boundaries and maybe doing harm. It may be that the wrongdoer does not want to be or see themselves as part of the dominant group; I do believe though that what they want is recognition of themselves as actors in their own lives. I think this is what respect, which is built into the restorative script, can do. It is a process of constructing a new story, one that has all of us present in it, and as such, it brings us into relationship. We do not have to want to be together and play together for this to be the case. However we think of it, there has to be room for openness and acceptance of diversity. At the same time, what we are all working for is absence of conflict, acknowledgement of harm, and agreed processes for living more peaceably together in our difference. But this may be moving too far from the idea of restorative justice practice. I wonder if it is.

Mo Felton

During this last year, as I have been writing my chapter for this book, people around the world have been remembering the sacrifices of the men and women who died in battle in 1914–1918 and in 1945–1949. I think for the first time, in my experience, there has been an opportunity to consider the experiences also of 'the enemy'. I made a special trip to see the spectacular scene of poppies tumbling from the Tower of London, filling the moat with a sea of red creating an impact that words alone cannot convey. To allow oneself to feel the emotion that this scene generated and to connect that feeling with the knowledge of events and cognitive understanding is what Dan Siegel in his Digital Journal describes as *Mindsight* (2014).

Writing my chapter on transactional analysis (TA) felt like a passion and a pain. I struggled with making the time necessary to write, and discovered new skills of procrastination as my impasse heightened to almost a full scale battle. Alongside this writing I was also completing a masters degree in TA psychotherapy, and in the year I turned 65 I was, I think, the oldest graduate at the ceremony. How sweet was the experience!

As I received the other chapters to read, believing I had almost completed the task, I decided to read through the other contributions on holiday. Light reading I thought! Not! For here was the greatest challenge. As I began to read I was surprised and fascinated to discover that other writers were using many concepts that I understand to be either rooted in TA, or very similar to established TA theories. I began to question what was derived from what in a search for authenticity and original ideas. Knowledge and experience can create a certain comfort and security in what is tried and trusted. Well-used neural pathways get easier to engage and aid speed and accuracy, it takes time to reflect on the value of difference, perhaps looking at the subject through a different lens or from another angle. I reminded myself of my own philosophy, that all parts of the system are important and valuable. It matters less to identify who was the originator of some ideas than it does to draw together what each of us finds powerful in a restorative encounter, because joining our strengths and our passion could continue to create an approach that is more than the sum of the parts. The emerging challenge was to take the time to explore together when as experts in our own fields there could be a pull to take the one up position and get on with the task. We seem to have discovered an amazing confirmation of a universal theme which each of us recognised and named in one form or another. Many authors used a grid to illustrate ideas, and it was my development of a grid or matrix as a tool for working with young people in care that first connected me to restorative approaches and the similarity in our model.

Many of the authors described processes using words that I wanted to have said myself. My background includes training in psychodynamic, Jungian and Gestalt programmes and currently I am hugely influenced by attachment theories and neuroscience, particularly Dan Siegel. I found myself more and more excited to dialogue with the other authors, and particularly those who quoted references for people and theories that had influenced me.

In conclusion I feel I have been privileged to be part of a team engaged in describing a healing process for humankind. However, for the reader the most important learning will be to bring these theories alive in practice by integrating the best of each into what works for the individual practitioner in their own setting, whether that may be at the level of individual conflict resolution to organisational differences and potentially even to aid national and world peace. The first step is for someone to have the courage to bring people together. When the editor Belinda Hopkins took that step in bringing these chapters together I believe she opened a door to a new order where this book can provide the fertile ground to create a meta-perspective on restorative approaches.

Belinda Hopkins

What has struck me most from having read everyone's contributions is how important it is to be conscious of the theory that underpins one's practice and of the way that this theory combines with one's own value base, connecting a 'theory of mind' with a coherent, internally consistent and congruent way to think and act. It is not enough to 'just' carry out one's practice. Indeed, I am more than ever convinced that there is in fact no such thing as a practice without a theory. Whatever we do or say is informed by what we think is happening in a given context, and this book has helped me to recognise the obligation in me as a practitioner to be more explicit with myself about what assumptions I am making, and what I am doing or saying based on these assumptions.

How we arrive at the theory that will help us with our practice may be an individual matter. The contributors in this book have chosen one specific theory to inform their own practice and this is why I have invited them to participate. Readers of this book may decide to choose aspects of the various theories and be eclectic, a stance I would admit to myself. However, there are three ways to be eclectic and they are not all necessarily effective:

> the highest form is *synthetic eclecticism*, which is an attempt to synthesise or integrate compatible approaches, resulting in a more complex and comprehensive theory than the original theories alone. The second form *technical eclecticism*, utilises one

organising theory and borrows some approaches from other theories. The third form is *atheoretical* eclecticism, in which the practitioner lacks a theory base and so uses whatever methods seem like a good idea at the time. (Porter 2000, p.13)

This last form should not be an option for restorative practitioners and hence the obligation to think carefully before integrating new ideas and practices into one's own approach. Are they consistent with one's own values, ethos, philosophy and core beliefs, and are they also internally consistent?

The individual contributors have done much of the work for us here. On the one hand they have clearly described the internal coherence of their own theory and its relationship to their practice and then, in this last Check-out section, they have explored the links – the shared themes, values and principles that they all have in common. For this reason my own work as editor has been made much easier. These last pieces are beautifully and thoughtfully constructed. Each one is like a mini-editorial. I do not think I can add much more and so instead I am going to finish by focusing on what I have learnt as an editor.

Being the editor of a book is a new role for me and so I have learnt a great deal from this task. The book was my idea, as was the original notion of making it open-ended and dynamic, involving all the contributors in reflecting on each others' contributions. In this regard it has felt almost like an action research project. The inspiration for the design of the book emerged as I discussed its interactive nature with a colleague.[1] It did increasingly sound as if what was emerging was a 'circle process in book form'. So in a sense I have been learning about how one might design a book that reflects restorative principles – namely: inviting and valuing different perspectives; encouraging the expression of thoughts, feelings and needs; exploring the impact of each others' expression of all these on ourselves and then creating together the ways we will move on from the experience.

As the chapters came in I was almost overwhelmed by the breadth and depth of wisdom and experience in them, and the beautiful, heart-felt ways in which all this was being expressed. My

---

1   I was encouraged to be more explicit about the book's Circle design after a conversation with my friend and colleague Joelle Timmermans in Belgium. She recognised the Circle structure in the way I was describing what I wanted to do and I am grateful to her for this.

first impressions were very positive and I was able to give positive feedback to everyone. I enjoyed my role well as cheer-leader and enthusiast, remaining positive and keeping us all going even when deadlines for each stage approached. I knew how much pressure people were under in their busy lives.

The importance of relationships in restorative practice has emerged as a strong theme in all the chapters. I have learnt that the relationships between me as editor and each of the contributing team is vital – and I have enjoyed my exchanges with everyone immensely. And of course the relationships between members of the contributing team have also been important to nurture – and I have thought of us as a team from the outset.

I have learnt how important it is to be open and transparent, to stay in touch with everyone, to be positive and encouraging, and to keep everyone updated with how things are going. I designed an Action Plan with dates by when each stage should be complete, and contributors were brilliant at meeting deadlines, by and large. We had to shift the goal posts at times, but the final deadline date has always stayed the same.

Everyone has engaged with the tasks in different ways, and this individual creative process has been a delight to witness. It has not always been easy – we have all been open and interested in each other's approach and yet it will be clear from reading all the contributions that there are differences in opinions. Not everyone would agree with each other, that is for sure. But it is in our differences that we learn and grow, and this has been my biggest learning, and the reason I came up with the idea for the book in the first place. However everyone has been gracious and I look forward to a chance to invite everyone together for real-life discussions. One day we may meet, in one room, and have a circle together, followed by breaking bread (or cake) together.

It has been a wonderful project to be involved in and I want to thank everyone for contributing from the bottom of my heart. What an adventure it has been.

One final word to you, the reader. You will, I am sure, have your own ideas about what other theories you would have liked to see represented here. Some people were invited and were unable to get involved, for health reasons or because they had too many other calls on their time. I already have a list of people I would love to invite next time. You are encouraged to get in touch with me with

your own suggestions, or even offers and perhaps there will be a
'Volume 2' in the future. And should you wish to find out more
about any of the theories in this book and communicate with the
author then contact me and I can pass on your queries.

belinda@transformingconflict.org

References

Brown, B. (2012) *Daring Greatly: How the Courage to be Vulnerable Transforms the Way we Live, Love, Parent and Lead.* London: Penguin Books.

hooks, b. (1994) 'Theory as Liberatory Practice.' In *Teaching to Trangress: Education as the Practice of Freedom.* New York: Routledge.

Denicolo, P. M. (2003) 'Elicitation Methods to Fit Different Purposes' in F. Fransella (ed.) *International Handbook of Personal Construct Psychology.* Chichester: John Wiley and Sons.

Llewellyn, J. (2012) 'Restorative Justice: Thinking Relationally About Justice.' In *Being Relational.* Toronto: UBC Press.

McNamee, S. and Gergen, K. J. (1999) *Relational Responsibility.* Thousand Oaks, CA: Sage.

Palmer, Parker (n.d.) *The Myth of the Individual.* Available at http://fetzer.org/resources/parker-palmer-myth-individual, accessed 17th November 2014.

Porter, L. (2000) *Behaviour in Schools: Theory and Practice for Teachers.* Buckingham: Open University Press.

Sampson, E. E. (1993) 'Identity politics: Challenges to psychology's understanding.' *American Psychologist 48*, 12, 1219–1230.

Sampson, E. E. (2003) 'Unconditional kindness to strangers.' *Theory and Psychology 13*, 2, 147–175.

The Scottish Government (2013) *Better Relationships Better Behaviour Better Learning.* Available at www.scotland.gov.uk/Publications/2013/03/7388, accessed 22nd December 2014.

White, M., and Epston, D. (1992) *Narrative means to therapeutic ends.* New York, NY: Norton.

Subject Index

Author Index